THE MOTHER I NEVER KNEW

Diana Moss

Published by New Generation Publishing in 2016

Copyright © Diana Moss 2016

The author asserts the moral right under the Copyright, Designs and Patents Act 1988 to be identified as the author of this work.

All Rights reserved. No part of this publication may be reproduced, stored in a retrieval system or transmitted, in any form or by any means without the prior consent of the author, nor be otherwise circulated in any form of binding or cover other than that which it is published and without a similar condition being imposed on the subsequent purchaser.

www.newgeneration-publishing.com

*Many loving thanks to Jim, my husband
for all your love, patience and understanding.*

*This book is dedicated with my fondest love to our
children,
Simon and Hannah,
also their children, Esther, Rayan and Amena.
Here is a little bit of your heritage!*

Acknowledgements

My heartfelt thanks go to my mother who shared so much of herself with me in her later years.

I must acknowledge Bettie Tapper's part in this by her meticulous saving of newspaper cuttings and letters that have been reproduced exactly as they were written.

NB All family names remain the same, but some of the names of my mother's friends have been changed to preserve anonymity.

Introduction

Just after her 80th birthday in December 1988, my mother suffered a severe subarachnoid haemorrhage (stroke). I was told that in the unlikely event of her regaining consciousness, it was doubtful that my mother would be much more than a vegetable. However, against all the odds, and with some good nursing, after just three weeks she came out of a coma and was eventually discharged home to her little flat three months later.

During that time I visited her daily. She reminisced a lot about the past, telling me many things I already knew. However, when we were on our own, she also revealed more details I hadn't previously known about her or myself until that time.

I found the events she talked about to be fascinating, as I began to understand how she 'ticked'. I wrote everything down with a view to piecing it together in chronological order sometime.

Eventually I typed it into manuscript form and gave it to her on her 85th birthday. She was thrilled with it and promptly wanted me to get it published. I realised that it needed a lot more polish and much more dialogue before it was even vaguely interesting to others.

It was only after my mother died in November 2003 that I came across the manuscript again. I made it my business to feed it into my laptop, editing as I went along. I suppose I was working through the grieving process.

By the middle of 2005 I paid to have the manuscript published by *Bound Biographies* in honour of Mum's memory as this is what she wanted me to do.

Now, over ten years later, I have made other additions, added more dialogue, changed the title, and hopefully made this an interesting book for you, the reader.

Diana Moss, 2016

PART ONE –

HUMBLE BEGINNINGS

Chapter One

"Oh, come! Come quickly! The baby's coming!"

Walter ran in from the garden where he had been trying to keep their two little girls entertained and out of mischief.

"Let me help you, Lottie." Putting his arm around his wife, he struggled to help his wife up the narrow twisting stairs and into their bedroom.

"Better send for the midwife now," said Charlotte as she flopped, groaning onto the bed. "Oh, it feels as though my insides are being ripped out of me!"

Her husband wrung his hands. "Lottie, my dear, I feel so helpless."

Walter's face buckled with concern, but he clattered down the stairs to send for the midwife. Going into the garden again he called his two small daughters, urging them to be extra good. Filling the kettle, he set it on the old range to boil before stomping upstairs again.

"How are you, Lottie, sweetheart?"

"I've never known pain like this before."

"Sit forward a little then I can plump up your pillows. Would you like a cup of tea? I put the kettle on to boil."

"Thank you dearest, but having cold water to sip would be better.

Charlotte moaned as another pain gripped her, and she squeezed her husband's hand. Not for the first time he admired her beautiful titian hair as he stroked it, but was reluctant to stay. The birthing room was no place for a man.

"Is there anything else I can help you with, sweetheart?"

"Towels, we'll need towels. Old ones," she gasped as another pain engulfed her.

Walter did as he was asked, then checked on the children. Both girls were tottering about in Charlotte's flower bed.

He ran his fingers through his hair. "Oh dear, you're

not picking all Mummy's flowers are you? She planted them to make the garden look pretty."

"No, Daddy, we're just picking the best ones especially for Mummy," Grace called back.

He couldn't argue with them. "Not too many. Mummy likes to see them growing as well."

Walter was distracted by the arrival of the midwife. By this time Charlotte was screaming in pain and terror.

Scratching his head, he asked the nurse, "Ought I to send for the doctor?"

"No, no, I can deal with this. You keep the children amused and everything will soon be over." The midwife bustled off, shooing Walter and the two girls outside.

It was at the end of February 1910 and the weather was cold but sunny. Walter tried to interest Grace and Marjorie, aged three years and fifteen months, in things outside in the garden, not understanding quite how to amuse them without Charlotte's encouragement.

Together they put the squashed snowdrops and crocus in a jar of water.

Worried about his wife, Walter somehow got through meal times with the children and eventually managed to get them to bed and to sleep. Something must be wrong. She had been delivered of Grace and Marjorie easily enough.

After eleven long hours, the midwife announced that Walter was the father of another lusty baby girl. Forgetting his tiredness, Walter rushed upstairs, then, remembering the flowers the girls had picked, went back to collect them. He was warded off by the midwife.

"Your wife is extremely tired, so you may only look in on her very quickly."

He slowed his step, peeped round the bedroom door to see his adorable wife lying pale, exhausted, but triumphant, nursing a small white bundle.

Lottie looked up and smiled a wan smile.

"She looks just like her Daddy."

"Can I see her?"

"Of course, don't be shy, come and look!"

"The midwife said ..."

"Bother the midwife, it's you I want to have near me and tell me how clever I've been!"

"I'm sorry but Grace and Marjorie raided your flower bed. They wanted to please you." He placed the jar of flowers on the chest where she could see them.

Lottie looked up at her husband. "Please thank them for me. They can see their new little sister tomorrow."

Together they admired the small child with her button nose and closed eyes, their lashes forming half moons above her round rosy cheeks.

"Let's call her Jessie. That's a nice name."

"Well, my dear, *I* think she looks just like her pretty mother. What could her middle name be?"

Charlotte screwed up her face. "We gave Grace my first name and Marjorie my middle name of Louisa ..."

What about calling her Jessie Benjafield Heath? Then her middle name will carry on your whole family name."

"Oh Walter, what a wonderful idea!" Charlotte smiled up at her husband.

As if in agreement, a small snuffle came from the bundle in her arms, but the baby didn't wake.

* * *

Walter became worried about his wife as the days passed. The midwife didn't seem too concerned when he voiced his thoughts to her on her visits. Upstairs his energetic wife seemed to be fading away before his eyes. She still seemed to be bleeding far too much for Walter's peace of mind. He paced the floor then sent for the midwife again before she was due for her regular visit.

The midwife was annoyed when she arrived. She frowned, made a cursory examination, sighed and told him not to worry.

Upstairs Lottie thanked him for his concern, squeezing her husband's hand to reassure him she would soon be all right.

Unconvinced, Walter sent for Charlotte's mother who would know about such things. Phoebe Benjafield arrived that afternoon, having only had to travel from nearby Wincanton to their small farm in Charlton Musgrove. She soon assessed the situation and sent for the doctor.

Grace and Marjorie, her grandchildren loved her and she was able to entertain them in ways that Walter never could. Pheobe soon had the girls helping her make cakes and a warm aroma of baking floated out of the kitchen.

Grace dragged her father to the kitchen table. "Look Daddy, I helped Granny make some jam tarts."

"Jam, me did jam," added Marjorie.

Phoebe had only been in the house a few hours and everyone was feeling better for her soothing and unruffled presence. The doctor examined Charlotte and wanted to know why he had not been asked to attend her before. He administered medication, promising to visit again the following day.

The situation worsened.

In her weakened state, Charlotte contracted pneumonia which eventually led to emphysema as she became too weak to sit up in bed and fluid collected on her lungs. A nurse was called in to be with her day and night.

Phoebe wrote to her son telling of her concern for his sister.

Pear Tree Farm
April 1910

My dear Harold

You will be sorry to hear that the news today is no better. Charlotte has been unconscious since yesterday, and we cannot quiet her.

The doctor drew 2 quarts of fluid from her lung today, and he says it will probably collect again in a few days when some more will have to be drawn out of a tube inserted, if she can stand it, but it does not seem possible that she can last so long. She must be completely exhausted, for she is quite raving at times. It is most distressing to see and hear her.

She often calls for you in her delirium but I don't think she would know you. Sometimes she keeps calling Walter, then when he goes up, orders him down – poor girl, it is sad to see her.

Nurse will not leave her at all today to take her much needed rest. She can seem to soothe her better than anyone. She has been singing to her for the past hour or more to try to get her to sleep.

Love from
Your affectionate mother

Phoebe Benjafield

Phoebe worked hard to keep the house clean, cook meals, entertain the children, look after the baby, and trying to calm Walter.

"We must live in hope," she would often say.

Early one morning Walter went downstairs to find the kitchen deserted. He had become accustomed to his mother-in-law rising early to prepare breakfast. Perhaps she had overslept; after all, she had retired from this pace of life years ago. Maybe he ought to ensure she was all right? Returning upstairs he tapped gently on her door. Silence. He knocked louder, eventually opening the door a little. Phoebe was lying in bed.

"Are you all right?"

There was no response. Stepping inside he made to wake her. Touching her hand, he discovered it to be cold as marble.

Going downstairs, Walter sat, stunned, cradling his head on his folded arms on the kitchen table. Then, realising that the girls would soon be awake and how much there was to be done, he busied himself like an automaton.

The doctor soon came to examine Charlotte. He certified Phoebe's death from a heart attack in the same visit.

"Your wife must not be told about her mother's death as the shock of it might affect her own will to live. That is most important," he said.

Walter sighed and sat with his head in his hands as the undertakers arrived and bore Phoebe's body away.

Grace, Marjorie and Walter all wore black armbands after that, but Walter removed his every time he visited the sick room.

"Where's Granny?" demanded Grace.

Her father then had the painful task of explaining that Granny had died in the night.

"Has she gone to heaven?" she asked, still in awe of the situation.

"Oh yes my dear," he assured them, and turned away in his sorrow. The girls turned tearfully to one another as the seriousness of the situation began to dawn on them.

Walter took Charlotte some soup at lunchtime while the nurse had a short and much needed break.

She looked at him weakly and whispered, "Where's mother?"

"She had to go away," he replied awkwardly. "Something to do with chapel matters I think. She'll be back when she can." He bent to kiss her forehead, with fingers crossed behind him. He had never lied to her before.

Walter struggled to maintain the household and family over the next forty-eight hours before Charlotte lapsed into a coma.

The doctor told him that she was too weak and ill to be moved, even to be transported to Wincanton hospital.

Hilda, a local woman from the village was brought in to look after the children while the nurse continued to oversee all of Charlotte's needs. Walter attempted to till the land once again, but his mind was not on what he was doing. All the while he worried about his darling wife. He loved her so much and knew he would never love again with such passion.

Exactly a week after her mother's death, Charlotte herself lost her grip on life and died, leaving three small girls and their grieving father.

Walter was devastated, his mind numb and frozen with shock.

On the day of the funeral when everyone dressed all in black filed to the local chapel, Hilda made Grace and Marjorie sit on chairs round the kitchen table while she read to them from the Bible. In the background the tinny tolling of a bell could be heard.

* * *

Walter Heath had married Charlotte Benjafield in the spring of 1906 and had taken her to back to his little fruit farm with its stone walled cottage covered neatly by a tiled roof. It was made private by having just one entrance door at the back of the house and a blank wall where the building met the thoroughfare, to the nearby village of Charlton Musgrove. Looking at the house from the road, it seemed as if it cherished beloved secrets. The house faced a sizeable walled garden, beyond which was the farm.

Their marriage, although short, had been an extremely happy one. It was in this cottage that all three of his daughters had been born.

Walter's anguish was like an exposed nerve that he tried to deaden by concentrating on his work.

His love for Charlotte had bloomed late in life and had been blossoming with such promise. They had wanted children so badly and had them in quick succession. He was forty-one now. Charlotte had been thirty-seven when she died. He wondered whether three pregnancies comparatively late in her childbearing years had been too much for her. How he wished he had ignored the midwife's assurances that she could manage Jessie's birth on her own and gone for the doctor anyway. If only…

Charlotte had lost so much blood. It was remarkable that she had lasted so long in the circumstances. Walter winced as he remembered her lying there in that bed, suffering because of his deep love for her. He should have called the doctor sooner. He could not bring himself to spend very long with the girls now. They were all too keen reminders of Charlotte whom he loved so dearly, and had lost as a result of that love.

Charlotte's body was buried in the churchyard of St Mary's parish church, Wedmore, Somerset.

*In loving memory of a dear wife and mother
Charlotte Louisa Heath (nee Benjafield)
1873-1910*

* * *

After their mother's funeral the three little girls were distributed amongst three of Charlotte's sisters for some months. Marjorie presented quite a pitiful sight as she hugged herself, saying "Nobody loves me!" She would then totter round the garden chanting the three words she knew of the hymn 'Trust and Obey'. These were the only six words she spoke for many weeks.

Meanwhile, Hilda had become Walter's housekeeper and they eventually married. This meant the family was reunited, but things were never the same again. Soon after that the family moved to Broadstone in Dorset. Then Ronald was born, although his actual birth date was always shrouded in mystery. Two years later Bettine was born in 1918.

During the Great War Hilda became very nervous of zeppelins and the possibility of enemy aircraft even though they lived a long way from any city. She would ensure each child removed their clothes and had laid them neatly in exact order so they could all be dressed quickly during any emergency in the night. Fortunately this never happened.

As they had moved away from Somerset, Walter, having relinquished his fruit farm, had found work and would cycle nearly twelve miles each way to the munitions factory in Wareham, thus providing his family with two pounds a week to live on.

Hilda was devoted to her own children who now took precedence over the older three. Her step-daughters were hardly old enough to do much for themselves before she gave them tasks to do around the house. They were ordered to creep about the home so as not to wake the younger children and were also told that if they made any sudden noise this would spoil a cake should one be baking in the oven. On Saturdays Grace would have to clean the bedrooms. She also had the unenviable task of blacking the stove each day and lighting the fire. Then Marjorie would dress Ronald and Bettie in front of it. Grace also fed the dozen hens that strutted and clucked at the bottom of the garden, collecting the eggs they obligingly laid in return. When she was a little older she cleaned them out and did everything in connection with them. Marjorie was only seven when she had to walk Bettie and Ronald in their pram until they went to sleep. (If she was honest with herself this created an excuse to get out of the house and away from the disquieting atmosphere.) In addition she would have to change their nappies and feed them, a task that would take ages, as they were fussy eaters. On Saturdays her additional duty was to cook the lunch, which was not easy with two little ones clamouring for attention. Jessie had to polish all the family's shoes each day. On Saturdays her task was to clean the silver as well. Every Saturday all three of them would have to clean and tidy their bedroom.

Hilda had an obsession with manners, even with such young children. Her step-daughters were not allowed to be finnicky with their food even though her own children were fussy. Friday lunch was regularly steamed fish that Marjorie hated however hungry she was.

"Come along Marjorie, finish your dinner. Everyone

else has." Hilda would goad her.

Marjorie would stare at the pale cod cutlet beribboned by grey skin squatting in a pool of congealing liquid that looked most unappealing.

"I don't want any more thank you," she would whisper.

Hilda would sound threatening, as she said, "What you don't eat now you must eat at tea time."

Marjorie's stomach would churn at the prospect. Horrid, horrid fish!

She still felt hungry, even though she had eaten the potato and peas.

"No pudding either until all that's gone." warned Hilda, indicating to the others that it was time for the plates to be collected. Marjorie sighed and pushed the fish round her plate again summoning up the courage to eat it.

Winter would bring coughs and colds, meaning chests would have to be rubbed with *Wintergreen.* Marjorie would always associate the strong smell of it and with a runny nose and a cough. Having her chest rubbed with such pungent stuff seemed to her to make her snuffles worse rather than better. Cleaning their teeth involved dipping a damp finger in salt and rubbing them whilst trying not to swallow.

Grace, Marjorie and Jessie all shared a double bed and once sent upstairs in the evening they were not allowed to talk or even whisper amongst themselves. After a few hissed mutters between them, their stepmother would call up the stairs.

"No jam on your bread tomorrow – and that goes for all three of you!"

They decided she must have incredible hearing, as even *they* hadn't been aware of making a noise when she would shout up the stairs again.

"Silence, all of you! No jam *or* margarine on your bread for two days!"

After suffering these threats, they invented a game when they would scratch rhythms of music hall songs or hymn tunes on the pillow for the other two to guess the title.

Their stepmother never showed them any sign of love or affection. It seemed that they had been reduced to servant status.

The three older girls always wore clothes that had been handed down between them until they were worn through and full of holes. However, Ronald and Bettie basked in the privilege of being Hilda's mother's only grandchildren. She ensured they had nice clothes and went to fee-paying schools, whereas Grace, Marjorie and Jessie were educated at the local village school which was a two-mile walk away. To get there they had to cross a small brook by means of a broad flat stone. They decided that this was how the village of Broadstone got its name.

Life was hard as the older girls rushed through their duties at home before setting off for school, needing to get there before the bell sounded tolling their lateness. It was a small village school with two teachers and two classes. The youngest child would find it hard to understand everything whereas the older children often got bored. Nevertheless Grace, Marjorie and Jessie enjoyed their school life and did their best there. At least here they were rewarded with praise.

One Saturday the next door neighbour banged furiously on the Heath family's front door. Hilda answered the door.

"I want to see your son! He's done no end of damage in my garden. This is not the first time he's kicked his football over the wall and flattened most of my fragile lettuce plants!"

Hilda simpered. "Oh dear, Mr Wilson. I'm sure he didn't mean to do it."

The neighbour shook his fist in Hilda's face. "You bring him here! I demand to see that son of yours so I can personally tell him what I think of his stupid behaviour!"

Hilda gave him her most winning smile. "He's a very nice lad when you get to know him. But you know what boys are – they have their boisterous side."

"Just you bring Ronald here so I can give him a piece

of my mind. This is not the first time he's done this."

"Well in that case I apologise on his behalf. I'm sure he didn't *mean* to do it,"

"I want him out here to apologise to me now!"

"I don't think that will be necessary, Mr Wilson."

"All that garden he's got to play in and he has to kick his ball over the wall into my garden!"

"Well, as I said, I'm sure he didn't mean to do it."

"I only just planted those lettuces out two days ago. He's damaged about half of them!"

"As I say, boys will be boys."

"It's not the first time this has happened. Your boy is costing me a fortune in seedlings!"

"He's busy with schoolwork at present, but I'll mention it to him."

Eventually Mr Wilson stomped off in a temper, still muttering, while Ronald, sniggering to himself upstairs, thought it was all a huge joke.

"Just imagine! Supposing one of us had done that!" Grace protested quietly, but vehemently as they heard his laughter float down the stairs.

"We wouldn't have jam or margarine *or* even bread to put *anything* on," replied Marjorie dully.

Grace went to live with Charlotte's sister and her husband as a live-in housekeeper when she was fourteen. They lived at Ringwood, a market town on the borders of Dorset and Hampshire. Marjorie and Jessie were quite envious of her being able to leave home, although they did miss her. Jessie eventually left school and found work, first, as a waitress in a café before moving on to be a sales assistant in a haberdashery shop.

Marjorie however was suddenly taken out of school just a few months before she was fourteen. A local minister, Reverend Howard, had a two-month old baby who was very ill and not expected to live very long. His wife already had two small daughters and two young sons to cope with. Hilda had offered Marjorie's services without bothering to consult her. She assured the couple that Marjorie was very good with babies. Hilda had written to the headmistress of the school to say that Marjorie would not be attending in future.

Marjorie was summoned out of her class one day to be sent home where she was told about her future. She was sent upstairs to pack a small suitcase. She dare not say anything to her stepmother, but was most indignant about her life being organised without her knowledge. It was too late for plans to be changed.

In just two days, Marjorie found herself installed at the home of the Howard family. She was surprised by enjoying her new live-in job, wallowing in the love that the family gave her, realising how much she had missed out on over the past years.

To everyone's amazement the baby recovered, and Marjorie was asked to stay on as the baby's mother was pregnant again. The family were moving to Peterborough. Marjorie became their live-in nursemaid, thrilled that she was earning money doing something she enjoyed.

The Howards were pleased with her.

Often the children would tell her, "I love you, Marjorie."

"You'll never leave us, will you Margie?"

"Stay with us for ever and ever, please!"

Reverend Howard and his wife were continually singing her praises to their friends and parishioners and she felt a glow of happiness rise within her as she realised she was accepted for who she was. This was what it felt like to be loved.

Marjorie stayed with the family for almost two years before Hilda summoned her home again. This time, Hilda's own sister Margaret was recovering from flu and needed someone to look after her while she convalesced. Marjorie resented having her life ruled by her stepmother, but there was nothing for it but to obey. Her stepmother had not even written to her directly, instead Hilda had written to her employer asking that he release her. Reverent Howard read the letter out to her and Marjorie knew it was no use trying to ignore or delay the command. She was grateful to him for reading the letter out to his family at the beginning of their evening meal that day. Without exception, faces fell and there were cries of "Oh Marjorie!" It was hard, but she must move on as her stepmother dictated.

* * *

Aunt Margaret was Hilda's sister who lived in Wincanton. She had suffered a particularly bad bout of influenza and had been quite weakened by it. Once they had shared their first meal together Marjorie realised that Aunt Margaret was very fair-minded. Before long they were to become closely bound together sealed by a true understanding of one another. Hilda was never mentioned.

Marjorie worked hard to cook and clean for her aunt. She even tended the garden as well. One day Aunt Margaret had a suggestion to make while they ate lunch together.

"Have you thought what you would like to do with your life, my dear?"

"Well, no. I just do what Mother tells me to do."

"As you seem to be so good with tending to people's needs, have you thought about taking up nursing as a career?"

Marjorie thought for a while. "Do you really think I could? There would be an awful lot to learn."

"I have every confidence in you, and if that's what you would like to do, then I will do all I can to help you."

"Would you? Oh, thank you! That would be wonderful."

Aunt Margaret helped Marjorie to apply for a nursing position at Bristol Children's Hospital. Following a daunting interview, Marjorie received a letter two weeks later telling she had been accepted for training there. A dress pattern was enclosed with instructions that she must supply two regulation uniforms before the hospital would provide her with more.

Aunt Margaret owned a treadle sewing machine which she showed Marjorie how to use. She took Marjorie's measurements and loaned her the money to buy fabric. Together they cut, pinned, tacked and sewed to make the necessary uniforms prior to her starting date early in 1927.

Chapter Two

Marjorie started work at the Bristol Children's Hospital two months ahead of schedule when she was just eighteen, because a nurse had been laid off with typhoid.

So it was on New Years Day 1927, she arrived at the main door with her suitcase. The building was relatively small for a hospital, but it towered above her as she plunged into it and was swallowed up by the tall Victorian corridors with their high windows, almost too high to allow any light to pierce the gloom.

After a short interview with Matron, another nurse was summoned to show her to her room which was off a long corridor. It had the bare essentials, but at least she had it to herself. Marjorie started to unpack, laying out her uniform ready for the next day. Once she got used to it she began to feel quite proud of it.

The clanging of a bell jerked Marjorie from a deep sleep. The noise grew louder and then passed on down the corridor. Shivering, she sat up in bed and rubbed her eyes, fighting sleep before putting her feet to a cold linoleum floor. It was six o'clock.

Doors slammed and feet pounded along the passage while Marjorie scrambled into the unaccustomed striped uniform and thick black stockings. She trod into her shoes, laced them quickly and tried to fix her muslin head-square in the regulation way, anchoring it with hair grips. Following the stream of nurses to the canteen she noticed that they *did* look smart and different when they were all massed together and began to feel that she belonged.

After breakfast Marjorie did not take long to find the ward she was to report to. It was girls ward and divided into two sections by the sluice, bathroom and lavatories.

Marjorie was first given the task of sweeping and then dusting the ward. She had always been quick and efficient, so she then went in search of someone to enquire what she should do next. Everyone looked busy. A pile of bedpans were in the sluice, all apparently emptied, but not washed. She decided to take the initiative and tidy them away.

As she was about to plunge the first one under the tap to rinse and empty it, Sister marched in and shouted at her.

"What do you think you're doing, nurse? Those bedpans have been emptied and are waiting for the rest of their contents to be tested for typhoid! If you find yourself infected, then you only have yourself to blame!" She turned on her heel and marched out.

Marjorie, who had so longed to leave home, now ironically felt herself to be terribly homesick and she leant on the sink and burst into tears of self-pity.

Later on, she was told to clean out the wash basins, shining all the taps. Then it was time to empty the steriliser, scrub that out and refill it. As soon as those tasks were done, the Staff Nurse took Marjorie into the sluice and gave her detailed instructions on how to deal with the bedpans. Afterwards she said, "Now watch what I do and I'll show you how to give a bedpan."

Staff Nurse grabbed one and ran it under the hot water tap before drying it. "Awful to have a cold thing like that to sit on." She grimaced.

Leading Marjorie up the ward, she instructed her to pull a wheeled screen round a bed. In it lay a pale young girl in her early teens who focussed them with huge dark eyes.

"Don't worry, you'll soon feel better," Staff Nurse assured her, then to Marjorie, "Watch now, Heath."

Marjorie watched as the nurse slid her hand under the girl's back and wedged the white earthenware pan under her buttocks. Immediately there was a small responding splash of urine.

"Well done!"

The Staff Nurse removed the pan, covered it with a cloth while Marjorie folded back the screens. Staff Nurse took it to the sluice where she tipped it down the shallow glazed sink, flushed it and handed it to Marjorie.

"Give it a rinse with hot water and a dash of disinfectant,

then hang it to dry. Now you know what to do for next time. Wash your hands; it's nearly lunch time!"

After lunch Marjorie was taught how to make a bed with mitred corners. She had never realised that a sheet could be inside out, and tried to catch her side of it as Staff Nurse whisked it efficiently through the air and worked wonders at whipping draw-sheets in and out. Pillows had to have their open ends away from the door. Simple things like water jugs and cutting bread and butter alternated with alien phrases like 'getting specimens' and 'gastric feeds' amongst other peculiar sounding things which would all become second nature to her.

Half way through the afternoon Marjorie was told to go to the sluice where she found Staff Nurse piling bowls, towels and soap onto a trolley. She stood by, hands hanging, overawed by all the activity.

"Come along Nurse, we've got a new admission to attend to. She must be washed and put to bed."

They put the bowls of hot water on the locker beside a bed where a small child was perched, gasping for breath.

"Screens, Nurse."

Marjorie hauled the screens round the bed and Staff Nurse started to yank the clothes off the poor confused girl. Together they washed her and clothed her in a sterile hospital gown, lifting her, smelling of carbolic onto the bed. The child was whimpering by then, "I want my mu-mummy." Marjorie's heart went out to her, but she was called away to another task.

Her feet felt as thought they were treading on hot coals as she trotted backwards and forwards with the patients' supper trays that evening. After that she was told to sweep up again. The work seemed never ending. How on earth would she get through a week of this, never mind months?

Sister grabbed her arm.

"When you've finished that, go through the linen cupboard. It needs sorting and checking."

The closeness of the cubby hole became a refuge as it shut out the hustle and bustle of the ward. Marjorie almost gave way to tears as she clumsily tried to bundle the large sheets into some semblance of order. Finally, out of sheer weariness, she just stayed leaning against the shelves in the cupboard waiting for her liberation at the end of her duty.

She was still preparing for bed when she was plunged into darkness at ten o'clock. At first Marjorie thought there must be some sort of fault, until she realised that this was institutionalised living. If she didn't put her light out by the appointed time then it would be put out for her. She scrabbled around in the dark, and as she lay in bed that night she wondered how long she could keep up nursing.

During the next few days, Marjorie staggered through the pattern of hospital life, emerging from a storm of new impressions, baffling orders and mystic phrases. Routine eventually rose up through the initial chaos.

Tidying lockers, kicking bed-wheels into line, ensuring that bedspreads were straight, almost afraid of the bodies beneath them, she was entrusted with more responsibility and given a closer liaison with the little patients, if only to give them a bedpan. Slowly the bodies beneath the bedclothes became young people – children in need of her care, and Marjorie was able to respond by giving love as well. She would help by bathing them and changing their bedclothes, occasionally helping a small child to walk some small shuffling steps, relieving its little body of some weight.

Each of the six wards had a coal fire that had to be stoked and kept alight every day during the winter months. As she was the most junior nurse, this task fell to Marjorie.

Visiting times were on Sunday afternoons only. When their parents had gone, all the children on the ward cried for their mothers and families to come back. Marjorie surprised herself by getting used to this cacophony of noise and came to regard it as part of the Sunday routine.

She would never forget one young patient, a girl called Gladys Pugh. She had a dislocated hip and was encased in a plaster cast that forced her into a somewhat bizarre frog-like position. She was meant to be on complete bed rest, but nevertheless enjoyed having the nurses chase after her when she got out of bed and somehow managed to run all over the ward. She came from a poor, run-down home and simply loved staying in hospital; so once she was discharged she would do her utmost to get back in again, once more with a dislocated hip. Everyone knew Gladys Pugh!

The next few weeks were chaotic and sometimes humiliating. Everything had to be done so speedily and Marjorie found it hard to keep up. If she slowed, uncertain of what to do next, she would receive an angry prod from a more senior nurse. If she tried to rush about like the other nurses did, someone would pull her up sharply and warn her not to run. As she worked in the sluice, the sickly smell of disinfectant filled her nostrils along with many other awful smells.

After about eight weeks the haze began to clear and Marjorie could use a thermometer, record the temperatures on a chart, make beds, wash helpless patients, and even give an enema, although she could not disguise her revulsion of this. She was also allowed to feed the children who could not feed themselves, although something was often spilt when she was feeding unwilling patients. She still felt clumsy when she compared herself to other nurses. Now, though, as she looked back to her first day there, she could see her progress for herself and she determined not to slack. She was going to be a nurse, and not only that, but a good nurse. She owed it to Aunt Margaret.

Enid Saxton had fully recovered from typhoid. On her return to duty she was put to work with Marjorie. They took an immediate liking to one another. She was so full of life, despite her recent illness, yet had a calm efficiency about her. Enid was tall and slim with a pale face and beaky nose. If it hadn't been for her gentleness and sense of humour she could have appeared somewhat severe. Her stature was the opposite to Marjorie's who was short and had a round face with rosy cheeks.

"You have a pretty face with such rosy cheeks, like a rosy apple." She told her.

"Like a Cox's Orange Pippin!" chortled someone.

Saxton nodded. "Can we call you Pip?" The name stuck.

Enid Saxton already had a nickname. Her friends called her Saxy.

Marjorie was thankful for Saxy's calm easy-going nature and capable attitude when Rosemary was found dead. She was more upset by the fact that the body was a child's. As soon as the doctor had been, Saxton took Marjorie behind the screens and showed her how to lay out a body in death. The staring eyes were closed. The corpse was undressed and the limbs were straightened. The orifices were plugged with cotton wool and the dropped jaw had a pillow propped under it to close it. The emaciated body was washed for the last time and the jaw became fixed after about half-an-hour. Having done all this Marjorie rushed straight to the sluice and vomited into the sink.

Edward was a little lad and at just five years old, he couldn't understand why he was in this awful place, feeling so ill and with no mother to comfort him. He would often cry to himself, and if a nurse passed by, she would try to divert his attention and cheer him up. One weekday his mother got through the security doors and actually came in the ward with a pile of comics for him. She was just about to embrace her son when Sister bore down on her like her steamroller. Edward screamed and tried to get out of bed and run after her, but Staff Nurse laid a restraining hand on him.

Marjorie was moved to witness the scene and fought back the tears as she went to the sluice and started to clean the trolley. Staff Nurse came in and laid a sympathetic hand on her shoulder.

"He was only a young boy," sniffed Marjorie. "Just a sick child crying for his mother. Why can't parents visit their children?"

Staff Nurse sighed and patted her shoulder comfortingly. "It's easier for us if we have complete control of a child while we are treating them. Rules are rules. Sometimes they are hard to keep."

Time seemed to speed up when there was a lot of work to be done. As the sun sank in the sky, Marjorie had sometimes nowhere near finished her work, yet she got more efficient as the weeks and months went by. She and Saxy would sometimes spend their off-duty time together, and Saxy would pass on tips which would lessen her workload a little without bring the wrath of Sister upon herself.

Aunt Margaret was very hospitable and enjoyed having Marjorie to stay for a couple of days when it was too far to travel home to Broadstone.

It was 1930 and examination time was approaching. Marjorie was feeling jittery. She was spending some free time with Aunt Margaret and studying there.

"Don't take things too seriously," said her aunt. "You have your whole life before you."

"But my whole life depends on it! I don't want to let you down after you've put so much faith in my success!"

"Now, don't be silly my dear. Should you fail, which I'm sure you won't, you can always take the exam again. It's not the end of the world! Just do your best!"

Realising that her aunt wasn't expecting perfect results helped her to put things in perspective. A few weeks later, Marjorie learned that she was a qualified State Registered Children's Nurse and left hospital that day with her head held high.

* * *

Enid Saxton was leaving Bristol. Marjorie realised how

sorry she was by her departure and how friendly they had become.

"Why not come with me?" said Enid. "It can only be good for you – promotion, I mean, by becoming a fully qualified nurse."

This was something Marjorie had not considered, certainly not for the immediate future, anyway. She wondered if her father would allow her to work in London. Being a countryman he was wary of the 'Big City' and its dubious influences. However, she had survived Bristol, so why not London?

"I may well do that," she said.

Marjorie received several encouraging letters from Enid, each one telling her what a wonderful place the Middlesex Hospital was and describing all kinds of aspects to the work. Eventually Marjorie applied there herself but was turned down because their training facilities were over-subscribed. Not to be put off at this stage, now that she had plucked up the courage to get this far, she wrote and asked to be placed on their waiting list for future consideration.

In the meantime she heard about the Infant Hospital in Westminster needing a Staff Nurse. Wanting to be near her friend, Marjorie applied for this post and secured it.

On arrival, this turned out to be a quaint building, being four storeys high, each story housing one ward of twenty children.

One child Marjorie would never forget was a very ill baby called Jennifer. She was about eighteen months old and extremely small for her age. Knowing that she was about to die apparently upset her mother so much that she couldn't face visiting her baby. By contrast, Jennifer's father came to see her every single day and sat by her cot, talking to her occasionally, his big hand always ready to hold her tiny one.

One day Marjorie was so concerned for the child that during her off-duty she telephoned the hospital to enquire about her. Sister was furious with her and informed her angrily that she should not be so involved with any patient that led her to being worried or even thinking about a patient in her own time. She regaled her about being unprofessional. Marjorie, somewhat ashamed, crept into the ward next day, relieved to discover the child still hanging onto the threads of life.

Jennifer's father asked Marjorie to go out with him soon after that. She hesitated, but then realised he needed someone to talk to, and anyway, Sister would never know. They went for a long bus ride before going to a teashop for afternoon tea. He told Marjorie he was a caterer by trade, otherwise she knew nothing about him. He just wanted to talk about Jennifer and Marjorie was his sounding board. The little girl died a few days later and she never saw him again.

Chapter Three

Along with twenty other new nurses, Marjorie started training at the Middlesex Hospital in September 1931. She was impressed by the hospital, being one of the first to live in the new nurses' home with its indoor swimming pool and tennis courts, not that she found time to use either. They worked hard for long hours and had to attend lectures in the mornings. If one had been on night-duty it was very hard to keep awake, especially when the lecturer tended to have a soporific effect on a person anyway. The most memorable times were the snatched social times with one another in each other's rooms with different nurses taking it in turns to supply tea and biscuits before lights out at ten o'clock.

Day duty ended at ten minutes before nine o'clock when everyone was supposed to go to the hospital chapel for evening prayers until nine o'clock. People would take devious routes to avoid Sister standing like a sentry to herd the nurses into the service. Their stomachs called them to better things such as being first in the queue for supper that was served on the dot of nine o'clock.

During her first year Marjorie wore a uniform of mauve stripes with long sleeves. She had a stiff collar and cuffs to button plus a huge apron with a bib that had wide shoulder straps which crossed over at the back and fastened to her waistband. The cap had been specially designed with a pleat at the back. Once she had mastered how to fold it properly, Marjorie became quite proud of her distinctive-looking headgear.

After she had been there two years, Marjorie would graduate to wearing a blue striped uniform. Staff Nurses were identified by their black belts while Sisters wore a plain blue uniform with a different style of cap.

Now she was a junior nurse again, Marjorie was given junior type jobs to do, such as cleaning the sluice, laying the patients' trays, cutting bread and butter, making beds, and everything else that wasn't really nursing. One thing she never liked doing was the 'back round'. Every four hours all the patients who were bedridden would have their backs washed thoroughly with soap and water, dried, and then surgical spirit would be rubbed in to ensure they didn't suffer from bedsores. Woe betide anyone who was discovered with a patient displaying the smallest spot on their back. Marjorie lived in dread of a more senior nurse discovering that she hadn't massaged properly, or not dried the patient sufficiently well.

It was good to be with Enid Saxton again. Marjorie made many friends during her first few years at the Middlesex, but the closest were those made at the start of her time there. She also formed bonds with other nurses as they sat next to one another in lectures. One was Ruth Saunders, a pretty, but serious girl with auburn hair who came from Sussex, and the other was Beatrice Talbot whose family lived near Bath. She was dark with a long face and a ready toothy grin, often turning quite solemn moments into a joke. The four of them were to develop a lifelong friendship, albeit a lot of it by correspondence at times.

Marjorie was never lonely. She was a popular girl and never short of company. Being loyal she always thought of her close friends first such as Enid, Ruth and Beatrice. Olive Benson was always good for a laugh and she and Marjorie would occasionally have coffee together along with Dorothy Bates, Olive's friend, who had been doing her nursing training for a year longer. The most popular meeting place was at *Lyons Corner House* for a cup of coffee and after pay-day, they would stretch to a bun or a hot buttered teacake, feeling rich indeed.

She had been there some while when she was transferred to the Private Sector. Marjorie felt rather lost as everyone else seemed to know where they were going.

Then Saxy grabbed her arm. "I think you're on the private wards with me. Come on."

The bells were a hazard there. Some patients would

ring by mistake, others wanted something they had dropped picked up from he floor, someone else would want to chat, not realising how much the nurse had to do beyond their little room. Even just entering the room of a private patient, nurses felt that they could not just do what they needed to do and then leave. These patients were fee paying, so they felt entitled to discuss the latest news, or a family grievance. It was difficult not to edge nearer the door when there was so much more to do.

Sometimes these patients would pass on gifts they had been given and did not want. One memorable time a patient gave Enid Saxton a whole fruit cake which she generously shared with the other nurses.

Marjorie was grateful that they all had a name on their door so that remembering who they were was one less thing to worry about. It also meant that their symptoms could be studied out of sight, meaning she could breeze into the room.

"Good morning Mrs Ramsey, how is your chest today?"

This hopefully added to the patient's confidence in her nursing skills, despite the fact that she was starting all over again. She was glad of her experience at Bristol. Children had confidence in her just because she had been their senior to start with. Now she had some nursing experience to bring here and Marjorie knew she was going to enjoy her stay at the Middlesex.

Just as he had done when she was working at Bristol, so her father ensured that Marjorie would continue to attend chapel whenever she could by giving her the address of a suitable place of worship and also writing to ask the minister there to make her welcome. Marjorie felt obliged to attend if only to ensure a favourable report of her.

Marjorie had been at the Middlesex for some months, but the minister whom Walter had contacted must have decided that she was young, naïve and fair game for his affections, despite the fact that he was already married. His wife was often very involved with parochial affairs and presumably did not give enough time for him. She often took the Girl Guides away to camp and frequented ladies' meetings. These were the times when the Reverend Sullivan took the opportunity to wine and dine Marjorie.

The first time she was invited for a meal, she naturally assumed it would be round the Rectory table in the company of Mrs Sullivan. However when Marjorie arrived, Reverend Sullivan shook her hand and took the opportunity to draw her close to him.

Marjorie froze.

"Don't worry, pet. Nothing will happen to you."

"A-aren't you going to introduce me to your wife?" Marjorie spluttered the first thing that came into her head, even though she had often met Mrs Sullivan in chapel.

"She's not here, my dear. She had to go to another of her women's meetings – so come on, we'll dine out in town. You must call me Jack."

He summoned a taxi, and they sat in the back. Marjorie left a gap between them, watching the mannequins in the shop windows under their spotlights in the store windows. She saw the tiers of windows in the houses and flats and wondered about the lives behind them, and of her own, and the rights and wrongs of what she was doing.

At first the restaurant posed something of a threat with its crisp white tablecloths and faded décor. It was almost full of people – obviously a crowd waiting for them to get lost in.

"I'll order for you, if you like," he offered. After studying a large menu he spoke in French to the waiter. Marjorie was suitably impressed.

"I was over in France in 1918 at the end of the war. I can only just about remember how to order food now." He laughed and his eyes twinkled at her.

The high quality and difference of French cuisine stunned Marjorie. She tried not to appear too hungry. The thick wedges of garnished steak melted in her mouth and the accompanying sauce was perfect. A waiter came to their table, gave a little bow and held out a little wicker basket that cradled a bottle of wine with its neck wrapped in a white napkin. Jack Sullivan tasted the drop that was poured into his glass and nodded his approval. For dessert they had profiteroles. Marjorie had never tasted such light choux pastry oozing with cream and smothered with rich dark chocolate. She chased the final fragments round her plate and sighed with guilty pleasure.

She smiled "Thank you so much. That was delicious." Taking a deep breath she added, "I'm sorry if I'm spoiling your evening, but I must be back at the hospital before the curfew at ten o'clock." Unsure of his intentions she was glad of an excuse to make a hasty exit.

He paid the bill, hailed a taxi and courteously ushered Marjorie into it, thrusting some money into the driver's hand to cover the fare. As they pulled away from the kerb, Marjorie leaned back into the worn leather seat, confused.

Jack Sullivan took Marjorie out for several meals, all at different restaurants. He said he intended to look after her and introduce her to London. Marjorie didn't know what to do for the best. The outings seemed innocent enough on the surface, but she felt guilty about each one. If she were to stop attending chapel, or even transfer to another, she was sure the situation would get to her father's ears and cause trouble. He may even stop her from nursing.

To her relief, Mrs Sullivan saw her after a chapel service one Sunday. "You must come and have a meal with us sometime." She suggested a day. At least this invitation would be all right.

Marjorie went to the Sullivans' home believing she would be dining with both husband and wife. To her horror, Jack Sullivan was alone. This time his wife had been called away to counsel a depressed young mother.

He looked at her closely before stepping towards her and holding her against him. He liked Marjorie. He was used to her now. She didn't nag him. She was good-humoured and predictable, which calmed him. He smoothed her hair with one hand. She squirmed.

"Come and make yourself at home," he said, leading her towards the sofa.

Marjorie twisted out of his grasp and sat on the edge of a chair, trying think up an excuse to leave early while Jack Sullivan was in the kitchen making coffee for them both.

"My wife sends her apologies," he called from the kitchen. "She's left a casserole in the oven."

"Mr Sullivan, I ..."

"Call me Jack," he interrupted, coming to sit on the arm of her chair. "Now what were you about to say?"

She leaned away from him as her mind groped for a suitable reply.

"Er, just that I don't think I shall be able to come to church for the next few Sundays as my duties have been changed round."

He bridled. "Well then, we shall have to see more of you during the week then, won't we, so that I can write a favourable report to your father."

His arm slid round her. Marjorie wriggled. She knew she was trapped.

"I think I ought to be going."

"Come, come my dear, you've only just arrived!"

"I – I have to be up very early in the morning."

To Marjorie's immense relief the doorbell rang at this point. Jack Sullivan went to answer it and she grabbed her coat. He was deep in conversation on the doorstep.

She slipped quickly past him saying, "Thank you, see you one Sunday. Goodnight!"

She walked blindly into the lighted street, unaware of where she was going, so was surprised and relieved to find herself outside the hospital again.

Such an awkward situation. This was like blackmail. She decided never to go to the Rectory again. If she did receive another invitation she would take Saxy or another friend with her. It would save her embarrassment and surely a minister couldn't refuse the possibility of another soul to add to his congregation.

Then, one evening, Jack saw her in her off-duty time as

she was out for a walk.

"Well, if it's not my little nurse from the country!"

Marjorie bared her teeth in a reluctant smile.

"Would you like to accompany me?" he asked, offering his arm.

"Well, actually, I was on my way to meet some friends."

"Fine, then I will come with you. We can't have young girls wandering about on their own all over London. Your father would never forgive me if he knew."

Marjorie bit back the obvious reply with a sinking heart. How was she going to get rid of this man without getting them both into trouble in more ways than one?

* * *

Marjorie had been at the Middlesex hospital for just three months when she learned of the Annual Grand Ball due to take place at Christmas. This was exactly as described – grand.

Full evening dress was to be worn by all and everyone seemed to have a suitable dress except Marjorie. She saved from her meagre salary and then went to the market where she found some inexpensive satin fabric in a pretty shade of green. When she next went home to Dorset she spent most of her time there sewing and making up her ball gown. Marjorie was pleased with her efforts and especially when she discovered there was enough fabric to make a little Dorothy bag to match.

"Pip, you'll outdo us all in that dress!"

"That looks amazing!"

"You *made* your own dress? How clever you are!"

"You'll be the belle of the ball!" were just some of the comments made by her friends.

They were used to this kind of occasion but Marjorie wasn't. As they admired her efforts, so her confidence grew.

Marjorie noticed the sun sinking in the glory of a red

and gold sky towards the end of that day. The evening promised to be perfect in more ways than one.

As she changed into her dress a tingle ran down her back when she caught sight of herself in the mirror. She had developed into a pretty and attractive young woman. She kept her dark hair in a short manageable bob that curled prettily around her jawline. Her round face made her look younger than her years, and her hazel eyes always looked vividly sparkling with life. Tonight they were enhanced by the green dress.

She had never worn make-up before but Beatrice and Ruth persuaded her to use some of theirs. She dabbed on a little rouge and gave her lips a smear of lipstick which served to brighten her face to just the right degree.

There was a knock at the door.

"Come in!"

"Marjorie, you look superb!" admired Beatrice.

"Just wonderful," agreed Ruth. "But have you got a necklace? That would set everything off nicely."

"I've got a cross and chain."

"No, you need something more than that," Enid chimed in. "Come on girls, let's see what we can find."

Ruth remembered she had a necklace with green stones and they went to examine it.

"I'm sorry it's not the real thing," she apologised. "Just green glass really, but it does match your dress very well."

"Tones in beautifully," agreed Beatrice.

They all nodded their approval, then began to hustle along the corridor.

"Come along, we ought to be getting a move on now."

As the ladies entered the large room they were each given a little tasselled card so that the men could book their dances in advance. Marjorie was surprised to find that her card filled up remarkably quickly; she could have easily had almost twice the number of names had there been enough dances.

Matron arrived to make sure everyone was behaving themselves. All in all it was a very regal affair and much enjoyed. Marjorie was thrilled to discover the new experiences of lavish food, sniffing the blend of the ladies' perfumes, gliding round the floor in time to a live band, seeing the way all the different colours twirled around the floor, the gentlemen looking very dashing in their white tie and tails. Above all she was amazed at how different everyone looked out of their usual uniform. Dragons of Sisters looked surprisingly human, even feminine.

Marjorie glided round the room in the arms of several different doctors and medical students before Dr Timothy Powell bore down on her.

"Ah, there you are. I believe I am entitled to claim you for the next dance, fair maiden."

Marjorie pretended to be coy as she consulted her card. "Yes, I believe this dance has been reserved for you, kind sir."

Timothy clasped her firmly round the waist, waiting for the band to strike up again; then he spun her into the sea of dancers, a rainbow of colours whirling against the bandstand.

"May I tell you how beautiful you look tonight?"

She had never been told that she looked beautiful before. Fortunately she caught his flirting mood before she'd blushed with embarrassment.

"Yes you may!"

"You're looking beautiful tonight," he declared as they careered round, negotiating a spin turn almost crashing into Ruth as she danced with a second-year medical student.

All too soon the dance ended and it was time to sample the sumptuous supper. Marjorie tried to taste a tiny bit of everything on offer, as a lot of the food was new to her.

Timothy had booked her to dance immediately after the buffet and again at the end of the evening.

The Annual Ball passed by all too quickly. She only caught glimpses of Enid, Beatrice and Ruth; they were all popular people. All too soon Marjorie was in Timothy's arms once again ready for the last waltz together. It was almost midnight. They stood very close, hands clasped, one of Timothy's arms about her waist, Marjorie's hand on his shoulder, waiting for the music to begin. Then she raised her head to look at him and gasped at what she saw. If at any time during this evening she had convinced herself that the attraction she felt for Timothy was not returned, her doubts were dispelled in that moment by the look of tenderness she saw in his eyes. Before he could disguise it with joviality she saw the deep longing he had for her.

Time stood still for them as they stood silent in the midst of the hubbub around them. Somewhat embarrassed, Marjorie broke away.

As the dance started, Marjorie said, "Thank goodness I'm not on duty until late tomorrow." The spell was broken.

"How can you be so mercenary, thinking of work in this setting?" Timothy remonstrated.

"Sorry, I'm a realist."

"I'm a romantic; we're the two Rs."

The music slowed to the last couple of bars and then the lengthy final chord echoed around the room. Timothy held on to her hand as everyone stood straight and still while the National Anthem was played before drifting off to their quarters after Matron had thanked people who needed to be acknowledged and urged them to be off to bed in order to get as much sleep as possible.

"That brings us back to earth with a bump!" moaned Beatrice.

"I don't feel at all like sleep."

"I feel more awake now than when I'm on nights!"

Marjorie wished Timothy goodnight, whereupon he made a princely bow as the four friends linked arms and headed off towards the Nurses' Home.

Men's surgical was the ward Marjorie enjoyed the most, partly because Sister there was kind and patient, and partly because the men themselves were generally so cheerful.

She began to gain more confidence and to believe she would make a good nurse after all. The lectures she had attended at the beginning of her time at the Middlesex all began to make sense now, and became not such a lesson to be learned, but more a way of life.

There was always some thing going on here. As well as surgical cases, there were casualties from factory or road accidents. Most days would bring someone new on the ward. It was hard work, but all worthwhile.

One man could not swallow after an operation on his throat. Marjorie was shown how to oil rubber tubing and poke it up his nostril then ease it down into his stomach. A glass funnel was attached, then liquid food of beaten eggs and milk were poured in until he was fed. Nursing began to be fascinating now.

Soon after this, Marjorie was told she was being transferred to night duty. On the day prior to her first night on the ward she was sent to the nurses' home at noon so that she could get some sleep. She hardly slept that afternoon and her first night passed in a haze of exhaustion. She longed for the morning when she staggered, almost drunk with tiredness into her bed and slept soundly.

She soon got used to living the upside-down life after a few days. Supper in the morning and breakfast in the evening began to feel normal.

Chapter Four

Marjorie had been at the Middlesex for just over a year when she was transferred to the Biochemistry Department. This meant the luxury of regular hours from nine to five. She was also attracted to Dr Timothy Powell whom she had met at the ball. They worked together for a fortnight before he asked her out. Marjorie was thrilled and sorted through her meagre wardrobe, wondering what she should wear.

Timothy Powell always had an eye for a pretty girl. He and his pal Stuart were known throughout the hospital as being lads about town, never having a serious relationship and leaving a trail of broken hearts behind them. Neither could really help themselves. Both were good looking and had charismatic personalities that attracted people, especially women, like iron filings to a magnet.

When Marjorie joined the Biochemistry Department Timothy was fascinated by her devotion to work and lack of attention to the frivolities of life. He was determined to get to know her better. The very way she seemed to distance herself from him heightened his awareness of her.

He was surprised by her nervous reaction when he eventually asked her to go out with him. She reacted like a shy schoolgirl on a first date. Instinctively Timothy felt protective towards her. If he and Stuart had been together they would have goaded one another on until they had a story of some sort with intimate details to hint at to the other next day. He was amazed that his feelings for Marjorie already went a lot deeper than that. Here was a girl who was beyond sniggering in doorways and cheap cuddles in the back of a car. She trusted him and he in turn must be trustworthy. He felt proud of this new responsibility thrust upon him.

The evening came when Timothy and Marjorie had their first date. It was darkening outside, a spring dusk that was overtaken by the lights of London. They met in the appointed place. He took her to the theatre. The auditorium was almost full. Marjorie glanced up at the ornamental plasterwork around the blue velvet draped boxes. There were many nodding faces all round them. She stared ahead at the two huge blue velvet curtains that would surely part at any moment. Timothy saw her looking round and felt for her hand, squeezing it to reassure her.

Then, without warning, the house lights dimmed and silence fell. The fringed edging on the velvet folds of curtain swept majestically back to reveal the set. The play began and Marjorie was transfixed. So taken was she by all that happened that tears were running down her face by the end. There was a short mercifully dark few moments before the lights came on again.

The applause increased and the audience continued to clap. Eventually everyone stood as the National Anthem crackled through a speaker. Then the curtains came together one last time before the audience reluctantly took their leave.

"Thank you so much. I really enjoyed that. It was very good." Marjorie felt her comments were lame after such an outstanding performance.

"Yes, it was good. I hadn't realised how brilliant until now."

He took her to eat at a small, noisy, but fashionable place. Marjorie was tired but she tried to be lively for Timothy's sake. He watched her face in the candlelight seeing the darkness in her eyes and placed his hand gently over hers. They laughed a lot over their meal and later joined some mutual friends for coffee. They were also from the hospital and had been dining a few tables away. Marjorie recognised Stuart Percival, the comic of the Biochemistry Department, together with his current girlfriend, Sheila. There was a lot of banter and laughter between them. Marjorie sighed happily. It had been an excellent evening.

Glancing at the clock, her face changed to one of horror

when she saw how late it was. Now she was faced with the problem of getting into the Nurses Home after ten o'clock, and made to leave.

"Oh no! I should have been back by ten o'clock. It's way past that."

Sheila waved her hand airily. "Don't worry. My friend always makes sure there's a window open to a ground floor bathroom."

Sheila and Marjorie left then and made their way back to the nurses' home. Sheila led the way round the back of the building. With a lot of shushing and giggling, both girls were soon safely inside and nobody else was any the wiser. Marjorie occasionally used this route at other times if she were out after curfew.

Timothy and Marjorie saw each other regularly after that. He also became a saving grace from Jack Sullivan. She and Timothy went to chapel together sometimes, so to Marjorie's relief, the Rector left her alone.

Timothy was very generous to her. Marjorie once admired a dress in a shop window.

"Three pounds!" she had exclaimed. "Imagine paying that much for a dress!"

"Go in and try it on," Timothy had urged her.

"Good gracious no! I couldn't possibly afford it. That's more than my monthly salary."

"Don't argue, just try it on for fun," he suggested

The shop assistant had removed the froth of pale pink chiffon from the window display and Marjorie had meekly gone into a cubicle to try it on. To her surprise the dress fitted perfectly.

"How are you getting on Madam?" asked the shop assistant.

Marjorie stepped outside the cubicle.

"Give us a twirl then."

She did so.

"You look amazing! It must have been made for you." Timothy said to Marjorie, then to the shop assistant, "Thanks, we'll take it."

Marjorie gasped, then stepped back in the cubicle to get dressed.

"Oh Tim, you shouldn't have done that. Thank you so much," she said gratefully when they were outside the shop.

"Nothing is too much for you," he smiled down at her, kissing the top of her head. "Now don't say you have nothing to wear at the next Middlesex Ball! Not long now."

It was a sunny autumn morning when Marjorie read in its slanting golden light that she was to be transferred to Theatre work. She was prepared to enjoy the excitement and drama there, but she had not reckoned on being in the sluice and dealing with all the gowns and towels that threatened to bury her as time went on. Bowls containing bodily parts would be brought in on their way down to the Laboratory for testing. She also had to sterilise all the surgical instruments, ensuring that the sterilisers themselves were scrupulously clean.

As the weeks dragged by, Marjorie decided that this was the work she hated most. The Theatre Sister had a quick temper and commanded such exactness and speed from everyone that Marjorie was terrified of her from the start of her time there, understanding it was possible to do more wrong things here than anywhere else in the hospital. Sister would bark out an order from behind her mask and Marjorie was never sure which was the worst crime; to ask her to repeat what she said, or to trot briskly away and return with what may well be the wrong item.

Operations were enthralling, each one a scientific drama. Marjorie was amazed at how much the human body could stand. She was prepared to be squeamish about things at first, but discovered that by standing close enough to see what was going on, interest would overcome nausea. Nevertheless, although able to handle inner bodily parts when necessary, she was to discover that familiar sights, such as an amputated toe or finger, once separate from the body, would cause her to faint, thus bringing more disgrace upon herself from the stern Theatre Sister.

Marjorie and Timothy began to see quite a lot of one other. Even when she was transferred back to ward work they saw one another when they could, although it was difficult when their hours were not the same.

One evening they were walking companionably along the Embankment. A wispy mist hung round the light from the Victorian styled street lamps. They stopped and leaned side by side on the cold smooth stone wall and looked out over the River Thames. Below them its depths seemed very dark, almost black. However in midstream and on the opposite bank, the surface rippled with reflected lights looking like shimmering jewels on black velvet.

A riverboat plunged through on its way up river, scattering and distorting the reflections as it passed. Another boat chugged by, but it passed them unnoticed.

Timothy took Marjorie in his arms and studied each of her features in turn as if he wanted to ensure they were imprinted on his memory for ever.

"I love you," he said with meaning.

Marjorie blinked. *Did I hear right?*

"Let's get married," he said simply.

Marjorie sighed and leaned against him. She needed no time to think over her reply.

"Yes," she said breathlessly, looking up at him. "Let's!"

A boat swept by, its bows slicing through the water. The traffic bowled over the bridges on either side of them, the lights on the buses seeming so different and bright compared to the river's murky depths beneath.

They kissed to seal their agreement.

The next day was Sunday. Timothy had driven Marjorie to Epping Forest in his battered old Ford car. They followed well-worn paths between the trees and crossed a wide grassy space by a lake fringed with reeds. He took her hand and held it there as they sat on a log talking in low voices. They watched the coots and moorhens as they trailed ever-widening ripples behind them across the water. There seemed to be so many important things to discuss, yet they couldn't bring themselves to, contenting themselves with chat about things of no real consequence, leaving the rest to find its own time.

When at last it was too cool to stay still, Timothy put his arm around Marjorie and they meandered back to the car.

"We'll have to keep our engagement unofficial and secret to the time being," he said as their time together came to an end. "After all, your State Finals are only a few months away and you are going to need all your energy and concentration to study for them."

She smiled. "Not only that, but Matron wouldn't hear of such a thing."

"Once your Finals are behind you, we can make it public."

"Don't you realise, Tim that a nurse may not be married? She is either married to her husband or her profession!"

"Surely getting engaged will be OK?"

"Yes, but if that happens before my Finals the Hospital will realise they won't be getting much work out of me afterwards and I shall have to leave immediately."

"Really? That seems such a waste when you've had so much training."

"You'd think so. Still it's the hospital's loss, then."

"Their loss is my gain."

Marjorie raised her face to receive his kiss, looked up at him and smiled. She felt that her dreams were coming true.

Six weeks after later, their off-duty weekends coincided, and they both thought it best if Timothy was introduced to Marjorie's father and stepmother.

As the train puffed out of Waterloo Station, Marjorie was surprised by the feelings that chased around inside her head. She was so thrilled about Timothy, yet also fearful of the impression her family might give. She prayed that everything would be exactly right and that everyone would like one another. She glanced out of the window as they left the filthy smoke-covered terraced houses behind and the scenery gave way to a scrubby grey wintry landscape further south.

Timothy took her hand in his. "Don't worry old thing, I'll be on my best behaviour!"

"It's not so much *your* behaviour I'm concerned about, it's my family's."

"Oh, I'm sure they're wonderful really. It's just that they don't always seem that way when you live amongst them."

How understanding he is! She threw him a grateful glance.

"I'm sure you'll like my father. He's a wonderful man and he's always worked so hard." She presented as many positive points as she could, more for her own peace of mind than Timothy's.

The meeting with her family could not have gone more smoothly. Everyone seemed to mind their manners and seemed impressed with 'Marjorie's Young Man' as her stepmother referred to him. "A young doctor, eh? Fancy that!"

They all attended chapel together on the Sunday morning and Marjorie took Timothy for a walk on the heath after lunch.

"You certainly live in a beautiful part of the country," he remarked.

"It's beautiful, yes, but you've only seen a tiny bit of it this weekend."

They stood on a high point of the heath with a carpet that had, until recently been covered in purple heather. Away to their left stood a mass of whispering pine trees standing upright like an army of soldiers silhouetted against the pale blue sky. Through a haze of happiness Marjorie realised that the weekend had gone well. Her family had accepted Timothy. Words were almost unnecessary.

He kissed her. She closed her eyes and savoured it.

When they got back to the house there was just time to pack and say their goodbyes before catching the return train to London. Bettie and Jessie sat on the bed urging Marjorie to tell them more about Timothy as she collected her things together. Until then, she had wanted to keep everything of him to herself, but now she was so elated the story spilled out of her without much prompting. Her sister and half-sister clasped their hands together and their eyes shone with glee.

"So are you really engaged?" asked Jessie in awe.

"It seems like a fairy tale," breathed Bettie.

"How romantic!" sighed Jessie.

"Now forget what I've told you," Marjorie warned them. "It's top secret until *we* choose to release the news, so don't you dare tell a soul, not even down in faraway Dorset!"

"We won't." They solemnly shook their head, then simultaneously licked their forefinger and drew it across their throat as a reminder of their childish pledge. Marjorie was both amused and assured of their promise.

Hilda gave them a packed tea to eat on the train and they insisted they could walk the short distance to the station on their own, refusing offers to escort them. As she stepped outside Marjorie became aware of how cold it had become. Overhead the sky was the colour of pearl and to the west the bright red ball of a sun sank in a pale pink sea.

She stopped daydreaming.

"Come on!" Timothy was making some last minute farewells when Marjorie took him firmly by his arm. "We'll miss the train!"

They leaned into one another on the way to the station then waited on the station propping one another up like bicycles, each gaining warmth from the other. Once seated in the carriage, they shared their sandwiches. Later, so relaxed was she that Marjorie was not sure if she dozed off or was merely comforted by the sound of the carriage as it rattled over the rails. Then Timothy's arm went round her and she slept.

Timothy opened the letter carelessly. He thought he recognised the handwriting, but could not be sure. Receiving letters from past girlfriends had often happened. As he read the neat copperplate script, he sank into the nearest chair as the news hit him like a battering ram. Surely not! He couldn't believe this!

He frowned. Claire had written to tell him that she was pregnant. Timothy rubbed his furrowed brow as if to erase the news he had just received. What to do now? He couldn't just abandon her. He didn't have enough money to buy her off. There was sure to be a scandal. The words stood out from the page as if to shout at him. *You are the father.*

She reckoned to be over six months gone, but goodness only knows why she hadn't made contact before now. He did some mental arithmetic. The timing could be about right. As his energy returned he began to pace up and down the room, grinding his fist into his forehead. It was then that Stuart found him.

"You look awful, old boy. Have a drink."

"I've just had some rather upsetting news, actually."

Stuart's expression softened as he led Timothy to a chair.

"I-I've just had a letter from Claire. She's p-pregnant; or so she says. Apparently I-I'm the father."

"Oh lord, I see what you mean. Can you sort out an abortion?"

"How can you even suggest that? You're a trained doctor, trained to save lives not do away with them! If anyone found out I'd be struck off!"

Stuart took a step backwards. "All right just a suggestion. Calm down and be rational."

"Anyway she's six months gone." Timothy was near tears.

"God, she's left it long enough before telling you. Are you sure it's yours?"

"W-well, it m-might be."

"There was this other bloke after you."

"If she really is six months pregnant then although we were only actually had sex twice, then that baby could be mine," said Timothy miserably.

"On the other hand, if her other bloke ditched her when he heard the news, she may well be wanting anyone to make an honest woman of her." Stuart tried to raise Timothy's hopes then patted his shoulder.

"Look, I'll scout round and make a few enquiries. Hold on, don't do anything and I'll see what I can find out."

Stuart returned after lunch.

"I can't find out any more than what you've already told me."

"But what shall I do now?"

"Suppose you'd better marry the girl. Stand by her. Make an honest woman of her."

Timothy hesitated, thinking of Marjorie. Stuart saw his uncertainty and urged him.

"Well, we can't be bachelors gay for ever, can we? Sooner or later we'll all take the plunge!"

Timothy gulped, on the point of explaining about his relationship with Marjorie, but thought better of it as Stuart had never had a serious romance with anyone and he wouldn't understand. Besides, it was something too precious to be laid bare and risk his scathing remarks.

He sighed and knew he was going to think hard about his final decision, as somebody was likely to be badly hurt by it.

The day of the State Finals dawned. Marjorie looked out of the window at the surrounding buildings bathed in a thin murky sunlight. So many probationary nurses had been rushing around saying things like "I'll never pass."

Now that time had come, some realised with horror that those lightly spoken words might well be true.

As Marjorie walked towards the examination room she tried to quell the fluttering butterflies in her stomach. Stuart Percival passed by.

"Wish me luck!" he called airily. "I'm off to be a best man."

Marjorie laughed. "I should have thought the groom deserved those sentiments, especially with *you* as best man."

"Precisely." Stuart grinned. "I hope I don't loose the ring – or the groom come to that! Hey!" he added as an afterthought. "You'll know him, won't you – remember Timothy Powell in the Biochemistry Department?"

Marjorie felt the walls beginning to spin round her and leaned heavily against one to keep her upright.

"Timothy Powell is getting married?" she checked in a tight little voice.

"Yes, it doesn't seem possible, does it? Kept himself to himself lately, but before that I always thought he was a confirmed bachelor. Well, mustn't be late. Tootle-pip!"

He left her slack-jawed as the implication of what he had said dawned on her. Marjorie buckled beneath her sorrow. She shut her eyes against the sunshine streaming in through a nearby window and heard a motley of cheeky sparrows squabbling in the branches of a nearby tree. When had she last seen Timothy? It had been two weeks since their off-duty times had allowed them to be together, although they had snatched coffee together in the canteen since then, all the while playing down their relationship for the time being to enable her to study.

She heard the rumble of traffic in the street below and wondered how the world could go about its business, so cruelly indifferent, when the bottom of her own world had just dropped away.

Nurses hurrying along the corridor brought her to her senses. She felt a touch on her arm. It was Beatrice and Ruth.

"No time to daydream today!" Ruth indicated the exam room at the end of the corridor.

"The rest of our lives depend on these next few hours!" added Beatrice dramatically.

Marjorie could not hold back the tears any longer. They spilled down her cheeks as tried to contain her sobs.

"Oh I'm sorry, is it something I said?"

Marjorie shook her head and bravely tried to explain the situation through her emotion. Her friends exchanged glances and looked horror-struck by the news.

"Oh Marjorie, how awful!"

"My dear, I'm so sorry!"

"Couldn't be a worse time for you to hear that."

Both Timothy and Stuart only have thought for themselves – I'm sorry Marjorie, but they do, and this proves it."

"But Timothy and I – we weren't just going out – we were secretly engaged. He was going to buy me a ring when I passed my Finals to celebrate."

Ruth tried to be practical.

"Look Marjorie, you have my full sympathy, but there just isn't time to express it now." She took her arm and steered her towards the examination room.

"Just be thankful that you didn't marry him and discover the sort of bounder he is afterwards. Now, go to the nearest washbasin and splash water on your face before coming in – there's just time. Oh, and good luck, Pip!"

She squeezed Marjorie's shoulder and was gone along with Beatrice, leaving her to follow her advice.

Marjorie made her way blindly to the examination room and sat down heavily in the appointed place. When the paper was produced she stared unseeingly at it for quite five minutes before making any attempt to read it, let alone tackle any of the questions. She struggled to concentrate and bring her thoughts under control. By the end of the day her mind was in a daze. She was sure she had failed.

On her final release from the room, exam completed, Marjorie felt a tight pressure round her chest like a tight band. Something was threatening to burst out of her. She felt a weird, wild gaiety and laughed rather too loudly, saying to nobody in particular,

"I want to go out and have some fun!"

As she increased her pace she felt as though her feet might have lost contact with the ground. She was about to break into a run when a heavy hand clamped itself onto her shoulder as a Sister brought her to a halt.

"Nurse!" she bellowed. "You should know by now that a nurse should never run in any circumstances! What is your business?"

Marjorie looked shamefacedly at the floor. "I've just taken my State Finals. Sorry Sister."

The senior nurse's mood relaxed as she smiled. "I understand your need to let off steam, but kindly do it *outside* the hospital." She walked on.

Marjorie sighed and shook her head. "She doesn't understand. Nobody understands."

She went to her room and slumped miserably on the bed, watching the heavy iron-grey clouds build up as the wind blew them across a darkening sky. Even the weather seemed to match her mood. The rain began to fall in large teardrops against the window, each leaving a colourless globule to drizzle down the glass. The shower eased off and Marjorie left the room, determined to leave the hospital complex.

Outside the weather had worsened again. The temperature had dropped and as the rain began again, the wind drove heavy gusts of it into her face like handfuls of needles. It could have been a winter's day.

Inevitably, like an automaton, her route to nowhere took her past *Lyons Corner House*.

Her arm was grabbed in a vice-like grip. It was Ruth. "Come and join us! We're celebrating the end of exams."

"Oh no, no I couldn't," protested Marjorie.

"Don't be silly. Drown your sorrows in a cup of coffee."

"No really, I …" Marjorie tried to wriggle free.

"I'm holding on to you until you agree, and in this

weather it's not nice for either of us!"

The rain beat against the coffee shop window making a bleak and lonely sound. Beyond it was welcoming warmth.

Marjorie concurred. "Oh, all right then."

Ruth promptly dragged her inside and reluctantly Marjorie joined a large number of her set all giggling round a table full of coffee cups. She approached them with a fixed smile pinned on her face and a heart like lead. Dragging a chair from another table she sat between Beatrice and Ruth.

Several weeks later Marjorie was amazed to discover that she had passed her exams and was now a qualified State Registered Nurse. At least she had achieved something, and it took away something of the sting of being jilted by Timothy although she did sometimes catch herself glancing reflectively at her own left hand.

Now she was a qualified SRN Marjorie wanted to take her nursing qualifications further. She decided to include Midwifery in her achievements. This training would have to be paid for, so she applied to be a private nurse under the umbrella of the Middlesex Hospital.

Chapter Five

When nursing private patients, Marjorie would generally nurse patients within the hospital complex, although she could be sent to their homes. She met so many people in differing situations. She became familiar with those who were dying yet wanted to spend their last few days in their own home surrounded by the people and possessions they knew and loved. Then at the other end of the scale were those extremely rich people who summoned a nurse and took to their bed as soon as they had a sore throat.

Her first payment from the private sector came after she'd been sent to a boys' public school where a flu epidemic was raging. She and Beatrice were both sent there to assist the overworked Matron, as almost half the school were sweating it out in the Sanatorium, all in various stages of the illness. However, by the time Marjorie and Beatrice arrived, the worst appeared to be over and they had only been there for three days when Matron sent them off to the cinema one evening.

They stayed at the school for a fortnight, and the number of boys in the sick bay slowly diminished. Matron was extremely grateful for their help, but the two friends did not feel they had been overworked. Coming to such an establishment had shown the newly qualified nurses how the children of the upper classes lived in their expensive school with its old, but nonetheless beautiful surroundings. Despite this, the school was renowned for strict discipline and a chill atmosphere leaked into the corridors that could have been due to a lack of heating.

Marjorie was glad to return to the warmth of the hospital even though she had to nurse a seventy-year-old patient who was already suffering with cancer before she had a stroke, necessitating urgent admission to hospital. Mrs Roper was very confused about her surroundings and who Marjorie was. Keeping her confined to bed was a major task as, despite her paralysis, Mrs Roper insisted she should be up and about so was frequently found to be wrestling with the cot sides of the bed. It was only about ten days after being admitted that she suffered another stroke and died as a result of it.

It was 18th January 1936 and the country was in mourning for its king, George the Fifth who had died that day. People were wearing black armbands. Flags were flying at half-mast. Life had slowed to a respectful pace as England's citizens lamented.

However at the Middlesex Hospital a quiet panic was spreading as the Union Jack could not be found to fly at half-mast in honour of the late sovereign. Eventually it was discovered in the hospital chapel, draped over the coffin of the eminent story-teller, Rudyard Kipling, who had died earlier the same day in a private ward near to the ones where Marjorie had worked only hours before. The honour given him was only short-lived but at least he had been considered distinguished enough to lie under the national flag, if only briefly, before his monarch took precedence.

Marjorie's next patient was also in the hospital. She was a spinster of 58 who had fallen and fractured her femur. Her leg was encased in a Balken's frame and extension for several weeks before showing any significant sign of improvement. Marjorie enjoyed her company. She was a sweet lady who was afraid of being too much trouble, forgetting that she was paying Marjorie to care for her. She would often give Marjorie little gifts, mostly things that visitors had brought in for her.

"But I can't take this," Marjorie would protest. "Your visitor wouldn't like to think you were giving your gift away to someone else."

Miss Tanner would draw her eyebrows together and jut out her chin to ask, "Well, who's going to tell them? I'm not. If anyone tells, it will be you!"

Marjorie was duly silenced.

Another of her private patients was Edith Tindall. This lady was not a good patient. She had always been blessed with a lot of money that she had used to buy just about everything she wanted throughout her life. Unfortunately, although she had her own private nurse in Marjorie, her money was not buying her the good health she valued. The wasting muscular disease from which she suffered had progressed to a stage where she could no longer walk, even with assistance. She sat in a wheelchair when she was out of bed with a rug tucked round her knees. She looked a lot older than her 64 years.

"I don't like this," she complained when Marjorie had been there a few days.

"I know." Ignoring the rules, Marjorie knew she had to demonstrate her care for this crusty old lady and she held her head, cradling it to her. She looked down and saw the thin strands of grey hair revealing the scalp beneath.

Mrs Tindall had hated hospital so much that she was prepared to pay for a private nurse. Her flesh felt papery as if it would just flake away. Mrs Tindall refused to face up to illness and would simply talk about getting old. She survived longer than the doctors had predicted. Marjorie found those six weeks very trying.

Her next case was nursing a middle-aged gentleman in his own home. He was suffering from a gastric ulcer. He was painfully thin with a long drawn face and a prominent nose. His wife was quite the opposite in every way, being plump and cheerful, and was no doubt preparing foods for him that aggravated his complaint.

So it was that Marjorie found herself to be something of a cook as she ordered food for Mr Atkinson that was apparently quite alien to anything he had eaten before. He and his wife had previously indulged in full cooked breakfasts and all sorts of things he should not have eaten because of his condition. The Cook-General who worked for them took a great dislike to Marjorie at first, complaining that nobody had ever objected to her cooking before. When it was eventually explained to her that Mr Atkinson needed a special diet to help his stomach complaint, and possibly avoid an operation, she became sweetness itself and went out of her way to assist. At first she would cook husband and wife separate meals but then Mrs Atkinson decided that her husband's diet looked a healthy one, so as she ate similar things, she began to lose weight much to her delight. Marjorie was proud when Mr Atkinson's ulcer had been cured by a combination of diet and medication, thus avoiding surgery. She left, them, urging the family to continue with the same recipes. Mr Atkinson's face managed to split into a cheerful smile.

* * *

The wedding had been hurriedly arranged. Claire had borrowed a dress from a friend and a weekday was chosen for the wedding when the register office was not so busy with other ceremonies. Her parents, once the initial shock was over, were pleased about the match and offered the couple the use of their spare room until something more suitable could be found. Timothy was dazed by it all; everything had been taken out of his hands and he just became a cog in a well-oiled wheel. Dimly he recalled saying his vows; dimly he recalled a mass of friends and relations wishing them well. Only too well he recalled the embarrassing closeness of being in bed with Claire, knowing that her parents were in the next room.

Later came the arguments as they hissed about the feasibility of it all. Eventually the baby was born, a girl. Timothy and Claire's fraught relationship became more strained as the child cried, and its frantic parents rushed to soothe its sobs before the wailing disturbed her grandparents. Their baby was a fractious child.

Timothy was suffering from sleep deprivation which began to affect his judgments at work. He began to take sleeping tablets so that he could at least shut out the noise of the screaming baby and sleep himself.

His jangled nerves became shattered as the depression closed in on him. Marjorie's face often passed before him in any dreams he might have and he would awake with a sense of guilt. He was too ashamed to contact her now, even to apologise. Was this to be his punishment?

Eventually he sat at a table, chewing the end of a pencil while he composed a letter. When it was finished, he left it where it was, swallowed the remainder of the sleeping tablets with a glass of water and laid down on the bed awaiting eternal sleep.

The hospital staff were agog with the news, yet as always, the person most likely to be affected by it was the last to hear. Marjorie was just finishing her lunch when the gossip began on the adjoining table. Ruth and Beatrice realised that Marjorie was unaware of the scandal, so they exchanged meaningful glances before attempting to tell her.

"It's about Timothy."

"Oh yes."

"Have you heard…?"

"Why he dumped me, you mean?" Marjorie was curtly disinterested

"Not that…"

"That he's married now?" Marjorie stirred her coffee, eager to be away.

"Did you ever find out why he …"

"What about him?" Marjorie did not really want to know now that their relationship was over.

"He married a girl because he got her into trouble."

"You mean she was pregnant?" They had her attention now.

"Yes, but the sad thing is that he couldn't cope with family life and living with her parents."

"So he took an overdose."

"H-he what? I-is he all right now?" Marjorie was shocked out of any apathy.

"Well no, he died yesterday morning right here in this hospital."

"He knew what he was doing, you see."

Marjorie felt tears dribble down her cheeks. Ruth and

Beatrice each put a comforting hand on her shoulder from either side of her.

"I thought all that was over for me now," she squeaked in a voice quite unlike her own. As she struggled to gain composure, she asked "How's his wife taking it?"

Her friends glanced at one another.

"Typical of you to be concerned for someone else – but we hear she's being quite brave. Maybe she had her suspicions about his character. One never knows a person until you live with them."

However brave she appeared on the surface, Marjorie was shaken. Timothy's sudden marriage explained a lot, yet she could not understand how he could have got so carried away. His behaviour with her had always been impeccable. It still hurt to think that she had been two-timed in this way, whilst promising Marjorie their engagement. Her own reaction was to revert to hard work.

Marjorie's next assignment was to stay with a couple whose only daughter was 10 years old. She was a precocious child with long thick plaits, and Marjorie had been sent to look after the girl while she suffered from tonsillitis.

Fiona Forsythe ensured that everybody was aware of her smallest twinge of pain and left Marjorie in no doubt as to what her role was. Marjorie was not merely a nurse in this household, but a nursemaid, employed to look after every single one of Fiona's whims. Just encouraging the girl to gargle regularly was a major task in itself. Mr and Mrs Forsythe were devoted to their darling daughter and their world seemed to revolve around her. Marjorie was only too glad that the tonsillitis was a mild bout and did not last long, although even when she decided it was time to take her leave, Fiona invented another sore throat, thus persuading her mother to ask Marjorie to stay on another couple of days. She conceded just that once. When it happened again, she finally took her leave, pleading urgent duties elsewhere.

Marjorie worked for some months nursing private patients before she had amassed enough money to pay for her Midwifery training.

Despite her previous experience, she found the work confusing at first, because there was no smooth routine as on other wards. Babies come when they think they will. Babies cry and babies are demanding. Their nervous mothers were not sure how to do the correct things with them, and all the babies needed seemingly endless attention. Some would be sleeping, but there was always one who would be restless and fretful, waking up the others, to create a cacophony of noise.

Each one would have to be bathed, changed and fed. Mothers had to be shown how to do these things for their babies too, and screens were constantly being shifted around beds. Nurses would have to make frequent visits to ensure mother and baby were doing all the right things.

Babies varied in temperament and looks from wrinkled apples to delightful cherubs, yet all were beautiful in its own way.

Every birth was a miracle and she enjoyed the delivery of each baby, no matter how challenging. Afterwards she joined in the joy of the happy parents, pleased to have been a part of it all.

Marjorie was notching up her qualifications one by one. She was a State Registered Children's Nurse, a State Registered Nurse, and before long she became a State Registered Midwife. Having completed all these various forms of nursing, she now knew what she really wanted to do was to nurse overseas. She didn't know why, apart from the fact of it being one way to see something of the world beyond Britain.

Overseas Nursing meant another training course to qualify for, and this also had to be paid for. Yet again, Marjorie moved into the Private Sector in order to pay for the fees. This time these included some Maternity cases.

One of her first duties in the private maternity sector

was at a huge mansion house with at least twenty servants to run it, situated in a village on the south-east coast. The Kingsley-Fforbes family had lived here for generations, and so, it seemed, had their servants, as they were all very loyal to the family. Mrs Kingsley-Fforbes had sent for a nurse-in-waiting as soon as she reached the 36th week of her pregnancy. Nothing was to be left to chance. Marjorie got lost several times trying to find her bedroom during the first few days. She was glad she had taken some embroidery to sew as well as some knitting, or life could have been boring. There was a first nursery for the young babe about to be born and the second nursery was used by the older child who had a nanny to supervise him.

Marjorie was embarrassed to be waited on hand and foot and she found it hard to get used to this sort of living. She was not allowed to do anything for herself. When she arrived downstairs to breakfast with the family, as they insisted she did, the sideboard would be covered with silver tureens, each containing a different dish to choose from, whether grilled bacon, fried eggs, poached eggs, scrambled eggs, kippers, kedgeree, or whatever took her fancy.

The family would also hold the most wonderful dinner parties which Marjorie was asked to attend. She was grateful for the dress she had made for herself as well as the one that Timothy had bought her. Both were perfect in this situation.

At last the waiting was over and the baby arrived, greeted by regal splendour. It was a little girl, and the family and servants alike were thrilled with her. Marjorie was congratulated and treated as if the child was all her own work. She was quite sad to leave that household, not just because of all the grandeur, but because everyone had been very friendly and kind towards her.

The next case she was sent on was a complete contrast. It was located in a house located in the back streets of London where a lady was dying from cancer. Her husband wanted his wife to have the best possible attention during her last days.

Marjorie was glad she could complete he journeys to and from the house in daylight, as she wouldn't want to be seen on her own after dark in this downtrodden area with its narrow streets. The house was shabby and dim, with worn carpets and brown paint everywhere. The grubby curtains were permanently drawn together, making it difficult for Marjorie to see what she was doing. However Mrs Williams only lasted a week before she died. When Marjorie laid her out, she was surprised to discover she wore a wig. Mrs Williams looked quite incongruous without it.

The final private patient she nursed during the last five weeks of 1938 was one she would never forget. He was a twelve-year-old boy with cancer of the jaw. He was in Middlesex Hospital for a large part of his illness then was moved into a flat nearby, to live with his father. His parents were separated. The lad's face was literally being eaten away by the disease, which apparently had started as a little sore on his lip during his first year. Had it been attended to promptly, he would no doubt have been all right, but it turned cancerous.

Marjorie would nurse the boy, Graham, during the day, and his father would return from work and look after him from the evening until morning. Latterly he moved the boy into his own double bed so that he could attend to the dressings during the night.

She was disturbed by the fact that for as long as Graham was able to sit up, his father would take him in a wheelchair to the Fascist Movement meetings held in a hall down the road. Quite apart from the politics of it all, Marjorie's heart would go out to the lad as his father got him ready to go out, looking so pale and ill, accentuated by his black clothes. The best place for him was resting in bed and not propped up in a wheelchair.

Graham's father would do anything to cheer up his son. Graham had everything he wanted from one of the first television sets to a budgerigar. Where all the money was coming from to buy all these things, Marjorie never knew as his job didn't appear to be a highly paid one. She sometimes wondered if he was some sort of spy, then felt very guilty for even thinking it. She felt embarrassed when she was presented with an expensive bottle of perfume that Christmas.

As the cancer devoured his jaw, sounds became too much for Graham to bear and he would have screaming fits that seemed to pierce Marjorie's very soul. When the doctor next visited he sent Marjorie to the hospital to collect an additional prescription for Graham. Glancing at it, she saw it was for quite a high dose of morphine and tried to point this out to the doctor who waved her away.

Marjorie wasn't surprised when she went in next morning to discover that Graham had died in the night as he slept. His father reproached himself for being asleep himself when it happened in case Graham had wanted something. Marjorie reassured him that this wouldn't have been the case; after all he was used to hearing the slightest noise from his son during the night and responding to it.

Graham's father gave Marjorie the budgerigar when she left, giving her a memento with which to remember his son. She was due for a few days off duty she carried it in its cage on the train down to Dorset much to the amusement of the other passengers.

Her father was fascinated by it and bought another to be its mate. From those two budgies, he bred many more over the years, even building a small aviary in the garden for them all.

It went against all that she had been taught, but she couldn't help herself, and Marjorie unburdened herself to her father about her last patient, telling him how the family seemed to support Oswald Mosely and go to meetings dressed all in black, even when the young boy was dying. Walter told her very definitely that as soon as she returned to London she was to go to the Police and report him. It was something she hated to do, but her father had impressed it upon her that it was her duty.

Once back in London, she did go to the Police, trembling as if she herself were a wanted criminal. She told them her story just as she had confided in her father. She was relieved, to hear that although the Police had known about Graham's father, he had appeared to change his ways since his son's death. Although once prepared to betray his country, the Police had never been able to gain evidence of this. Now all was well. Marjorie felt happier.

When she next reported to the Middlesex Hospital, it was to receive her discharge papers plus all the paperwork that was required to take her overseas to the West Coast of Africa. Marjorie's last day at the hospital was 1st January 1939 and although she was embarking on an exciting new life, she could not help but feel saddened to leave many happy memories behind her, even though they had been underlined with such hard work.

She had a month to have all the necessary injections and this enabled her to visit different relatives saying farewell. Everyone congratulated her on her courage at leaving England to travel so far away. Forthcoming war in Europe was mentioned, but then discounted, as it was not likely to last very long. She enjoyed the weeks of anticipation for the ensuing voyage, alongside getting things together for her eighteen months trip abroad. Secretly Marjorie shrugged off people's concern, glad to be free to be herself, to get to know herself, to discover for herself how the real Marjorie would react in situations when she was away from stifling rules and regulations.

Aunt Margaret could not help but show her pride in her niece. "And to think that not so many years ago you were anticipating just being a nanny!"

Marjorie smiled. "I've got you to that for all that."

"For the inspiration possibly, but you did all the hard work and study."

"I could never have done it without your encouragement."

"And now we're losing you."

"I'll only be away for eighteen months."

"Yes, and that time will pass quickly, especially with all these rumours of a war."

"If that happens, I'm sure it will soon be over. Anyway, West Africa will be well out of the way. You look after yourself."

"You too, and you'll keep in touch, won't you?"

Marjorie hugged her. She was fond of Aunt Margaret.

"I will. I'll write as often as I can. I'm planning to write different letters to everyone so you can all share each other's. That'll save me having to write the same news several times over!"

"Don't you worry about us. Just you concentrate on doing a good job of work and enjoy exploring when you get the opportunity."

"Thanks Aunt Margaret for everything."

By the time she was about to leave England, Marjorie was thirty years old. Jessie was twenty-eight and nervous about her sister's venture. She clung to her arm as she said, "Are you sure you're doing the right thing? You're going such a long way away."

Marjorie tried to brush her concern aside light-heartedly. "Come on, Jessie, where's your sense of adventure?"

Conversely Grace, now thirty-two was still in Ringwood working as a housekeeper. Currently she had stars in her eyes as she was walking out with a young farmer named Jack Antell. Marjorie began to wonder if she had actually taken in the news that they wouldn't see one another for eighteen months.

Next day Jessie was still worried. "It's not like going away on holiday for a few days. You're going to the other side of the world – well almost."

"Don't worry, I'll be all right."

"Then they say there's this war brewing in Europe."

Marjorie spoke lightly. "Well, I'm going to West Africa, so I shall be safely out of the way then!"

Her stepmother was very chilly about Marjorie's adventure to the unknown. Until that time, even when in

London, she knew Marjorie would return home when she had a few days off. Now the family would not see her for a long time. Any sign of affection from her was out of the question.

"So you're about to leave us in our hour of need, then?"

"Whatever do you mean?"

"You know there's talk of another war."

"Oh, that's just talk. I've heard it won't last long if it does happen."

"After all I've done for you, you just up-sticks and run away to Africa to look after the natives there without a care for your own family!"

"Oh mother, that's not true. I've worked really hard to get as many qualifications as I can. It's only natural that I want to put them to use now."

"You can use nursing qualifications in this country just as well."

"I want to get more experience, that's all."

"Oh yes, always what you want, never mind us, your family. I worked my fingers to the bone for you and this is the reward I get."

Marjorie felt exasperated and did not want to give in to her stepmother. Fortunately her father came into the room at this point and the conversation ended.

After that Marjorie tried to ignore her stepmother's remarks and concentrated on her farewell to her father. She did love him. He had always worked so hard, and was such a saintly man, always working to please someone, generally people other than himself. Her only consolation at leaving him was that she would not be a financial burden any more; not that she had been for some years, now that she had gained her independence during her nursing career.

The big day arrived when Marjorie finally left home. The ship would be sailing from Liverpool, so taking a train to Lime Street station, changing trains at London was the first stage of her journey.

Her stepmother stayed at home pleading a headache,

but the rest of the family went with her to the little station at Broadstone.

The train puffed into the station like a furious black dragon, its carriages creaking to a stop as it slowed to a halt. Once aboard, Marjorie leaned out of the carriage window as far as she dared, waving until they were lost in a cloud of steam. Hauling the window up by its leather strap, she sat back on her seat watching the plumes of white clouds puffing by from out from the engine. The carriage swayed rhythmically along the rails, clicketty-clack, clicketty-clack.

Now she was on her own. What did the future hold?

PART TWO –

AFRICAN ADVENTURE

Chapter Six

It was a cold grey day in January 1939.

The train chuffed across the countryside leaving a trail of steam in its wake. Outside the landscape was bare and wintry, giving her a chilly send-off. Marjorie began to look forward to warmer climes. As they slowed and rattled through a steep bank on either side, she saw clumps of luminous looking snowdrops clustered here and there amongst tangled damp brown leaves and twigs close to the earth. Momentarily she was touched with regret, knowing that for her, the brash, harsh colours of a hot climate would no doubt replace these tiny delicate flowers and the pastel shades of the coming spring. Soon it began to rain, needles of it slanting across the window. Skeletal trees bowed in the wind as a cloak of rain enveloped them. Marjorie shivered. Soon she would be free of this raw dampness that seemed to seep into her bones.

Eventually she reached the dockside at Liverpool, and was directed towards customs where there was the rigmarole of registering her luggage with the Elder Dempster Shipping Lines. She was to sail on the 9,000 ton ship SS *Accra*. Eventually Marjorie walked up the gangplank and stood on board the ship. A steward examined her ticket and showed her to the cabin that was to be her home for the next couple of weeks. Although there were two bunks one above the other, Marjorie had it to herself. The space was small, as most ships had confined personal space, but everything was surprisingly compact. She had her own private washbasin, shower and lavatory. Her bunk looked as though it had been made out of walnut and the little fitted dressing table and wardrobe were constructed from the same wood.

Marjorie explored the ship before they left Liverpool and discovered the passengers' lounge where there was also a dance floor, the dining room, the swimming pool, and several kinds of deck games such as deck quoits and table tennis. She shouldn't be bored.

Towards evening, the ship became a mass of lights towering up to the sky, and shortly afterwards the ropes that bound the ship to land were untied and she was unleashed onto the open sea.

The throaty throb of the engines beneath, along with several small tugboats persuaded the liner to sail down the River Mersey before heading south. Marjorie leaned over the rail and waved for all she was worth, even though there was nobody she knew on shore to wave to. She couldn't help herself when all around her people were almost throwing themselves overboard in an effort to attract attention to the ever-decreasing crowd of faces on land.

She kept the shoreline in sight for as long as possible, from the aft of the ship, contemplating her past and her future. The propeller churned up a white froth of water that showed a marked contrast to the dark silken sea around it. An echoing voice from the tannoy system told the passengers that dinner would soon be served in the dining room. Realising how hungry she was Marjorie left the scene.

At the end of an enjoyable but uneventful two-week sea voyage they arrived at the town of Accra on the Gold Coast. However the ship could not moor very close to land as the water was too shallow to accommodate such a large vessel. Therefore Marjorie and other passengers needing to disembark were met by launch and transported to the jetty.

A tall gentleman with thinning dark hair and brown eyes stepped forward from the crowd. "Marjorie Heath?" he asked.

"Oh, yes, that's me." Marjorie was startled to hear her name spoken in a refined English accent.

"Welcome to Accra! My name is Hugh Beaumont."

"How did you know I was coming?" asked Marjorie.

"Your father, Walter Heath, wrote to me and asked if I could make sure you are all right. I'm the local Education Officer and my wife and I are also missionaries covering this area."

Marjorie smiled but sighed inwardly. Was she never to be completely free? Moreover, how did her Father get hold of all these names and addresses? Still, that was not Mr Beaumont's fault; he was only doing his duty. She should feel grateful.

Hugh Beaumont took the largest piece of Marjorie's luggage and strode away.

"My car and driver are just here, so I'll take you to the hospital." he called over his shoulder.

"That's very kind of you."

Marjorie was impressed by the large amount of various species of palm trees that grew everywhere, although the shrubs seemed stunted and even the shape of the grass-blades were different. Most memorable was the red dust that settled all over her as she walked, and in the first instance, this fascinated her, just as an African might have been when seeing snow fall for the first time. From the back seat Marjorie stared at the crinkled black hair of the driver beneath his official hat and the glossy brown neck beneath.

As they pulled away, Hugh Beaumont said, "My wife, Rosemary, would normally have come with me, but she's currently in England recovering from typhoid."

"Oh, I am sorry."

"Thanks, but she's doing well; should be back here with me in about six weeks."

"Did she have to go home especially?"

"Fortunately we were on the way home when the ship's Doctor made the diagnosis, so she was confined to medical quarters for the voyage and was in good hands there."

"That must have been frightening for you both."

Around them were many cyclists, young men in shorts and singlets. Across the bicycles and, most surprisingly, on the riders' heads, were bundles, baskets, and even live chickens. The town rushed by, shacks, then rows of wooden shops, white houses with verandas, all glaring in the bright light. Even the sounds were different to those in

England. They were disembodied, frantic horns from cyclists, shouts and laughter, tinny music and the clatter of work all seemed to burst on the air beside them. As the scenes rushed by, they created riots of vibrant colour. The dark skinned people all wore brightly patterned clothes, especially the womenfolk. Olive green leaves on the palm trees showed up against a multitude of dried scrubby looking plants and bushes.

"Here we are, just turning into the hospital drive now." As they turned the car wheels threw up more red dust in their wake.

Marjorie was amazed by the differences in scenery. Although largely scorched and barren in appearance, trees grew to three or four times the height of those in England. They dwarfed the buildings all around them.

Hugh Beaumont's chauffeur drove the car to the main door of the hospital and opened the car door for Marjorie. Hugh showed her to Matron's office then he held out his right hand and gripped her's firmly.

"Welcome again to the Gold Coast," he said. "I'll leave you for now, but I'll be in touch. I'm sure you'll settle in all right."

"Thank you very much – and goodbye!"

Marjorie knocked on Matron's office door.

"Come in!"

She opened it and saw a nurse sitting writing at a desk.

Matron looked up. "Ah, you must be Miss Heath," said the plump, dark-haired lady as she rose from behind her desk, extending a welcoming hand to Marjorie. "I'm Maureen O'Rourke, Let me order a pot of tea before I show you round."

She rang a bell and shortly afterwards a soft padding of feet could be heard followed by a rap on the door. A barefooted young African with gleaming black skin stood in the doorway. He wore a white tunic and shorts.

"Could you bring us a tray of tea for two, please Kofi?"

"Yes Matron!" He disappeared, returning with the tea.

"Thank you Kofi, that is all for now; oh, except that

Miss Heath's luggage will need to be taken over to her bungalow." She raised an enquiring eyebrow at Marjorie.

The youth bowed reverently and said, "If it please you Matron, the chauffeur man and me – we already take suitcases and leave them in the nurse's house." He beamed a smile, pleased with his own initiative.

"Very good Kofi, thank you. You may go now."

The hospital was all on one level, although built on brick pillars, partly to keep the building cool, and partly to prevent animals and creepy-crawlies from finding their way in. There were wooden shutters at all the windows to keep out the glare of the sun. It was a European hospital, having just one men's section and one women's section, plus an out-patients' department. Marjorie was required to work twenty-four hours on duty and twenty-four hours off duty from two in the afternoon, until two in the afternoon next day. In her off-duty time she would live in her bungalow in the compound.

Miss O'Rourke was a tough Irish lady who didn't actually do any nursing unless this was urgently needed, but saw to the overall running of the hospital. Each patient had their own room, and all the nurses, whatever their rank, were coolly dressed in white cotton dresses with a white muslin head-square folded to a triangle and tied round their head; otherwise it was very similar to an English hospital.

When Marjorie was eventually shown to her bungalow the first thing she did was to have a cold bath. She had never experienced such heat before, and dreaded to think that she would have to work in it. She turned on the electric ceiling fan and its blades moved the air a little.

As she was unpacking a few items, Matron appeared with a young boy in tow.

"Miss Heath, this young man is your house-boy. His name is Bicycle. Anything you need and Bicycle will see to it. In fact, if I were you, I would let him do the unpacking for you. He is more used to this heat than you are!"

Bicycle nodded happily in agreement, so the two women left him to it.

When they were out of the boy's hearing Miss O'Rourke explained to Marjorie, "You'll find that some natives just love anything that has an English sound to it, hence some peculiar names. Actually, I believe he *does* own a bicycle, but I don't suppose he did when he was born!" She laughed merrily and Marjorie joined in, already beginning to feel at home in this strange land.

"Now, make sure you always use your mosquito net at night," warned the Matron. "Those little creatures can be quite lethal! Malaria can be prevented."

So saying, she departed.

Bicycle provided Marjorie with a much-needed iced drink before she dismissed him and decided to turn in for an early night.

The hour felt much later than it actually was, because there was no dusk in this part of the world. Being so close to the equator the sun rose and set very quickly. Marjorie found she was perspiring enough to need another cold bath before climbing into bed. Even the one sheet felt as though it was a heavy blanket on her. The sounds of the night outside were eerie and unfamiliar. Night birds called to one another and there were even stranger cries from beyond the bush; monkeys chattering perhaps, against a background of crickets urgently serenading one another.

Marjorie woke early next morning and decided to go for a walk before the heat of the day. Many Africans were already going about their business, and the women taking goods to market. The African women had a designer fashion of their own as they paraded by draped in a limitless variety of colours and designs, many with no apparent regard for which colours blended best together. The patterns on the different fabrics were large and bold. Most women wore elaborate bandeaus on their heads as brilliant as butterflies, and topped by the bundle they were carrying; moving with effortless grace.

The men wore various forms of robe or long jacket, but

the most striking seemed to be the simple, single cloth worn by the farmers, which was draped over one shoulder and swathed about the body.

Returning to the bungalow, Marjorie found Bicycle serving iced paw-paw for breakfast, which made up for the heat several times over.

She was not due to start work for another couple of days and Miss O'Rourke had invited her over to the bungalow where she herself lived for drinks that evening. Marjorie was to discover that after sunset, the Europeans would sit out on their terraces enjoying the air as it grew cooler. The drinks would be cold and people would talk to strangers as they would on board ship. It certainly was a whole new world out here.

During their brief time together on the veranda, Maureen O'Rourke tried to enlighten Marjorie on some of the apparently peculiar customs of this country that was so new and alien to her.

Continuing a previous conversation, she said, "You'll find that the Africans have some peculiar names," she began. "Some of them might be named after the day of the week on which they were born, such as Tuesday. Some would not want the English version, so this would be translated *Kobina* for a boy's name or *Abina* for a girl. Generally, they prefer to use the English though. That is likely to be the child's only name, although sometimes they do take on their father's name for a surname; otherwise there are no regular surnames. Then this is sometimes made confusing by being altered from time to time. You see, if the man after whom the child had been named had done something wrong, the child's name must be changed to avoid any *Ju-Ju* or evil coming to that child. The idea behind it is that if the child still kept the surname, the same *Ju-Ju* that forced the man to do wrong might get into the child."

After sipping her drink she continued. "The Africans rise at dawn and go to bed at sundown. This means their day is from six in the morning until half past seven in the evening. The women will first draw water, sweep the compound and prepare the first meal of the day. The Africans cook on an open fire, so the women will also hunt for firewood. Most of the food is in the form of soups or stews of vegetables and fruit grown on their family smallholding. Men and women eat separately, sitting round a common dish into which they all dip their fingers. The men then go to work on their farm at about half past eight. Sometimes the women accompany them with their babies (or *picanninnies* as they called them) strapped to their backs. Alternatively they work around the house. These are generally constructed using mud for the walls and palm leaves for the roof. Either that or go to the morning market."

Marjorie placed her glass on the table. "This is a lot to take in."

Maureen continued. "The most common food (or *chop* as it's called) is *fou-foux*. The women pound plantains and yams into a thick stodgy paste with huge pestles, about four feet in length. This forms a base for their meal that always seems so thick and stodgy by European standards. Meat is always very expensive so will only be eaten on special occasions. Most families have a scrawny chicken or two running about and very occasionally a sheep, goat or turkey. Many families keep a pet dog and a bird in a cage."

Marjorie smiled. "Oh dear, I don't think I'll remember all this."

"You soon will. It will become part of your life."

They paused to listen to the sounds of the night. Then Maureen continued. "The men return from their labours at around mid-day for a rest and then go back to work for two or three hours in the afternoon. Let me tell you, they all love a chance to celebrate, and if there is any excuse to stay away from work, you could be sure they'll take it, making merry for as long as they can. Anyway, enough for now. You'll learn all kinds of things as you stay here."

Later Marjorie learned that Africans enjoyed playing

games and most villages had its own football ground with bamboo goal posts. The boys would play almost every evening, always in bare feet. Everyone bathed twice a day before each meal. Even if there was only a trickle of a stream near a village, it would be lined with boys covered in soap suds, washing as if their lives depended on it.

The Africans also had an amazing talent for re-cycling things. Petrol cans were one such item. While she was in Africa, Marjorie saw them being used to build walls, or hammered flat and used to tile the roof of a hut. They were used as water carriers, billy-cans, makeshift buckets, and even as little open air stoves.

When she had been in Accra some while, Marjorie was amused to see old motor car tyres utilised as window frames in a mud hut; another time an old bicycle wheel had been put to similar use.

Children in most villages had the opportunity to be educated. It was not compulsory for them to attend school, and it had to be paid for. A child could be educated from nursery school until the age of 15 years if his or her parents could afford the two shillings and sixpence (12 ½ pence in our metric money) per month. About 15 out of every 100 children did go to school, arriving from far and wide on foot, each one carrying their slates and books on his or her head.

Not every day was a workday. A European once made a survey of just how often the Africans worked. It was discovered that actually only 148 days in the year (that was less than three days a week) were spent on the farm. Then 117 (that is two days a week) were spent in village work, religious holidays or travelling; whilst 100 days were feast days or holidays.

Maureen O'Rourke had fed this gem of information to Marjorie and she later asked Patricia Burt, with whom she was to work, if it were true.

Patricia laughed. "I should take it with a pinch of salt," she said. "But at the same time, the longer you stay here, the more you will realise what a large grain of truth there is to it!"

As time passed, Marjorie discovered more of the festivals and customs peculiar to the Gold Coast. She was amazed by its romantic past and by the fact that so little of its history had filtered through to people in England.

Important events in life would be marked by special rites and rituals, such as child naming, puberty initiations, marriage and death all meant family ceremonies. Seasonal festivals often brought a whole people or clan together in a spectacular fashion. Many of these included durbars (kings) or chieftains when tribal leaders and Queen Mothers were transported in decorated palanquins, (a large box for one passenger carried by means of two poles resting on the shoulders of several men). Others held traditional umbrellas, all this colourful panorama of movement would be backed by the sound of drummers to which the warriors would stamp out their rhythmic dance whilst discharging muskets.

Marjorie had arrived in the Gold Coast towards the end of the dry season, so everywhere looked very dry, dusty and parched compared to the damp grey English winter she had left behind. She was told that the rainy season would begin in mid-March and continue until September.

Patricia Burt was the other Nursing Sister at hospital and Marjorie's equal. They fell naturally into a friendship that was to last for many years. Patricia was a tall, graceful woman, about the same age as Marjorie. She had dark, naturally wavy hair that swung round around her open, friendly face. She tried to explain a little of the African ways to Marjorie and took her to the local market place, which played an important part in West African life and was all organised by African women. On the ground there were pyramids of groundnuts piled onto mats of woven grass, red and green peppers and purple aubergines. Marjorie had not seen any of these strange vegetables before. Alongside these were oranges, limes, paw-paws, green plantains and yellow bananas. There were wide calabash bowls, each containing a different spice; cones of powder, all rich in colour and aroma. Gradually colours of hand-woven cloth and African fashioned jewellery appeared from further along the gaudy row of stalls. Voices called to one another in a strange language, sometimes in Pidgin English. These would be mixed with squawking chicken from wicker cages, and the sound of tinny bells.

Many items on sale demonstrated the Africans' ingenuity to improvise as they displayed old motor tyres given new life as soles for sandals, old round cigarette tins with a few additions welded on made little paraffin lamps. Then there was a typically African stall luring one to the charms and spells of witchcraft. Marjorie cast her eyes over the mummified frogs and lizards, shrivelled claws and bowls of weird looking seeds and roots. A shiver ran down her spine and she passed quickly on.

"You can buy just about anything at the market place," said Patricia, as they passed some tortoises and live snails alongside some rush matting and stuffed leather pouffes. Fish and meat were also on sale, hanging up in the sun with flies flocking all over it. Some cuts were actually crawling with maggots. The market sights and smells could also be quite distasteful.

Patricia followed her gaze. "Never go into a kitchen if the cook's at work," she warned Marjorie.

Marjorie's stomach heaved. It was truly amazing how people survived sometimes.

Nevertheless she enjoyed her first trip to the market. It was certainly awash with colour; the womenfolk adding to it by wearing the long flowing robes.

"The women's dresses are called *boubous*," said Patricia. "You can see that when a woman has a child she will use an extension of it to tie her baby or even a toddler on her back." Patricia indicated two such women as they passed. "See, they sleep there quite unconcerned whilst the mother gets on and does what she has to do!" Patricia pointed out another lady's head-dress. "See that woman has all that vivid fabric round her head into a kind of turban – well that's called a *mousor.*"

As they were about to part following the trip to market, Patricia said, "Look, come round to my bungalow for dinner this evening and perhaps I can explain more of the local way of life to you. The more you know, the quicker you'll settle in."

"Thank you, I'd like that very much."

After the meal they relaxed on the terrace.

"Most people round here are small time farmers," explained Patricia. "Believe it or not but in a typical African village a man will have at least two wives."

"Don't they get jealous of one another?"

"Strangely enough, no, they regard one another as sisters."

Marjorie laughed. "Oh surely not!"

"Yes really. I suppose their way of life is very hard, so it's a matter of all hands to the pump as it were. They have to collect water from the nearest river every day and that may be several miles away. They need to gather wood from the forest to make a fire for cooking. The women also make a lot of clay pots similar to those you saw on sale in the market. Once they have been baked in the sun they are coated with some kind of liquid from the locust bean to make them black and shiny."

Marjorie was amazed by all the work that the women did. "No wonder the men take more than one wife!"

"Yes, then weaving is another job generally done by the women, and having a length of cloth she will either use it for her family or take it to market to sell."

"And you say the men are mostly farmers?"

"Well, yes, but some do other things like wood carving. A lot of Africans believe in herbal remedies and witch doctors who they call *ju-ju* men. You saw some of their weird stuff on sale at the market. A few of their medicines are OK, surprisingly enough, but most are not. That's where we have our greatest battle. We must get these people to realise that more often than not they are doing themselves more harm than good. It's an uphill task because most of them are so steeped in tradition that they live in fear of all kinds of evil spirits. Still, at least we're in the European Hospital, but if you get moved to an African Hospital, then be prepared!"

"You certainly are a mine of information. I don't think I'll remember all this very quickly, but thanks anyway for telling me about some of the customs and traditions before I actually encounter them."

Patricia smiled. "There's a lot more to learn, but one thing you must realise is that time is something that is quite alien to an African. It can be very frustrating to us, but they are very laid back about it all. Their attitude is that they never had clocks or watches before, so why start now? Be warned, it can be very frustrating to make an appointment and be almost certain that they will be very late. There are Europeans out here who refuse to understand the culture and grumble about unreliability, but if you are really bound by time, then ask a European to help you out!"

Marjorie drained her glass. "Well thank you Patricia. You have been so helpful. That was a lovely meal and I have enjoyed your company. Now I must go to bed and let you get to yours. I start my first twenty-four hour shift tomorrow."

Marjorie trod lightly and swiftly across the compound to her quarters, sniffing the scented air that was so unlike home and wondered how she would fare in her new post.

Chapter Seven

Matron had a reputation for having a bad temper. She was always kindly disposed towards Marjorie and Marjorie was determined to keep it that way, having heard some of the tales that went flying around from time to time, most probably exaggerated. Cook never tired of telling of the time when he was on the receiving end of one of her rages.

"I wus jes a-beatin' ma eggs together an' a-mindin' ma own business. In she cum all a-shoutin' an' picks up ma basin. 'Why ya always so far behind?' she say. She snatch up de basin and tip it all over ma head! Well, dat put me even more behind, dint it! I had to wash ma head under de tap an' beat more eggs. I dunno, I really dunno!"

He would linger for a while and if no further interest was shown, would shuffle off to go about his duties.

As time passed, Marjorie realised that it seemed to be the Africans who mostly annoyed Matron. She had a very broad Irish accent, and some, only understanding Pidgin English would misunderstand her orders, consequently heaping her wrath upon themselves.

Dr Driscoll at the hospital was slight of stature with greying hair. He was polite, dapper and Victorian in character. Marjorie decided he must have stepped out of one of Charles Dickens' books. Every morning when he first saw her, he would bow slightly from the waist and say, "Good morning, Sister Heath."

He never called anyone by their Christian name for fear of appearing too familiar. Even Hitler was given a correct prefix to his name and referred to as Mr Hitler.

Dr Driscoll always took time with the patients and treated each one as if they were his only appointment that day. Everyone was made to feel important in their own right and loved him for it. Both Dr and Mrs Driscoll certainly set a wonderful atmosphere in Accra Hospital.

Hugh Beaumont was as good as his word. He asked

Marjorie to dinner, and she went to his bungalow one evening after the service at chapel. Other members of his congregation had also been invited. After the meal they drank ginger wine over a couple of games of Lexicon. Marjorie decided that perhaps this idea of her father wasn't such a bad one after all. It was a helpful way to meet new people.

A few days later, Hugh Beaumont suggested a game of golf. Marjorie had never played before, but it seemed that most Europeans played golf here and it was a good social activity. She agreed to learn. He organised a game against other members of his chapel and they all tried to help Marjorie with her game.

"Not bad," they agreed. "Not bad at all, especially for a first try."

Marjorie was enjoying the friendly encouragement that enlarged her social life. She had attended chapel several times by this time and was getting to know more people through Hugh. Everyone was looking forward to the time when he would be reunited with his wife who was due back in West Africa very soon. It was about a week before her arrival when Hugh arrived at Marjorie's bungalow late one afternoon.

"Are you off duty long enough to play a round of golf?" he asked.

"Why yes, thank you. That would be nice."

Shortly after they had teed off, Hugh said, "I've really wanted to talk to you for some weeks now."

Marjorie had just spotted her ball in the grass and strode towards it. "Oh yes?" she said without interest.

"You see, I think ... no, in fact I know I have fallen in love with you."

She stopped in her tracks and almost dropped her club in surprise but Hugh continued hurriedly before she interrupted.

"Our marriage had always been a bit ... well ... um," he sought for a word. "Fraught – you know. I really think I must tell Rosemary – be honest with her. Then she'll no doubt divorce me and we can be married one day perhaps?"

"Mr Beaumont!" exclaimed Marjorie using his formal name in exasperation. "I couldn't possibly even consider such a suggestion!"

"Oh but …"

"No! Have you thought how your wife will feel next week when she arrives back from feeling really ill, then to be welcomed with *this* news! No doubt the poor lady would be devastated. Come to that, have you thought how *I* feel? Friendly we may be, but definitely, most definitely nothing more."

She turned on her heel and walked quickly back to the golf club, left the clubs there and walked back to her bungalow. Not once did she look back. Her heart sank. Why was it that she always seemed to attract the wrong people?

She received a telephone call a week later.

"Hello Marjorie, Hugh here."

She sighed.

"Look, I've had to tell Rosemary about us. I felt so guilty you see."

"I don't understand. What are you guilty about? You only asked me to dinner two or three times in the company of others." She was being hard, yet it had to be said.

"She's very upset. What shall we do?"

"I did warn you she would be upset. You shouldn't have said anything. Loving me must be your imagination. Leave me out of it. I'm sorry, but as far as I'm concerned you must mend your marriage. Goodbye." Exasperated, Marjorie slammed the receiver down and realised she was shaking.

Frightened after her London experience with Jack Sullivan, she couldn't risk any more similar situations. She didn't go to church or chapel any more and immersed herself in work.

Marjorie was in the act of pulling a screen round a bed

when there was a terrific clap of thunder, such as she had never heard before. The dirty ochre and black sky above the garden was split in several places by silver forks of lightning. Simultaneously the rain started and grew heavier, then poured down in a sizzling wet sheet. The combination of thunder, lightning and furious rain stopped all conversation for a few minutes.

"Seems like the rainy season's started," said Marjorie's patient as she adjusted the screen.

"Is it always like this?"

"This is mild my dear compared to some tropical storms. Just you wait!"

Marjorie soon understood that some tropical storms raged loud and long all through the night, giving the impression of living in a lighthouse. She was glad of the shutters to darken the room a little if she was trying to sleep; but the noise of the thunder was deafening at times and she would bury her head under her pillow to try and muffle it.

She wondered whether she would adjust to the extremes in climate of being either too hot or too wet, yet within a few weeks it all became just another aspect of African life.

The bonus side of the rainy season soon became apparent as flowers and foliage sprung into life from apparent deadness. Most arresting was the drive up to the hospital, lined with aptly named trees and bushes, called *Flame of the Forest,* (or Bougainvillea). Covered in red, orange or pink flowers, when the sun shone from a certain angle, the eye was deceived into believing that they were indeed on fire.

She witnessed flowers in the hospital garden opening and blooming extravagantly towards the sun. Everything seemed so big and bold here. Marjorie was amazed to see big Poinsetta trees growing wild and spreading out their scarlet leaves to the sky, hardly worth comparing with the little potted versions that had begun to appear in the English shops over the Christmas season, each bearing a huge price tag.

What an amazing place this was to work in, surrounded by such vibrant beauty.

The hospital garden had hibiscus, bougainvillea in a profusion of colours as it climbed and trailed where it willed. Pretty little pink flowers called Cats Whiskers waved their fernlike tendrils, and Woodbine scattered its white trumpet shaped flowers on the ground. Canna lilies added to the fiery effect, with their scarlet, orange and yellow blooms. Plants with ornamental leaves were also dotted about. Overall, was a most beautiful perfume from the Frangipani shrub with its little white flowers. Marjorie later learned that wreaths were often made of this.

The flamboyant birds were a fascination to Marjorie. Small parrots, often pale green or bright yellow would fly about her garden, and very small red fire-finches would run frantically about on the grass. She was thrilled when she first saw a tiny humming bird, plunging its long beak into a scarlet lily flower, its tiny wings invisible as they beat so fast, to enable it to hover steadily.

Patricia was giving a dinner party to which Marjorie had been invited. It seemed that the Europeans were continually throwing dinner parties and dances of one sort or another. It was in this way that she got to know a lot of people.

That evening Maureen O'Rourke was present, together with Dr and Mrs Driscoll, as well as one or two others whom Marjorie had not met before.

As they sat themselves down at the dinner table Marjorie commented on a small arrangement of pure white hibiscus flowers in the centre.

"I've never seen a white hibiscus at this time of day, only early in the morning."

"Yes, that's right," said someone. "The heat seems to draw out the colour in the flowers.

Dr Driscoll smiled. "Well, Miss Heath, you must keep and eye on these blooms then," He nodded to Patricia.

Conversation ebbed and flowed as the meal progressed and Marjorie watched in amazement as the pure white flowers slowly changed their hue to a deep crimson. She shook her head in disbelief.

"Are they real?" she asked. "Or are my eyes playing tricks on me?"

Patricia laughed. "Yes, they are real, and no, your eyes are not playing tricks on you!"

Mrs Driscoll explained. "We pick them first thing in the morning when they are still white before the sun has got to them. Then we store them in the refrigerator. As soon as the meal is ready to be served we put them on the table, then the warmth of the room helps their colour to change."

It proved to be a good talking point. Marjorie noticed that several hostesses used this trick of having white hibiscus on the dinner table. They always became the central topic of conversation as the colours deepened.

She had only been in Accra for a couple of months when an emergency call came through for Dr Driscoll. It seemed a young African man was ill with some unexplained disease, and the nurses at the hospital where he had been admitted could not cope with him. Dr Driscoll plodded over to the African Hospital, and in his calm, unhurried way, questioned the patient thoroughly. Eventually it transpired that he was in trouble at his place of work. Rather than interrogate him any more, Dr Driscoll went directly to the Manager of the firm in question, knowing that he would be better off with both sides of the story.

The Manager, Mr Todd, was an Englishman, a tall imposing man who was renowned for his good treatment of all employees, yet at the same time everyone knew that neither would he stand any nonsense from them. The doctor explained his problem to Mr Todd.

"So, there you have it," he finished. "I just cannot find any evidence of him having anything wrong with him, although he is obviously not at all well."

Mr Todd leaned on his desk.

"This is most interesting. You see that man in question was caught pilfering from the firm. I reprimanded him. Between you and me he is not particularly good at his work either, so I probably laid into him more than most. Anyway, he has not been seen at work from that day to this, just stayed away and sending in odd messages about feeling poorly."

"Well," confessed Dr Driscoll. "He most definitely is quite ill, but I just can't find anything wrong with the man. He just displays symptoms without justification of anything."

Mr Todd was no fool.

"All I can advise is that you discharge the man from hospital care then I myself will keep tabs on him."

They shook hands.

"I'll be in touch," promised Mr Todd.

Dr Driscoll discharged the man from hospital.

A week later he received a telephone call from Mr Todd.

"Good morning, doctor!" he boomed down the telephone. "Well, the situation is just as I thought. That poor man had been taken to the witch doctor by his relatives and been completely surrounded and overcome by their tomfoolery. The poor bloke gets weaker and more frail every time they dance and chant round him."

Dr Driscoll tutted into the phone.

"Anyway, my informant reported back to me so I went down there myself a few evenings ago."

"Oh, my!"

"Yes, marched right into their furore and gave the man notice to quit my firm."

"Oh dear."

"Would you believe it within a couple of days he was back on his feet, walking into my office asking for his job back!"

"Great Scott!"

"Of course a lot of Africans can be very unreliable, so I know now I must be firm with him."

"Good heavens!"

"Yes, Africans can soon spot a weakness to exploit, so of course I mustn't co-operate. It's all been a kind of blackmail really."

"Well, thank you indeed for your help, Mr Todd."

"Not at all, pleased to be of assistance."

"I hope you manage to find a replacement for him soon."

"Thanks, I'm sure I will. Goodbye."

Marjorie listened to this tale with fascination. Until then she had no idea of the power the witch doctors held over their people. She began to realise that although they may be simple in their ways, and indeed, some rather devious, the Africans must be treated with a lot more respect than she had, up until that time, credited them. Having thought this, she felt ashamed and narrow-minded as it dawned on her that she was working amongst human beings just like her apart from the colour of their skin and the fact that their culture was different. Annoying habits they may have occasionally, but then so did everyone, and whatever nationality they were, all people must be treated with the same amount of respect.

After this, Marjorie ensured she gained a good reputation as an employer, as all Europeans would have servants about the house as a matter of course. It became quite a joke that each would need a mate, however lowly their status, so the steward boy would have a steward boy's mate and the cook would have a cook's mate. Only the sensible people refrained from having a mate's mate.

Marjorie had been in Accra for just over three months when she received a letter from Grace telling her all about Jack, how she had met him whilst acting as live-in housekeeper to Uncle John and Aunt Louise in Ringwood, and that now they were engaged to be married. She described the sizeable farm and farmhouse they would be living in after their wedding, writing, *I am now in my seventh heaven!* Marjorie was sad that she would not be able to attend her elder sister's wedding, but was pleased that all Grace's subsequent letters reflected her obvious happiness.

Once the rainy season was over the highlight of Marjorie's week became a visit to the local cinema. It was open air, so could only be attended during the dry season. It was a new sensation to sit under a star spangled sky and watch whatever film was showing that particular Saturday. The films were generally ancient. She had seen many of them before in England, but being out of doors to watch them made for a wonderful romantic atmosphere, even when sitting alone in the auditorium.

On the 22nd June 1939 Marjorie was literally shaken out of her routine. Matron had gone out and Marjorie was serving the patients' evening meals. Suddenly there was a loud roaring noise, similar to that of an angry lion, but amplified many times. The hospital shook violently and the piles of thirty or so plates crashed to the floor ending in smithereens around Marjorie's feet. Screams and shouts could be heard. Food went everywhere and the floor became a sea of green peas carrying boats of lamb cutlets bobbing on top of them. The lights flickered then there was darkness. In a panic, Marjorie dashed to the telephone, not knowing who to contact. It was out of order. She felt her heart turn over as she felt the ground shuddering beneath her. So this was what it was like not to be in control of one's own situation and feel totally helpless.

"Get outside!" yelled someone. "Quickly! Everyone! Get outside!"

The cry echoed through the building and patients started to get out of their beds.

The African nurses started shouting and panicking. Eventually most of the patients who were well enough, were shuffling on their way to the exit, some needing help, eventually managing to get outside, calling to others to follow. Everyone did, apart from two typhoid patients who were too ill. The earthquake rumbled on for just over a minute and a half, although it seemed far longer.

Once outside, the situation could be assessed more calmly. The patients formed ranks, all chattering excitedly about the earthquake. Fortunately the hospital itself had not suffered any major damage. Soon Marjorie quieted the patients and was able to lead them back inside and to their beds.

Once the panic was over, Marjorie heard of some peculiar predicaments people had found themselves in at the time of the tremor, including one man who had been in the bath at the time and leapt out, even forgetting his towel. There were several other amusing incidents which provided light relief when recounted. Yet many people had been killed during the earthquake and Marjorie's own photographs of the large fissures swallowing cars and suchlike, bore out the seriousness of the situation.

One of her hospital patients at that time was a reporter for the *Daily Mail* in England. He was passing through on his way to East Africa when he contracted malaria, so had been admitted to Accra Hospital. Thrilled to be in the midst of such action, as soon as Matron returned to the hospital, he tried to persuade her to drive him to the Telegraph Office so that he could send off a report straight away to his Editor by cable.

"But Mr Parsons," she admonished him. "It is not the done thing to take patients sight-seeing. It is not at all customary. I am Matron of this hospital, not a tour guide."

"Oh come on," he pleaded. "An earthquake isn't a 'customary situation' as you put it."

"The roads out there are not in the condition they were when you were admitted Mr Parsons. Driving is quite hazardous, extremely hazardous."

"Come on Matron, live a little! This is a real scoop!"

"No Mr Parsons. You are under my care as a sick man and I can't possibly concur with this ridiculous notion of yours."

"I'm a lot better than I was, you must see that, so why not?"

"No Mr Parsons ...!" Matron quelled his questions with a stern look.

He walked slowly towards his ward. "But I may well get promotion. You wouldn't want to deny me that, would you?"

"Come now, stop all this nonsense and get back into bed." She steered him towards it.

"The only other way is for me to walk to the Telegraph Office. Look, if you take me in your car, I'll include your name in the report as a credit, how's that?"

"Oh, well, I don't know..."

He smiled a winning smile and winked at Marjorie who was waiting by his bed.

Matron put her head on one side "I suppose once patients improve we normally assess our patients by allowing them to walk round the grounds before anything else."

"Well, can't you assess this one with a drive in your car?"

Matron shook her head in defeat. "I suppose I must then, or I'll get me name in the paper for letting one of my patients abscond and walk off the premises."

He eventually got his way as Matron gave in for the sake of peace. He seemed to improve with the thought of an outing, getting dressed, only to return from the drive with a melon slice sized grin.

Having been outside and seen some of the damage for himself he would regale the other patients with exaggerated stories of the outside world, describing the massive cracks and crevices in the road that resembled ravines, how he had seen three or four cars swallowed up along with some market stalls. Most patients were too ill to care.

British people read in their daily newspapers a few days later:

2000 Homeless After Quake
(from our Daily Mail Correspondent)

Europeans at Accra, Gold Coast, are concerned about the problem of housing 2000 natives left homeless by the earthquake in which 16 Africans were killed.

Two thousand children were fed at food kitchens yesterday.

Churches and schools have been filled and 200 houses erected by the Gold Coast Regiment were available for women last night.

Meanwhile tremors continued throughout the night. Marjorie was on duty and sleeping in the hospital, but she didn't get much sleep, what with the after-shocks and needing to soothe frightened patients.

In the morning Maureen O'Rourke took Marjorie out in her car .They toured round Accra as far as was possible, and saw the damage for themselves. Many houses had collapsed. Wreckage was everywhere. Roads were closed as they were either blocked or had huge ugly fissures down them. The African people looked a sorry sight as they tried to salvage the remains of their market stalls, drag their meagre possessions out of half collapsed houses and shacks, trying to recover what few things they owned. Marjorie felt she was an intruder, being able to see so many people's lives laid bare just by them having only half a home left standing, sometimes trying to cover its privacy with what was left of the corrugated iron roof. It was never discovered exactly how many people had been killed.

Tremors continued throughout the night and up until ten months later in April 1940. By then, there were so many of them that people were blasé and didn't appear to notice them.

Overall, the hospital had a very relaxed and friendly

atmosphere about it. Nothing was as strict as it had been in England. Once she got used to the idea of visitors drifting in and out whenever they pleased, and having to make do just because they didn't have any specialised equipment, Marjorie enjoyed it and was challenged by her work here as anywhere else.

She had been in Africa for almost nine months when she was entitled to take three weeks local leave. She chose to visit Lagos, and stayed with some friends who had moved from Accra to Lagos a few months beforehand. She was thrilled with the combination of shops and the knowledge of being so close to the African bush. A visit to the hospital there left her quite envious, as it was situated close to the river and had a very picturesque outlook, so much so, that it was known locally as the Creek Hospital. It too had been built on brick pillars. Once she had been a tourist in Lagos for three weeks it was hard to leave and return to Accra to work, but she soon settled again.

Chapter Eight

Marjorie had been in West Africa for eighteen months. This entitled her to a three month long break and meant she could go home. The Second World War had begun by then, as it was spring 1940. In her letters to Marjorie, Bettie sounded excited as she had by that time, become engaged to Bill Tapper. This meant that Marjorie would be home in time for their wedding, planned in June. Bettie was hoping that she and Jessie would be her bridesmaids.

Almost as soon as she arrived home, Marjorie cut out, stitched and sewed both bridesmaids' dresses. She was also in the process of packing away just about everything she possessed ready for her next voyage to West Africa. Official advice was that she should take everything with her lest it be lost or damaged due to the bombing if it was left at home.

Bettie would sit on Marjorie's bed writing letters to acknowledge wedding presents then pause to tell her some more about Bill. Hilda seemed to resent their closeness and would frequently call crossly up the stairs to ask what they were up to. All too casually, Bettie would shout back quite rudely in a spirit that Marjorie envied, as she was too timid to say more than she was packing and would be down soon.

"Marjorie? Bettie? Are you both up there?"

"Yes, Mother!"

"Whatever are you doing all this time?"

"Talking!"

"I can't think what you've got to say to one another that can't be spoken about in front of everyone."

"I've got a lot of packing to do as well, Mother."

"I'm writing thank-you letters."

"You need peace and quiet for writing, Bettie and there's an awful lot of chattering and giggling going on."

Bettie raised her eyes heavenwards and sighed. "Just leave us be, will you? We'll be down eventually."

"Well don't stay up there too long."

"Leave us alone won't you Mother," snapped Bettie, making a grimace as she heard her mother leave the hall.

Bettie reached into a wardrobe and brought out a long white lacy dress. Holding it against her, she waltzed round the room. "Isn't this just a dream?"

Marjorie agreed.

Now all the children had matured into adulthood their relationship with each another had surprisingly deepened, perhaps nourished by temporary separation.

Bettie's wedding turned out to be a fractious affair as first one thing, then another, met Hilda's disapproval. In the beginning she had been against them having a public wedding at all. Apparently she had also held this objection to Grace marrying Jack, although Grace eventually got her way.

"There's just no need to go to such a fuss and bother."

"Whyever not?"

"Marriage is a private thing between two people and they only need the necessary witnesses to make it so."

"But a wedding is something to celebrate and have our friends to celebrate with us!"

"I don't think so, especially now when it's wartime so unnecessary expense must be avoided."

"Mother, how could you! My wedding is not an 'unnecessary expense', as you call it. Bill and I are getting married because we love each other and we both think this is a cause for celebration."

"I don't agree."

"Well, I'm sorry, but I'm not having a hole-in-the-corner wedding for anyone, least of all, Hitler!"

The girls could only assume that she was jealous after her own quiet wedding to their father, then a widower. Bettie insisted that it was her wedding, her day, and she would plan it as she wished.

Hilda had been horrified by the cost of the wedding dress. It was truly a beautiful dress.

"How dare you spend as much as thirty shillings on

your dress alone!"

"But it's such a gorgeous dress."

"Take it back! We can't afford it!"

"It was the only one I tried on that fitted perfectly."

"Too bad, it's far too expensive."

Marjorie eventually solved the problem by pointing out that with a few alterations it would survive as a party dress for years to come.

Bettie looked at her gratefully as Hilda reluctantly agreed to let her keep it.

Marjorie later reminded Bettie of the occasion ten years previously. "Timothy insisted on buying me this evening dress just because I admired it in a shop window," she said. "I remember feeling so embarrassed at the time."

Bettie was duly impressed. "I say, really?"

"He just made me go in and try it on, and when he saw me in it, he loved it and bought it, just like that!"

"How romantic!"

"Yes, but the point I'm trying to make is that it was not a practical dress, it was frivolous and cost three pounds; and that was all of ten years ago. That makes your find a dream of a wedding dress pretty good going by comparison, so don't worry about breaking the bank. Stand up for your rights."

"Don't worry, I will. Thanks for standing by me."

"That little revelation is just between you and me – I don't want anyone else to know that a man bought me clothes whatever the situation. After all, it's not the done thing, is it?"

"Agreed!"

The next argument ensued because Hilda thought the flowers were too much of an expense and wanted the bouquet to be put together from those grown in their garden.

"Mother, I want everything to be just right."

"Well, it still can be."

"I want the colour schemes to all match and tie in. We don't have half enough blooms in the garden, never mind the right colours and shades."

"However many do you want then?"

"I want a nice bouquet and Jessie and Marjorie must at least carry a small posy each."

"But the expense of it all..."

"Blow the expense! Bill said he would pay for them, anyway."

"But he can't afford to pay for things like that!"

"Keep out of it, Mother, and let us do things the way we want to."

Marjorie was surprised that Bettie and Bill didn't elope to avoid all the fuss. After the ceremony, she was pleased that Bettie had got what she wanted – a wedding to celebrate their marriage rather than a quiet affair.

At least she sailed to West Africa with a happy heart knowing that Bettie would be happy and well looked after by a man as caring and patient as Bill.

Her leave had been busy. Marjorie sailed again on 22nd July 1940, once again aboard the *Accra*. Due to the war and needing to keep a lookout for enemy vessels, this time they sailed in a convoy of 52 ships of various descriptions, all keeping to the speed of the slowest vessel. A plane circled round from time to time giving added protection.

The first day was spent in unpacking and recalling her way around the ship. As the weather was cold for the time of year most people spent the first few days sitting on deck wrapped in rugs or playing table tennis. There were only six other women on board and about 500 men, most of whom were returning to government positions in the West African colonies.

On the fourth day out Marjorie began to feel seasick due to the heavy swell. No sooner had she settled comfortably on deck to get some fresh air, there was a terrific bang and the ship shuddered as if trying to shake off the resultant shattered glass and debris falling all around.

The ship immediately listed way over on its starboard

side apparently about to sink almost at once, so heavy was the impact from not just one torpedo, but two. Then the ship righted itself a little and the crew began lowering lifeboats although some of these had been destroyed by the impact of the torpedoes.

A voice from the tannoy. "This is your captain speaking. All passengers and crew must put on your lifejackets and go to your appointed muster station immediately."

"Man the lifeboats! Prepare to abandon ship!" roared another voice.

Marjorie donned her bulky lifejacket and staggered along to her emergency station. People were scurrying everywhere. She felt her stomach lurch.

Lifeboats were hastily lowered into the heaving grey sea below. As Marjorie looked, her stomach churned with nausea and in terror. Being unable to swim very well she hated water deeper than her bath.

The women were ordered to get into the lifeboats first. There was no time to collect any belongings. With pounding heart, Marjorie clambered awkwardly over the side of the badly damaged ship. The wind clawed at her clothing causing her to falter. Her heart beat wildly. Unable to swim she was terrified of missing her footing and falling into the sea. Then she felt the lifeboat sway beneath her as she literally fell into it. Once it was overfilled with people it was lowered jerkily over the side of the huge parent ship which by now was fast taking in water. All the passengers in the little boat clung on for dear life as it went down towards the moving murky waters below by means of ropes and pulleys, first the forward end pointing downwards, then the stern.

Suddenly one end hit the waves whilst the other remained suspended in mid air. Marjorie disappeared under the water as people fell on top of her in a kind of watery rugger-scrum. She resurfaced again a little farther away. Unable to breathe she panicked as she faced death head on.

Her life seemed to flash before her eyes. She recalled

her father, Timothy, Jack Sullivan, her stepmother; what was the quality of her existence anyway? Then she recalled some of the wonderful things she had heard spoken about her own mother; Lottie, people had called her. People had always spoken well of her. Perhaps she would see her soon? But suppose her own mother disapproved of Marjorie's life so far? Oh, she couldn't bear that! She struggled violently in the freezing cold sea that threatened to engulf her. Her body disappeared beneath a huge wave and she swallowed what felt like a large proportion of it as it overwhelmed her. Fear set in as her mind pictured what sort of life was lurking in the ocean beneath her. With her arms flailing wildly, she desperately tried to keep afloat and thrashed around in the chill wintry sea until lifelines from the *Accra* were thrown. Eventually she managed to catch one that snaked near her.

"Hold on down there!" yelled a male voice as she found herself hoisted into the air, crashing painfully against the iron hull, now a welcome island in the midst of such an angry sea. Several other people were also hauled up and left dangling on ropes like strings of onions.

Marjorie felt as though her arms would be pulled out of their sockets as she strained to hang on to the lifeline. Her hands were losing their grip, she was very weary and was tempted to let go until she happened to glance down at the dark stormy waters beneath her. She could not afford to feel pain any more.

Desperately she clung on to her life itself until after what felt like an eternity she was told to slide into a lifeboat below. Marjorie lost her footing and badly grazed her hands on the rope. Even then her troubles were still not over as this lifeboat was already half full of water. Everyone frantically baled out with hats, handbags and anything they could lay hands on. Then an African boy bravely climbed a rope back to the *Accra* returning with a bucket. The men then took it in turns to bail out as much as they could with that. The water level in the boat was reduced to knee level.

Some of the men then took up the oars and began to hysterically row as far away from the scene as possible. Everyone was afraid and nobody wanted to be dragged down by the suction and swirling of the sea as it began to close over the mother ship's hull.

By this time there was no sign of any other ships from the convoy. When the *Accra* had been torpedoed, they had all scuttled and scattered in different directions for their own safety.

The lifeboat heaved upwards in the water, hung for a brief moment, before plunging back down again. Up and down they went, backwards and forwards and from side to side. Marjorie's head was whirling and her stomach heaved. She turned sideways just in time to vomit into the waves' raging green depths. The sea was extremely rough and it was difficult to make headway. The little boat surmounted one enormous wave only to crash down the other side of it and be mocked by yet another steep hill of water to overcome.

All around were lifeboats laden with survivors, as well as people sitting and hanging onto rafts of upturned tables and other pieces of wreckage. They were faced with yet another breaker as the wind grew stronger and the swell increased.

Four men were heaved out of the vast watery waste into their already overcrowded lifeboat. One was already dead, so was thrown back into an oceanic grave.

Suddenly someone in the lifeboat pointed. "What's that?"

People became nervous, craning to see, chattering, wondering.

Then a woman screamed. "A periscope!"
"Oh God, not a German periscope, please."
"Hush! Be quiet!" snapped a man's voice.
So terrified were they, people hardly dare breathe.
Someone laughed. "Oh look, it's just a table leg!"
Everyone gulped in relief.

The massive waves continuously tried to fill the boat

and the men used the bucket to bail continuously and keep the water down to knee level.

They were all saturated with salty water, many were seasick including Marjorie.

The mountainous watery walls that heaved around them and tossed them about should have instilled fear, but there was no time to think as everyone who could, scooped and bailed fast to keep the floods at bay. The boat creaked ominously as it negotiated each wave.

Everybody was exhausted.

An hour later they saw the damaged ship heave onto its side, before sinking quickly, stern uppermost taking all their worldly possessions with it onto the seabed. It was an emotional moment. All the people in the lifeboat were silent for some while after this. The *Accra* had been a popular ship with a convivial atmosphere about her. Now she was gone, never to patrol the African coast again. Marjorie promptly leaned over the side of the lifeboat and once more vomited violently into the water. Thereafter, continuing to feel ill, shivering uncontrollably she clung to its side in terror.

After about three hours later a ship was spied on the horizon. All they could do was wave hysterically and hope it wasn't the enemy. They were spotted. This ship, a collier, the SS *Hollingside* was on its way to Nova Scotia and had already picked up other survivors. Therefore the three dozen crew were hard put to rescue a total of 400 people who would severely limit their space and rations. Marjorie would always be grateful to the crew for way they rescued and looked after 249 drenched passengers.

She had collapsed by this stage and when it was her turn to be taken on board the larger vessel, a rope was tied around her waist and she was hauled bumpily up the side in a most undignified manner as she slumped over the lasso of rope.

By the time Marjorie was hauled up on deck she was unconscious. Sailors were trying to categorise people. Marjorie was left for dead and cast aside on the hatchway.

After twenty minutes, a crewman picked her up to throw her back into the sea when he noticed that one of her eyelids flickered. He alerted a mate and they had a whispered discussion. Together they carried her off to the Chief Steward's cabin to recover where they placed her gently on the bunk.

After a while one of the men returned and Marjorie came to by having her cheeks patted and a man's voice saying, "Come on me luv. Wake up, there's a good girl."

She eventually forced her eyes open. *Where am I?*

The voice spoke again. "Come on, luv, drink this. It'll help yer feel better."

His hand supported her head to drink from a tin mug.

Marjorie gulped and swallowed a liquid that burned her throat. Spluttering and choking, she eventually felt the substance soothing as it trickled down to her stomach.

"Oops, choke up chicken! A small sip this time."

Marjorie obeyed, still too weak to speak. Soon the tot of brandy was finished. She leaned weakly back against the pillows. The man backed through the doorway.

"I'll let yer sleep fer a bit an' come back in an hour or so. All right luv?"

He disappeared.

Marjorie's head throbbed. She still felt nauseous, but supposed this was exaggerated by a hollow emptiness in her stomach. She felt bloated too, as if she had drunk several bottles of fizzy drink. The brandy slowly began to settle her system. She had always told her patients that sleep was a great healer; perhaps she could sleep – but she was so cold. She moved a little under the rough grey blanket, wondering what time it was. Then she realised she didn't even know what day it was. To weary to worry about these things, she drifted into oblivion as she slept.

The crew member who had dosed her with brandy brought her a mug of tea and a ships biscuit about an hour later.

"Nuffink stronger than tea this time, luv," he chortled.

Marjorie's head was spinning, but she managed to prop

herself up on one elbow and drink the tea for herself. The man stayed with her for a chat.

"Gave us a right turn you did, luv. Thought we'd got a dead body on board. Me mate was just about to chuck yer back into the old briny when you gave 'im the shock of 'is life fluttering yer eyelid like that! That's why we brought yer in 'ere. This is the Chief Steward's cabin, an' 'e don't give 'is quarters up to just anybody, I'm tellin' yer!" He grinned down at her.

Marjorie gave him a faint smile. "I'm most grateful to you – to everybody," she murmured.

That evening when the Chief Steward came to bed down for the night, Marjorie was still in his bunk, sleeping peacefully. With a wry smile he collected some blankets from the ship's store and gallantly kipped down elsewhere on the floor. Others were not so fortunate, having to sleep just where they could. Nobody slept properly as depth charges were being dropped all through the night, aiming at submarines as they silently probed the fathoms beneath.

The following morning Marjorie staggered to her feet and thanked the Chief Steward for his hospitality. She decided she felt well enough to join her comrades up on deck by this time. Another convoy had joined the ship overnight as they started homeward for England.

At seven o'clock each morning, everyone was lined up and given two dry hardtack, or ships biscuits, which were barely more than wafers, plus an old tin can of tea together with some corned beef for breakfast. By this time, people were feeling a little better and began to relate their adventures to one another.

Later in the day, buckets of thin watery stew were produced and everyone sat round trying to eat this as best they could using either a ships biscuit or their fingers. On a ship this size, there were not enough eating utensils for so many extra people. In the evening, large jugs of pea soup were brought to the refugees, each containing just one spoon. These were shared round amongst them, and they marvelled at the circumstances they would normally shun.

Now in a life saving situation, everything was welcome. They were all grateful for anything after their narrow escape.

Each morning the dustbins were raided and tins of every description were salvaged to use for drinking purposes; the bigger the tin, the more early morning tea. Marjorie managed to get hold of a tin that had contained pineapple chunks.

Nights were cold and uncomfortable as they slept wrapped in rugs, squashed in every conceivable space on the collier. Days became monotonous as all books and hobbies had gone to the bottom of the sea with the *Accra*. Everyone passed their time idly watching other ships in the convoy signalling to one another.

One morning there was much excitement when a sloop ship signalled that they had picked up 63 survivors from the ship that had originally been appointed to rescue them, but had apparently been torpedoed just after the *Accra*. The sloop came alongside and provided a distraction while more refugees were transferred to the already overcrowded *Hollingside*. Marjorie watched this with interest. Now they all had a different set of companions to keep them amused by relating their escapades and experiences. Their 60 or so new acquaintances had fared well, having enjoyed four meals a day, plus alcohol and cigarettes. They were certainly not pleased to discover that they would be limited to bully beef and hardtack, nor was there any cabin space available for them.

The rescue-ship limped back into Liverpool and was welcomed with cheers from the quayside. Marjorie finally arrived back in England eight long days after she had set sail. Everyone was given a blanket and a hot meal, plus a much-needed wash on board a ship that was waiting to set sail. They still resembled scruffy tramps, because their clothes were so filthy and dishevelled. Eventually Marjorie was given ninety pounds *ex gratia* payment to replace her possessions, a first class rail ticket home and was allowed to send a telegram free of charge. A bus took a lot of them to Lime Street Station and from there she was on her own.

Bettie looked forward to receiving letters from Marjorie. She obviously led a hectic life, yet the tit-bits of news that she sent were really interesting. Bettie herself had no inclination to travel. She was satisfied with her lot of being an efficient secretary, and now being married to Bill. He was a loyal, dependable character, and they were so much in love. Mother had almost ruined their wedding by wanting everything done to her way of thinking. She had irritated Bettie no end, so that the two women had nearly come to blows. Thank goodness Bill had been so patient. He and his father-in-law were proving to be two of a kind and they got on well together.

Her thoughts turned to Marjorie again. She was amazing in her determination to nurse in Africa, especially after that awful earthquake which must have been terrifying. Bettie admired her for her courage to travel the world, especially now this awful war was increasing.

Here in the Dorset country towns and villages they didn't have too much to worry about. Yet, every day in the newspapers there were fresh pictures of bomb damage and lists of casualties.

On the other hand, Marjorie was quite timid when it came to family relationships. Bettie thought of when they had all grown up together. She appreciated now how badly her stepsisters had been treated, although at the time it had all seemed normal. Marjorie never stood up for herself to anyone. Bettie recalled the occasion when they had both been having sisterly exchanges and giggles in the bedroom just before her wedding. Marjorie was packing absolutely everything. Mother had kept calling up the stairs to ask what they were doing. Marjorie had sweetly assured her stepmother she would be down soon, whereas Bettie had told her mother in no uncertain terms that they wanted to be left alone. She smiled, remembering Marjorie had been quite shocked by this.

Bettie wondered where her stepsister was now. She

couldn't write yet as she was not sure where Marjorie would be posted. Everything was kept so secret. Bettie loved writing and receiving letters. Perhaps she would write a little in diary form each day and post it as soon she knew her address.

She would tell her how they had settled into their little flat and how it was more convenient to walk to work from there, saving a lot of money in bus fares. She would tell her that Ronald was now a civil servant working in Whitehall, but they hardly heard from him because he was so secretive about his job she began to wonder if *he* really knew about it himself. She would tell her how Mother had started to save the *Daily Telegraph* newspapers so that they could be sent out to Marjorie in Africa at intervals.

Bill and Bettie were having their meal together in the flat when the doorbell rang.

Bettie jumped up. "Stay there. I'll see who it is!"

She returned slowly with a yellow telegram in her hand.

"The boy didn't wait. You open it. I don't think I can."

Bill tore it open with trembling fingers. "It's from Marjorie. She must be all right as it *is* from *her*. All it says is *'MEET ME OFF LIVERPOOL TRAIN ARRIVING POOLE 5.50PM TODAY STOP LOVE MARJORIE.'*"

Bill glanced at his watch. "We've just got time to finish this before we leave."

"I wonder why she's back home?"

"I'd better attach the trailer to the car for all that luggage she took with her."

"The ship can't have sailed after all," mused Bettie.

"I'll go and sort out the trailer now. Be ready when I call you." Bill disappeared out into the yard.

* * *

Alan McKenzie leaned on the railings of the *Accra* watching the hustle and bustle on the docks below. He had been home on leave for three months, but the time had not gone well. He was looking forward to returning to the hospital and being back in the swing of things there. He really enjoyed his work, it was absorbing and satisfying. Seeing people come to him in pain and unwell, then diagnosing what was wrong and being able to cure them with modern medical and surgical means brought him great job satisfaction. He enjoyed people anyway, whether he was working with them or socialising.

Being a man on his own meant he often got invited to other people's dinner parties and social evenings, as hostesses tended to feel motherly towards a man without a woman in tow. He had his own house servants, so was able to put on a good meal and entertain others as well as anyone else. He was sometimes given gifts by grateful patients, or was able to buy something from a shipload of smoked hams, or some such delicacy to take along to his host and hostess by way of a contribution.

That's another thing about this war, he reflected. *After a lack of certain items, a ship would bring a load of identical items so that the region would be swamped by a glut of bicycles or typewriters, perhaps tins of baked beans or meat. There was no way of knowing what might come next, especially as ships were being torpedoed and a lot of supplies were being lost.*

He turned away from the dockland scene and went below with a sigh, finding his cases in the cabin. He unpacked the one selected to be sufficient for the voyage and dressed for dinner cutting a fine image in his dark dinner suit which fitted his tall slim body perfectly. However, he still was not able to fully control the lock of fair hair that had a tendency to flop over one eye.

They set sail that evening. Alan enjoyed the sea and settled down to the prospect of anything up to three weeks of luxury as the ship and its convoy criss-crossed the Atlantic in order to confuse the enemy's submarines. Although it was cold for July he took advantage of all the deck games on board ship confident that his healthy tan would soon return.

It was on the fourth day at sea that it happened. There were two deafening bangs when everybody and everything were jolted everywhere. Alan was in the dining room finishing off a leisurely luncheon and taking his time over coffee. The message came over the tannoy almost immediately, instructing everyone to abandon ship. People went as quickly as they could to their muster stations.

Alan ran his hand through his hair in a characteristic mannerism and casually sauntered up the carpeted stairs to the deck. He had never hurried anywhere in his life, and it was his inbred calm attitude that had made him the excellent surgeon that he was.

Once on deck, he saw one of the first lifeboats being lowered. Suddenly it was upended leaving its occupants struggling in the waters below. Members of the crew were throwing ropes to them to use as lifelines. "What a shambles!" he muttered.

All around him was a sense of fury against the enemy for jolting the serenity out of their lives with not one, but two torpedoes. Alan was eventually herded into another lifeboat that was lowered into the water without mishap. Although overloaded with people they got a good haul on the oars and soon left the sorry scene behind despite the sea heaving heavily all around. Along with two other men, Alan took his turn at rowing, and after about an hour, a ship was sighted on the horizon. Praying that it was friendly, they sent up distress flares.

To everyone's relief it was a Norwegian ship, heading for home. There were sleeping quarters for everyone and enough select cuisine to share with the unfortunate folk from the lifeboat who were treated like royalty for the remainder of their journey to Liverpool.

Alan did not feel inclined to go home again, especially after the tension of his last stay. He checked in at a Liverpool hotel to await the renewal of his passage to West Africa. He wouldn't worry his family – they would think he was safely there, and indeed he would be before he contacted them again.

* * *

The train left Liverpool behind, rapidly gathering speed and plunging into countryside. Marjorie stared unseeingly out of the grimy window. It seemed that even the fields and trees were soporific after the early morning rain. The animals in the meadows looked too drowsy to move.

Everything matched her mood.

At last she climbed down at the local station and passed through the dingy booking hall displaying war posters instead of the usual cheery ones advertising the merits of Bournemouth and other seaside towns. She was relieved to see Bettie's silhouette against the light from behind her. They fell upon one another in relief.

"Didn't your ship sail after all? Where's your luggage? Bill can put it all in the trailer." Bettie plied Marjorie with questions, not noticing her bedraggled appearance.

"There isn't any. It ... it's all at the bottom of the sea."

They were outside by now. Bettie turned to Marjorie and held her at arm's length as she took in her appearance.

"Oh no! What happened?"

"W-we were torpedoed."

"Oh, Marjorie, you poor thing!" Bettie hugged her warmly and Marjorie finally gave way to tears.

Bill came striding over. Before he said anything, Bettie explained the situation while Marjorie tried to get a grip on herself. They walked in silence to the car. Marjorie could not help but notice the trailer hitched up behind ready to take all her luggage. Nothing more was said.

An account of the disaster made front page headlines on the 8th August 1940.

TWO U-BOATS DESTROYED AFTER SINKING LINER

SHIP ATTACKED IN CONVOY: 19 LIVES LOST

Two U-boats which torpedoed and sank the 9,337 ton Elder Dempster Line Accra *off the west coast of Eire on Friday, 26th July, it was learned in London last night, paid the penalty for their act, being themselves destroyed soon afterwards.*

This information was given by one of the 450 survivors landed at a port in the north-west of England. Eleven of the Accra's *passengers and eight of the crew are missing.*

The only women on board were five nurses and two stewardesses.

Most of the loss of life was due to the capsizing of a motor-boat in a choppy sea and to direct hits on the liner.

Survivors said that the Accra *was hit by two converging torpedoes.*

"We had no chance of keeping afloat," said one of the men. "The U-boats paid for their audacity in attacking at short range, for both were sunk immediately after."

Capt. John Joseph Smith of Wallasey, said that the passengers were having luncheon when the torpedo explosion occurred. They filed out of the saloon in orderly fashion.

The men in the lifeboats sang 'There'll always be an England' when on the way to rescuing ships. The whole of the rescue work was completed in about half an hour.

Capt Smith stated that he had just reached the bridge when the explosion occurred.

"When I tried to blow the whistle signals for the lifeboat I found that the power had gone. The torpedo hit us amidships. It shook the ship from stem to stern. There was no trace of panic. None of us saw the submarine, but we understand that at least one was sunk later."

The Accra *figured in a race recently with three*

submarines. She was one of the largest of the Elder Dempster boats and was launched from Belfast in 1926. She had accommodation for 500 passengers and crew and had proved a fast and popular vessel on the West African route.

Chapter Nine

Eventually Marjorie bravely set sail again for West Africa aboard the *Apapa* at the beginning of September 1940. This voyage turned out to be a memorably happy one as well as promising fine and calm weather. Marjorie was sunbathing on deck during the third day out, enjoying the warm sunshine. Opening her eyes, she took a deep breath of the salty air that made her nose tingle a little. She smiled with pleasure, pleasure to be returning to West Africa, but best of all, pleasure at being alive.

She had already met a lot of people who had been on the *Accra* and had been torpedoed with her and once again they exchanged experiences. Some would always bear the mental agony of what they had been through, but others were content to accept their lot.

It was on this voyage that Marjorie first met Alan McKenzie who turned out to be the Senior Surgeon responsible for all the hospitals in the southern part of Nigeria. Marjorie was initially in awe of him, but his relaxed and friendly manner soon put her at her ease.

They exchanged tales of how each had been torpedoed and Marjorie was surprised to hear that he had been aboard the *Accra* at the time of the tragedy. He described how they rowed through heavy seas before being rescued by a Norwegian ship. As he described the wonderful meals they were provided with, Marjorie felt quite hungry at the thought of it all, plus the individual cabin space provided for the unfortunate travellers.

Marjorie told him something of her experience.

"Oh my!" he exclaimed. "When I first came up from the dining room, I saw that lifeboat tipped into the sea. You poor thing! That must have been awful for you."

His sympathy extracted more of the perils she had experienced at sea than she would otherwise have given. He certainly was a good and sympathetic listener. She enjoyed Alan's company and easy-going manner. He was a tall lean sun tanned man with an open good-natured expression. He certainly looked pleasant enough. She tried to guess his age; probably similar to her own, possibly four or five years older.

One evening she was leaning over the rail at the stern of the ship watching the frothy wash bathed in moonlight. The dark sea all around was calm, making the jetsam resemble a bubbly mountain stream. Up in the sky was a big paper globe of a moon surrounded by twinkling stars nestling in a sky of black velvet.

"Beautiful, isn't it?" A voice behind her startled her out of her reverie. She turned and saw Alan standing there, the moonlight casting his face as if in marble.

"Sorry to startle you. I came on deck for some fresh air, and I thought it was you."

They turned and leaned on the rail together in silence for some minutes, absorbing the enchanting scene spread out before them.

"It's so calm and so different from that day when we were torpedoed," remarked Marjorie.

"Well, no doubt the enemy wants to do his worst and chooses the worst weather for his victims and lowers morale even more." Alan replied seriously.

Marjorie laughed.

"They don't really, do they? I thought that in war everybody was out to kill everyone else, not analyse the weather!"

"The aircraft use the darkest nights to fly and surprise the enemy."

They were silent again, then Alan pointed. "Look, see over there! There's a school of porpoise!"

Marjorie saw them playfully leaping about on their port side. She watched in gentle fascination before Alan broke the stillness.

"You're posted to Lagos Hospital from now on." It was a statement, not a question.

"Oh? Am I really?" Marjorie was dumbfounded. "I thought I was going back to Accra."

"No." After a pause he volunteered the information, "I'm based at Lagos too."

Marjorie wondered how on earth he knew. Perhaps it was because he was in a senior position. She recalled spending three weeks there and how she had enjoyed it.

She shivered.

"Come on inside. It's getting chilly now," he ordered.

Marjorie meekly obeyed.

They went into the lounge bar where Alan bought drinks. They sat chatting quietly together at a table against a background hum of other conversations until the barman called out, "Last orders please!"

People thronged to the bar to be certain of another drink.

"Do you mind if I disappear?" asked Alan. "Noisy gatherings like this tend to grate on me!" He smiled, squeezed her hand briefly and disappeared away from the clamour of the crowd.

Marjorie stayed where she was for some ten minutes, trying to assess what could almost be the beginning of a new relationship. Yet she was afraid to even think about it – so fragile was it, that to reach out, then try to capture it would surely shatter its delicate beauty.

Sure enough, when Marjorie tried to disembark at Accra, she was told to stay on board ship to travel further on to Lagos just as Alan had predicted. She never did discover whether he had the foreknowledge because of who he was, or whether he had taken advantage of his status to ensure that she worked under him at Lagos.

Alan explained to her that Lagos is the Portuguese word meaning lagoons, and that the town of Lagos, the capital of Nigeria, was built on the site of many lagoons and islands.

As Marjorie was to discover when the ship sailed into Lagos harbour, one group of lagoons formed the harbour, and fishing canoes would glide deftly past the large cargo steamers loading palm-oil, cotton, groundnuts or cocoa.

The sea road ran along this shore shaded by palms with lawns and jetties on its seaward side, and on the other stood Government House and other large buildings of administration.

Behind such an elegant façade were modern shopping streets of big stores and warehouses, treeless, airless and scorched. After that the maze of this African town sprawled into masses of low wooden buildings. Lagos had been a crowded town for many a long year.

Marjorie took all this in during the taxi ride to the hospital.

She was allocated a comfortable bungalow on the far side of the hospital complex. It was similar to the one she had lived in whilst in Accra, but a little larger. As she settled down for her first night in Nigeria, the noises that had seemed so alien and threatening at the beginning of her stay in Africa were comfortingly familiar on her return.

The hospital in Lagos was much larger, as it accommodated both black and white people. It was like a small village of long brick built white painted bungalows, once again atop supporting brick pillars. A corrugated iron roof then joined each section. Again, Marjorie's uniform was a white cotton dress with a white folded muslin square on her head that flapped as she walked, creating a small draught in the heat of the day.

She was to thoroughly enjoy her stay at Lagos Hospital. It had a pretty approach to it over a little wooden bridge. Situated just by the river it had a beautiful outlook. Because of all this it became known as the Creek Hospital. Marjorie would also be nursing European patients here.

Toby Wilkes was the doctor here. He was a tall, well-built man with dark hair and bushy eyebrows. He also had a highly coloured complexion that was often matched by his language when things went wrong. His gestures of goodwill could be violent too, with his hearty back-slapping or cheek pinching, depending on whom he was addressing. Marjorie was never very sure of him and tried to steer clear of his unpredictable energy when she could. His wife, Ida, was tall with a generous figure and was obviously a good match for him, although she always managed to look austere in a gracious kind of way. Marjorie could never imagine them on their own together as they only seem to socialise with other people.

The Matron, Miss Henley, was wonderful. Her task was to run the hospital by doing all the administrative work, but she enjoyed nursing and often came to help out, almost welcoming a busy time when she could lay her pen on her desk and pick up a stethoscope or thermometer instead. She was a tall woman who was always in a hurry, yet she still managed to move with grace. Her chestnut hair was caught back in a severe bun when she was on duty, but when she let it swing round her face it was easy to see what an attractive woman she was.

Miss Glover was the other Nursing Sister. She was short and plump with mousy brown hair that she tried to keep in a fashionable roll. Her Christian name was Barbara She and Marjorie got on very well together. They often went out together socially if they had any off duty times that coincided.

On her first day there towards mid afternoon, Marjorie sat in the shade in the garden of her bungalow absorbing the beautiful view. The grass ended just by the gentle curve of the river. In the foreground were some bushy shrubs, one of which was the Frangipani, currently covered in white flowers that issued their heady fragrant, perfume all round. Some magnificent tall palm trees backed the scene. She sighed. Working in a setting like this was almost too good to be true.

A figure appeared in the distance. She shaded her eyes, but could not make out who it was. As he approached she realised it was Alan McKenzie who had befriended her on board the *Apapa*. He waved and she waved back.

"Hello there," he called. "I just thought I would pop over and see how you're settling in."

"I met the hospital staff this morning, just briefly, and

now I'm admiring all this beautiful scenery while the steward sorts out my luggage. I haven't taken it all in yet."

"Yes, this is an amazing setting," he agreed. "Have you got everything you need?"

"Oh, yes thank you. I'm pretty sure that I'll enjoy working here."

"Good." He smiled down at her. "I'll see you at the hospital some time then." With that, he turned and strode away.

Marjorie wondered again whether he had requested her posting to this, his own base. After all, she had been sailing back to Accra as far as she knew, until she had been told to stay aboard the ship and travel on to Lagos. It was wartime and many things were kept secret, but where she was to work would surely not affect world affairs to that degree.

She gazed into the distance long after he had gone, suddenly seeing a large collection of what looked like balls hanging onto a tree. They would be the nests of the sparrow-like weaverbirds. It was amazing how neat and spherical a job they made of their nests using just feathers and mud. Sitting still there for so long encouraged a couple of crown birds to be bold and strut quite close to her, their tufted heads held high on their dull brown bodies, looking similar to herons. Glancing at the time, Marjorie made a move to return to the bungalow and the birds stretched their necks and wings as they ran away.

Apart from seeing Alan around the hospital, Marjorie met him at one or two parties and dances. He seemed popular. After one such meeting, he asked Marjorie if he could meet her down at the Ikoye club the following evening. Happily, Marjorie realised she would not be on duty, hoping that he had not heard her heart leap with delight. The club was a building where Europeans would congregate in their off-duty times. It had a bar, tables and a hall with a raised platform at one end. Dances were sometimes held there, and occasionally a show was staged amongst themselves.

That evening they sat in a corner, enjoying a quiet drink together. Marjorie noticed for the first time the long dark lashes surrounding his amber-coloured eyes. He had brown hair that had been bleached by the Nigerian sun. His hands, with their long artistic fingers, moved as he spoke, making dramatic shapes in the air, as if to illustrate what he was saying. Marjorie felt fired up by his apparently endless energy even in conversation, and she was relieved when he finally asked

"Shall we dance?"

He led her onto the floor holding her right hand and as the music begun, she willingly stepped into the circle of his embrace and melted. His hand on her waist felt warm and light as he guided her through a sea of dancers. Tonight Marjorie only had eyes for Alan. She glided round the room on a cloud, feeling lighter than she had ever done before. They danced together for a long time, hardly speaking, but very aware of each other.

When they next sat down, Alan looked at her objectively. He decided she was certainly the prettiest woman he had ever met. Yet beauty was only skin deep. This was not so with Marjorie as he could tell by her eyes. A lot of beautiful women tended to be obsessed by their appearance, often needing constant approval, but not Marjorie. He had never met a woman quite like her before. She had an innocence about her that he found very refreshing.

When the evening came to an end, both realised they were too excited by the discovery of one another to be tired.

"Shall we walk a bit?" said Alan.

"The coolness of the evening is too good to miss," agreed Marjorie.

The sky was scattered with stars, twinkling in a different formation to those back home. A large platinum moon hung amongst them illuminating silhouettes of trees. They were surrounded by the noises of the night as frogs croaked to each another, and crickets chirruped. He took her hand and they began to walk.

Marjorie felt vitally alive and charged with an astonishing happiness. She had not even felt herself worthy of such wonderful loving feelings until now. Alan glanced at her fragility by the light of the moon. She wasn't just any girl, any nurse. She was really special. He stopped, cupped her chin in his hand and kissed her gently.

"I'd better walk you home now," he said softly. "But I want you to know that tonight has been the most perfect evening I've ever had."

Marjorie smiled. "Thank you. I've enjoyed it too."

Outside the door of her bungalow, Alan embraced her briefly and planted a kiss on her cheek.

"Can I see you again sometime?"

"Thank you, I'd like that."

Marjorie let herself into the bungalow and leaned on the door as it closed behind her, hugging herself with sheer joy.

Two days after that memorable evening, a bunch of roses was delivered to Marjorie's bungalow. They were large, red and richly perfumed. Wherever could such blooms be found in Nigeria? The attached card simply read, *With love – Alan.*

Marjorie caught her breath and clasped the bouquet to her, burying her face in the velvet petals. She almost made herself late for duty as she rummaged for a vase, fending off the steward boy's attentions, and arranged the roses in several different ways before they finally satisfied her. She propped the card against the arrangement and stood back to admire the blooms, feeling a warm glow inside. The room soon became filled with their heady scent.

When Marjorie next saw Alan, she thanked him for the flowers, adding,

"Where did you find such beautiful roses?"

Alan tapped the side of his nose.

"Magic," he replied. "After a magical evening."

Another evening after they had been to the Ikoye Club during another evening together, Marjorie and Alan walked the short distance to her bungalow, a silence between them as they enjoyed the musical night noises of the frogs and crickets. Suddenly above it all was a pure song of joy.

Alan stopped in his tracks. "Hark, a nightingale!"

"I didn't realise they lived this far south."

"Oh yes, indeed. Isn't that a beautiful song?"

They both stood enchanted by the bird's song as it sang from the depths of its little heart. The trees cast shadows on their faces as the moon slipped silently in and out of wispy clouds. For a long moment they stood with a delicate thread of attraction strung between them. It held them, almost unwillingly until Alan caught her to him.

"Oh Marjorie, don't try and deny what we both know is already there."

They stared at one another, both suddenly bewildered by their feelings, both overawed now that he had made them both aware of their emotions. Their silence lengthened, broken only by the nightingale's song and the noises of the creatures of the night.

Eventually he stepped towards her and their arms went round one another. Their friendship developed as they sometimes saw one another in the Club. At first their meetings were accidental, then by arrangement. Soon they were meeting at times and in places that were nothing to do with Alan being a surgeon or Marjorie's nursing.

From that time they knew that their friendship had deepened into love.

Alan was surprised when he realised that Marjorie had never actually explored the surrounding area of where she worked.

"Next time you have a day off, I'll show you something of the place," he promised.

Cook had packed a hamper of goodies. Alan drove Marjorie out of Lagos.

Away from the town and on either side of them was dry savannah with rough grass and clumps of trees dotted here and there. They passed a small village consisting of round mud huts, each one thatched, some with enormous palm leaves. Some skinny cows, sheep and goats wandered around on the end of long tethers. Scrawny chicken clucked and scratched at their feet, in danger of being trodden on. A group of young children (or *piccanninnis* as the Africans called them) came to stare, wave and smile at them as they passed by.

Some gazelle were startled by the noise of the engine, and although they were far in the distance, darted away, their tiny hooves kicking up clouds of dust. Further on a family of monkeys wandered lazily across the road and disappeared into the bush without appearing to notice them.

By now they were on the edge of a thickly wooded area, known locally as 'the bush'. Alan stopped the car and indicated some tall cotton and kapok trees. Then he pointed upwards.

"It's here that I've seen amazing little Turaco birds."

Marjorie looked around and vaguely upwards.

"No you must look really high up in the trees as they prefer heights. They are incredible little green birds – olive green really. When it rains their plumage turns red."

Marjorie frowned in disbelief.

"Yes really," he added. "I've heard that they're related to our cuckoo but have brilliant hues and colours with a crest of feathers on their head."

They both shaded their eyes as they craned their necks skywards.

Soon Alan pointed out a bird running along a branch quite high up. "There, isn't that quite spectacular?"

Marjorie gasped at the bright bird, similar to a cockatoo in shape but with a long plumed tail. She had to agree.

Shortly after that they came to what would normally be a large lake in the rainy season, but at this time of year was reduced to the size of a muddy pond. Alan pointed out a little egret that was pure white with a long black beak, and had filamentous plumes on its head and standing about two feet tall. He indicated another stork-like bird beyond it, explaining that it was a yellow billed stork and that the pink head was actually bereft of feathers. He was certainly knowledgeable about his surroundings.

As they drove further on, Alan pointed out the plants growing to one side of them. There were yams which were as tall as vines, but only their long fat tubers growing underground could be eaten and used like potatoes. They crossed cocoa and rubber plantations that were important crops grown for export. Most important were the palm kernels that would be pounded to a pulp in order to extract the oil for which Nigeria was so famous. Alan was proving to be a mine of information.

Marjorie became more dependent on Alan for many things as time went on. It wasn't just his seniority on medical matters, but other things too. He had a love for wildlife that she too had always enjoyed, having been brought up in the countryside herself. He enjoyed good food and knew which wine went best with which dish. He also knew where to buy quality food; something that was getting scarce these days. It was easier now to ask Alan than to find out by any other method. In turn, her reliance on him easily led to a more meaningful relationship.

Marjorie was with Barbara Glover enjoying some time off together in Lagos. They had been wandering round its largest store, more to keep cool than anything else, because it boasted large fans keeping the hot still air on the move. Emerging once again into the heat of the afternoon they had decided to go back home again when Marjorie came face to face with a young woman she recognised instantly. They both dropped their shopping bags and embraced one another in the euphoria of meeting so unexpectedly in so remote a place.

"Marjorie Heath!"

"Dorothy Bates!" they exclaimed together. Immediately

they both began chattering at once, then Marjorie laughed apologetically.

"I'm sorry, Barbara, this is Dorothy who trained with me at Middlesex, although she was actually in the set above me." She introduced them and they shook hands, all smiles.

Marjorie spoke next. "Let's all go back to my place for a drink. We're almost there anyway."

The heat forgotten, they fairly bounded back to the hospital complex where Barbara excused herself.

"I'll go back to my own bungalow now. I'm sure you two have a lot to talk about, and ..."

Marjorie interrupted her.

"Oh no, come on Barbara. We don't want to exclude you. Come and join us for a drink at least."

Barbara stayed. They all talked generally over a drink before she left, pleading that she had a pile of mending and letter writing waiting to be done.

"So, what are you doing out here?" asked Dorothy.

Marjorie explained, adding, "More to the point, what are *you* doing out here?"

"Well, I'm married now to Malcolm Bradford. He works for an oil company and he's in charge of its operations out here in Nigeria."

"So you had to give up nursing then?"

"Yes, you know, either one or the other, but not both!"

"Then you must find yourself at a loose end sometimes. We must get together more often during my off-duty times perhaps."

Marjorie's friendship with Dorothy was rekindled. After that they regularly saw one another in their free time on some pretext or other. Sometimes Dorothy brought Malcolm over for dinner, at others, Marjorie and Dorothy would go to the cinema together. A lifelong friendship developed out of what had previously been an acquaintance. Occasionally Barbara joined them.

Alan was giving a dinner party. Marjorie had heard about

these parties; their wonderful reputation had spread far and wide. Now she was invited as his honoured guest, because she was the most recent addition to the hospital nursing staff. She was quite nervous as she bathed and dressed that evening. What dress would an honoured guest wear? Marjorie wondered who else would be there. She knew a fair number of white people in Lagos by now, but surely Alan would invite others whom she didn't yet know – if so, what would they be like?

The taxi eventually left her outside Alan's front door. He had seen the headlamps sweeping up the driveway and was there on the doorstep to greet her personally.

"Hello, my love. I deliberately asked you a little earlier than anyone else to give you a chance to relax before they arrive."

"Thank you, much appreciated. Hopefully I will remember names better if they come in twos and threes!"

Alan kissed her and offered her what was fast becoming her customary drink of gin and lime.

"Yes please, but not so much gin as you usually do. I want to at least appear intelligent!"

He laughed and tried to deceive Marjorie that he was about to pour twice as much.

"No, no," she shouted, apparently just in time.

"Sorry, I thought you wanted twice as much to give you Dutch courage!" His eyes twinkled.

"Alan, any more, and I'll go home right now." she warned him with a grin that said she was enjoying herself already.

After about half an hour, other guests began to arrive. First came Bob and Mary Richardson, then Dr Toby Wilkes from the hospital with his wife Ida. Gilbert and Hilary Milbourne were the last couple to arrive. Marjorie had only been slightly acquainted with them all in the past, but they were so amicable and kind that it wasn't long before she felt as though they had been friends for years.

The house-boy entered, approached Alan, bending to whisper in his ear.

"Thank you very much Stanley. We'll come in now."

Alan stood and clapped his hands for attention. "Apparently dinner is now served in the dining room ladies and gentlemen, so if we could please make our way…" He encouraged people to follow the house-boy with a gesture of his hand.

Marjorie felt herself in a kind of bubble of peace as everyone sat down at the table, all apparently friendly and at ease with one another. The gentle clink of glasses and cutlery, the apparently orchestrated rise and fall of conversation, the hum and murmur of life responding to the coolness of the evening after the heat of the day; all these things, but especially Alan's calm nearness contributed to her happiness.

She was also careful to join in with the conversations going on near to her, thus getting to know a few more people a little better.

The meal was delicious. It was made all the more pleasant by Alan finding Marjorie's hand under the large white damask tablecloth and holding it firmly in his own between courses.

She belonged.

Alan persuaded Marjorie to stay on after the other guests had left. She wondered if any of them had noticed and deliberately asked Alan where her shawl was likely to be, as she ought to make a move for home herself. Once everyone had departed she needed no further persuasion to stay a while when they sat in a satisfied silence.

"Well, I think you ought to congratulate yourself on a wonderful evening," said Marjorie. "Everyone seemed to enjoy themselves."

"Do you think so? Good. It's often hard to gauge one's own party."

"I seem to have gone to quite a few parties so I suppose it's high time that I held a party of my own."

"Don't sound so worried about it, my dear. You won't have to do anything; that's what the steward boys are for. All you need to do is ask people, provide the food and dress up."

"No, I want to be different! I want to have a different kind of party with dinner beforehand, then we'll have fun dancing and playing silly games as well."

To her delight he caught the essence of her idea and tossed it back to her. They sparked ideas off one another and built up an outline of what the evening would be.

"I must warn you, though," admonished Alan with a raised forefinger. "You mustn't visit the kitchen whilst cook's in action."

"But I'll want to make sure he's got everything ready that I asked for," she protested.

"Ah yes, *after* he's cooked it, not *while* he's cooking it!"

"Why ever not?"

"I made that mistake once and found the cook with a circle of pastry stuck to his sweaty fat hairy chest while he floured the pastry board!"

Marjorie grimaced. "I don't believe it!"

"It's quite true! Scout's honour!" He stood and gave a mock salute. "Other people will tell you similar tales too. A lot of Europeans refuse to buy their meat from the markets because it's so high it crawls on its own. If they did but know it, their cooks get their cooks-mate to buy foodstuff there."

Marjorie wrinkled her nose in distaste.

"Surely we'd be laid out with the most ghastly diseases by now?"

"Maybe, but you and I have obviously survived well so far."

Glancing at the clock, he added, "But you won't survive tomorrow and neither will I if we don't get any sleep tonight."

She gasped as she noticed the time.

"Come on little lady, jump in the car and I'll run you home."

He kissed her lightly and smiled.

After meeting them at Alan's dinner party, Marjorie became friendly with Gilbert and Hilary Milbourne. Gilbert was in the Police Force and always the life and soul of any party. His nickname was the Laughing Policeman. Although they all worked hard, they also played hard, and when everybody came together socially, Gilbert and Hilary seemed to be in the middle of it, if not the cause of it all. Because of this they were very popular guests at parties and dinner-dances, so just about everyone knew Gilbert and Hilary.

The second time Marjorie met them was at a beach party early one evening. The heat of the day was just giving way to the relieving balmy, cooler air just prior to darkness suddenly wrapping itself round them like a curtain. They had just emerged from the water after a final swim when Marjorie pointed out to sea and asked Hilary,

"What is that island out there?"

"You should know my dear!" It's for your use as it belongs to the Medical Department. There's a staffed bungalow on it as well."

"Really? Well, I didn't know that before! Have you ever been there?"

"Yes, Alan took us out there a couple of times. It's not very big, but perfect for noisy parties as you can make all the commotion you want and nobody else will hear you or interfere at all; not that they do anyway, unless there's a real crisis on."

Marjorie towelled herself vigorously and hoped she might be able to explore the place for herself one day.

Chapter Ten

A few days after that Alan asked Marjorie if there was anything special she would like to do.

"Well, I've heard that the island is available to those of us at the hospital. Could we explore that sometime?"

"But of course, sweetheart! I'm sorry I hadn't thought of that before. Are you saying that you didn't know about the island?"

"That's right. It was Hilary who told me about it a few days ago."

"My dear, I'm so sorry. I assumed you knew about it. Next time we're off duty together I'll take you over there."

Alan handed Marjorie into a rather nice motor boat moored at the end of a wooden jetty. Waiting beside it was a young African man.

Alan introduced Marjorie to him. "This is Shiloh. He'll be captaining our ship today!"

As the engine roared into life they left Lagos behind.

Marjorie leaned comfortably back on a cushioned seat.

She sighed. "This is the life. Where did you hire this from?"

Alan didn't appear to have heard her as he peered cautiously over the side.

"I hope there aren't any submarines lurking down there!"

"The water is too blue and sparkling have any hazards skulking down there! Just see how pretty it looks!"

Indeed it was. The sun beat down out of a bright blue sky that merged with the bright blue sea at the horizon. The only discernible difference was the lack of diamanté sparkles.

After about half-an-hour the boat chugged alongside the island's wooden jetty stretching out into the sea. They disembarked and trod warily along the wooden planks that were far enough apart to see the waves beneath as they lapped gently around the supporting pillars. Soon they were on the pebble stretch of beach and Alan led Marjorie up to a narrow path lined with limp looking shrubs towards the bungalow.

The front door was opened as they approached and they stepped into the cool hallway as the house-boy half bowed in greeting to acknowledge them.

"Ah, hello there Bonus. Could you make a nice cold drink please? Anything'll do."

The young lad beamed, nodded and rushed off.

Alan turned to Marjorie. "Believe it or not his name is really War Bonus, but it's too much of a mouthful, so we call him Bonus for short. He is one too – a jolly nice chap."

They went into the lounge and sat down facing the French windows leading out onto the veranda.

"Ah, thank you," said Alan as Bonus appeared with a tray on which were two tumblers of lemonade and lime clinking with cubes of ice. "Oh, by the way, is lunch on the go?"

"Yessir, I give de message to Cook and he a-cookin' right now."

"Wonderful, many thanks." Alan dismissed the boy with a wave of the hand.

He took Marjorie out on the veranda. Apart from this, just dwarfed shrubs and bush land surrounded the bungalow. The island was small and Alan told Marjorie that in theory, one should be able to see the sea in any direction, but the trees stood in the way.

Lunch was Groundnut chop that left yellow stains on their lips after each mouthful. It was spicy, hot and filling.

Afterwards they went for a walk along the beach which was damp and sandy. They could almost walk right around the island, but the rocks on the far side prevented them.

"We could scramble over them, but a lot are loose and wobbly. It wouldn't look too clever if doctor and nurse needed to be patients in their own hospital!"

Marjorie nodded, then added, "At least we could advise people where we hurt and what they should do about it twenty-four hours a day!"

"No. they might give us something to keep us quiet!"

The shadow from the small cliff fell across his face so that when he smiled his teeth showed up in the sunlight. Marjorie raised her face to his and he slid his arm around her shoulders.

"Now you've seen the island, what d'you think of it?"

"I think it's wonderful."

"The bungalow's not very big – just large enough to house the staff with a lounge and a dining room for us. I reckon the Medical bigwigs wanted to make sure that no hanky-panky went on here! But no, actually they said that any more rooms or buildings would make the bungalow look out of proportion in its setting, which is quite true really. Everything is scaled just right as it is."

Marjorie agreed. "Mm, it's just perfect. What a wonderful haven to come to after a wretched day!"

They walked in silence for a while, enjoying the sun, the sea and each other's company. Returning to the bungalow they realised the time, so made haste to return to the main shore before dusk and darkness enveloped them.

Watching Alan as he interacted occasionally with Shiloh, she knew that she loved him, and that this was no passing passion, but the real thing.

Marjorie's first party became the prototype in everyone's memory for many others that followed it during those years in Nigeria. She had asked just about everyone she could think of so it promised to be a lively affair. The cook and steward boys had prepared the food and it was all laid out with silver and glassware, sparkling as it reflected the artificial light.

Instead of a sit-down dinner, Marjorie had chosen instead to lay on a buffet supper.

She and Alan sat on the veranda sipping drinks before the guests arrived. It was about half past seven and the hours of daylight had gone. Twilight was almost non existent in this hot country. Marjorie sipped her gin and lime nervously.

Alan patted her arm soothingly. "Don't worry, everything will be splendid, I'm sure it will."

"Do you think so?"

"Yes, now you can't do any more so just relax and enjoy yourself."

She turned to him and smiled, grateful for his understanding, even at mere pre-party nerves.

The first people to arrive were Gilbert and Hilary Milbourne. Marjorie was grateful. Now she knew the party would go well as Gilbert always seemed to set the atmosphere and charge it with just the right amount of *bon homie*. Malcom and Dorothy came soon after them, closely followed by Toby and Ida Wilkes bringing Barbara Glover and Frances Doyle. Then it wasn't long before people simply flowed in, filling the main room, spilling into her small dining room and overflowing into the hall. Someone wound up the gramophone and played records while the guests talked, danced and swayed into the night. Everyone laughed a lot, ate a lot and drank a lot, all together in a big swaying crowd, often spreading out into Marjorie's little garden.

She felt a bubble of joy rise up inside her as she realised the success of her venture. Her heart pounded with glee and she felt quite breathless as she swept up her glass and joined everyone in a toast. She wanted to drink, dance, laugh and celebrate all the events that culminated in her being here at this very moment in time.

She enjoyed being a hostess, circulating amongst her guests, chatting with each in turn before moving on to the next. She also found time to talk with Alan, laugh with him as they danced together.

"Hey!" called Alan. "The night is young. Let's play American Charades!"

So a trend began. They thought they invented it, but whether they had or not, the game provided endless amusement. People mimed song, film and play titles to one another, sometimes getting quite frantic as their friends came so close to the answer but were seemingly too dumb to say the exact word. As they improved, poems, proverbs and even quotes from Shakespeare would be included by quite devious methods.

When at last the party was over, and everybody had wrung her by the hand, hugged her or kissed her, or all three, assuring her how wonderful it had all been, Marjorie flopped onto the sofa and looked round at the chaos.

"I thoroughly enjoyed myself tonight but I'm so glad I've got a steward-boy to tidy up. I'm so tired it would stay like this for days."

Alan reassured her. "It was a really good party. In fact it was best I've been to yet. Anyway, I won't stay, as you'll be wanting to get to bed, and I'm on call in the morning."

They looked fondly at one another and Alan leaned over Marjorie's shoulder to kiss her cheek. She playfully pulled his tie and they both collapsed in a heap as he lost his balance and fell on top of her. They giggled, intoxicated with being alone together after sharing one another with so many people all evening.

Alan suddenly stopped laughing and took Marjorie's face in both his hands. "I love you," he said. "How I love you!"

They kissed one another, a long exciting kiss that stirred them both. Marjorie wriggled out from under him.

"Well, as you said just now, I must get some beauty sleep, and you're on call tomorrow."

"Point taken," he said, getting to his feet. "But you're beautiful anyway!"

He left, blowing her a kiss from the doorway.

Alan and Marjorie were often together, sometimes during the daytime, sometimes in the evenings. One of the most memorable times they had was soon after Marjorie's successful party.

It was evening and Alan had driven them in his car out of Lagos itself and soon he turned off the made-up road and on to an unmade surface. They could smell the night blossoms and the crooning cries of nocturnal birds above the drone of insects. Marjorie could just make out palm trees on both sides of them. Beyond the trees to their left was an endless blanched beach, set against the dark silky sea. Behind was a wake of swirling dust.

They approached a small wooden jetty, and it was here that Alan pulled up and got out of the car, going to open Marjorie's door for her with a courtly little bow. Stepping up onto the landing stage, Alan put his arms around Marjorie's shoulders.

"Fancy a night sail?" he asked, nodding towards the motorboat moored at the end of the jetty.

"Oh come on, we can't just sail off in that. Who does it belong to, anyway?"

Alan shrugged with the innocent nonchalance of someone who has always been able to obtain what he wanted. "It's mine."

"D'you mean we used your boat before to go over to the island?"

"Why yes, what did you think?"

"I thought you must have borrowed it or hired it from someone, or even that it came with the island."

She shook her head in wonder. This man was full of surprises. As they walked slowly down to the landing stage she glanced up and caught her breath. Never before had she seen the moon and stars apparently so near to the earth with the huge lantern of a moon outlining the palm trees. She could hear the slap and gurgle of water as the sea caressed the posts of the jetty beneath them.

Alan took her hand and they walked to the large white motorboat, already anxiously moving in the water as if straining to carry them somewhere. He jumped into the boat and handed her down.

They stared at one another, the moon picking out their faces in ivory.

"Let's go over to the island!" he said impulsively.

"But it's dark!"

"There's a moon – a beautiful moon!" He gestured towards it and began to untie the craft from its moorings.

He started the engine and it throbbed into life, bursting on the night air.

The prow of the boat parted the seawater sending up small trails of crystal droplets. Marjorie watched fascinated by the dark sea of indigo satin, small rippling wavelets folding away from the prow of the boat. She recalled the sea she had once known to be so huge and angry, but was now giving up these jewels for her pleasure. Almost immediately it claimed them back again as the small boat ploughed on. She trailed her hand in the water and felt herself to be totally at peace with the world, amazed at the intensity of her feelings. The soft magic of this calm moonlit bay had certainly worked wonders for chasing any workaday blues and pressures away and thus increasing her awareness of the love she and Alan felt for one another.

When they reached the island, Alan tied up the boat and they walked across the frosty looking sand to the bungalow. The sea was claiming more beach tonight than it had done on their previous visit.

Time had left them yawning spaces to fill, yet they talked about little things, that were of no real consequence. Important things were too sacred to be spoken of in case they spoilt their dreams.

Nothing else mattered. The hospital was in Lagos with a stretch of water between them and work. Nobody knew they were here. Even the World War was in another world.

In a dip before they approached the building, Alan took Marjorie into his arms. He kissed her forehead and laughed.

"You'll have to grow a bit, Shorty. We don't match."

He picked her up as if she were a child and set her on a rock. He kissed her again.

"There, that's better, you've come up to my level now!"

Marjorie smiled. She had often been teased for being

short and slight.

The humour died from his face and she saw only tenderness there as his mouth came down on hers, kissing her so suddenly and vigorously it left her breathless. His arms were about her, crushing her to him in a bear hug, so great was his passion. Marjorie's feet left the stone on which she was standing and became suspended in mid-air, dangling from Alan's hug. They both giggled, and then laughed out loud and long, far more than the situation deserved, because this was a crazy night. Eventually they collapsed into a heap to roll onto their backs and studied the night sky.

"Do you know, I have never felt like this about anyone ever before," said Alan after a while, putting his arm across Marjorie.

"I feel the same." The cool breeze was a tender caress.

They clasped one another closely and their bodies became moulded together. He kissed her with a passion she had never known before and she responded. Eventually they parted breathlessly.

She rolled over onto her stomach.

They lay in silence for a while, then Alan leaned on one elbow and said,

"If I had three wishes I'd roll them all up into one right now."

"Mmmm." Marjorie was almost asleep.

"I'd just want one big wish so that I'd be married to you and we could make love right here and now."

Marjorie was instantly awake.

"Alan!"

"Sorry, but that's how I feel."

"Quite apart from anything else we're out in the open, someone might see!"

"Rubbish! Nobody sleeps on the island. Even the staff have a canoe to get back to the mainland before nightfall."

Marjorie sat up. "You mean you brought me here to seduce me?"

"No, of course I didn't. I just wanted us to be

completely alone."

"And now you've got me here."

"Don't be like that. I'm sorry. I didn't express myself very well. I suppose I was being selfish in wanting you all to myself for a bit longer than usual."

They were silent for a while.

Then Marjorie leaned over and kissed Alan's forehead. "I'm sorry too."

His arms were about her and they caressed one another tenderly with the intimacy of lovers.

"Oh god, I'm sorry, we must get back before I do something I shouldn't," he said reluctantly.

They rolled away from one another, gazed long and hard into the other's eyes before embracing once again in the height of their passion.

Only the moon was witness and she smiled down on them as they clung to one another again.

After a while they slowly they got to their feet, tidied their clothing, brushing it free of sand. He reached for her hand.

"I believe I have found the most wonderful girl in the world," he said simply, moving her to an appreciation of him that went beyond words.

The local chapel was drumming up support and was holding a special service to attract more people to it. Alan was away in northern Nigeria and Marjorie was off duty that Sunday evening, so she went along out of curiosity.

A lady was at the door welcoming people and handing out hymn sheets. She looked vaguely familiar to Marjorie. After the short service which had consisted mainly of singing popular hymns, Marjorie plucked up courage and approached the woman to ask her where they might have met before. Eventually they realised she had attended the same school as Bettie and indeed had been one of Bettie's school friends. Her name was Moira Woolmer, and she was currently in Lagos as a missionary. Marjorie became friendly with Moira and was thrilled to discover another contact from home. She was eager to tell Bettie the news, and after her encounter with Moira she often went along to the chapel song time when she was off duty. Alan didn't appear to mind but he never accompanied her.

European Hospital
Lagos
Nigeria
25.11.1940

My dear Bettie and Bill

Very many thanks for your letter received yesterday. It was written on 3rd October, so has taken nearly two months getting here. I expect this one will have to last for some time too as we hear that the **Apapa** *has been commandeered by the Admiralty so that means there is only the* **Abosso** *left, and as that only arrived on Saturday it will be ages before it is out here again. Of course there may be odd cargo boats bringing letters, so it doesn't mean you must stop writing!*

I will send you a pre-paid cable from time to time so that you can let me know you are all right. I will send one to different people each time.

I sent dozens of Christmas cards on the ship which was sunk on the way home from here; in fact I sent a card to everyone I could think of and enclosed letters in a lot of them too! Could you explain to people if they don't receive a card or letter? Instead of buying more Christmas cards I will send as many visiting cards as I can before the ship sails again, which isn't much longer now.

Bettie, do you remember Moira Woolmer? She is out here in Lagos and I met her at the local mission hall. She has become a missionary now. In fact she didn't have a letter from home at all on Saturday, only a bundle of Bournemouth Echo newspapers. She had some last month too and lent them to me to read. I'm passing on my Daily Telegraphs to her when I've finished with them, but am keeping the crosswords! I notice Mother hadn't done any of them before sending them out, suppose she needs me there to encourage her!

Do you remember Dorothy Bates? She trained with me at Middlesex. She is married now to a man who works for an oil company, so she is now Dorothy Bradford and her husband is Malcolm. He is manager for the Nigerian branch, so I see them quite a lot. She comes here to see me once a week and I go there to dinner once a week. Sometimes we go to the cinema and last week we went to a concert which made a change. There was a warship in for a few days and the crew came ashore and gave us a variety concert – it was very good, especially the male voice choir.

Eight soldiers came into hospital on Saturday afternoon. They all arrived together and it took me all afternoon to sort them all out, the Majors, Lieutenants and Privates, and get them in their respective beds. I seemed to be running round in circles for ages. Your letters had just arrived and I was dying to read them but couldn't get down to them until after I'd gone to bed.

I have just written to Jessie, but haven't sent it yet, as I didn't know her address now that she is in the Land Army. However, I will send it now. All your letters from me are different, so you can read each other's.

I have just bought the enclosed from a Hauser (market) man sitting on the doorstep. They come down from Northern Nigeria to sell their wares. He said it was "Cheap, cheap, cheap." It is supposed to be a manicure set, but it is not much good really, I shouldn't think. He sits on the doorstep until we have finished our meal, hoping we will buy something. At present I am waiting for the other sisters to come over for lunch.

What a job you must have had preparing for the soldiers and things.

By the way, how dare you refer to Lagos as a 'bush place'! I'll have you know Lagos is one, if not the most civilised place in West Africa. I told a friend what you said and she said it was an insult to our beautiful town. Lagos is rather pretty in places. It is lovely and green and we are beautifully situated here at the hospital with an outlook over the river.

I hope you have been receiving my letters as people here say that their relatives haven't received letters in England for three or four months: and they write once or twice a week from here!

No more now

Lots of love
Marjorie

Alan and Marjorie had been to Toby and Ida Wilkes' for a luncheon party. The day was even hotter than usual, but they had enjoyed cocktails on the veranda beforehand, and then gone out there again for iced coffee afterwards. Beyond the veranda was a paved terrace that glared in the sun. Huge stone urns had been placed here and there, each spilling over with brilliantly coloured flowers. Nearby a hummingbird, like a miniature firework, stabbed its beak into the trumpet-shaped bloom of a hibiscus, hovering steadily as it sucked the nectar from within. A shallow semi-circle of white steps led down from the terrace to the swimming pool that sparkled like a flat sheet of sapphire. The garden beyond it was well kept and colourful, but beyond that again gave way to scrub land, offering privacy from neighbours. A shimmering haze seemed to hang over everything, casting a spell on everyone as they drank in the scene.

Alan leaned over to Marjorie and murmured quietly in her ear before standing up. "Well, I'm sorry, but I must leave you now. Ida, that was a grand lunch, thank you very much."

Toby replied cheerily. "Good to have you, Alan. One day, perhaps you can persuade Gwen to come out here. She would surely love all this." He waved his arm expansively round him and Marjorie froze inside while the sun beat relentlessly down on them. *Who was Gwen? His sister maybe?*

She couldn't trust herself to say anything for some time and just sat, apparently admiring the scenery, desperately trying to appear calm while within her thoughts churned around, in her head.

About twenty minutes later, she too made her excuses and left. Alan knew she would and was waiting for her at the end of the drive.

"I'm sorry." Alan squeezed her hand. "Please let me explain."

They went silently back to Marjorie's bungalow where Alan poured them both a drink. Her hand shook as she took it from him. It occurred to her that they had spent so much time together, but still they hardly knew one another, properly.

The tears stung her eyes, but she stared through them, avoiding his gaze as she sat tombstone straight.

"Who-who is G-Gwen?" she finally asked, tears coursing down her cheeks as she realised within herself who she was.

"She's my wife." Alan squeezed the words out with anguish as he held up his hand to forestall Marjorie's protests, the short speech having an effect on her like gunfire. "Please don't think badly of me, I'm so sorry you found out like this; I knew I should tell you, but the moment never seemed right, and I didn't want to spoil our relationship."

"But this is awful! I don't want us to part – but knowing this, we must."

Alan sat on the sofa next to her and took both her hands in his. "Look, "Gwen will not leave Wales. She has never travelled with me and never will. She says the girls need her."

"Girls?" Marjorie was incredulous. "You mean you have children?"

Alan nodded sadly. "Yes, two daughters, but I hardly

ever see them. Of course now the war is on, children are not allowed to travel abroad. I used to feel I was split in two, wanting to enjoy my wife and home life, also my job, which, as you know, means so much to me." He shook his head. "Then you came into my life, and without even trying to, I've fallen in love with you in a way I never thought possible."

Marjorie wiped her tears away with the back of her hand and Alan passed her his handkerchief. "Thank you for the times we've had together. I'll never forget them – or you."

"I'm sorry, I wish I could make things easier for you."

"Please don't." She shook her hands free of his and stood up. "I'm going for a walk."

After she had gone, Alan sat staring at his half-empty tumbler. He reflected on his own life and selfishly wished he wasn't married. It had been an arranged wedding by both sets of parents, but both he and Gwen had been attracted to one another. Once the girls were born, though, Gwen had become distant towards him and devoted herself entirely to the children. He was annoyed that he hadn't told Marjorie early on in their relationship before they had got so involved and fond of one another. Now he had hurt her, and hurt her really badly. Damn Toby Wilkes! No, he mustn't blame him entirely, it was bound to have slipped out sooner or later. His fingers drummed on the glass he held as he untangled the net of memories. He waited for Marjorie to return.

She had lingered outside, watching the palm trees wave their fronds against the cloudless blue sky, wondering whether it was wise to rush off in the heat of the day. Suddenly, she didn't want to be anywhere near her bungalow or the hospital complex and turned her back and walked quickly away. She eventually came to a small clearing and stood at the edge of it, looking up at the variegated canopy of trees. Her eyes took in the silver thread of a small stream that tumbled between them, and on through the yellow-green expanse of open grassland, rolling away in the distance. A couple of monkeys were playing in the trees, cavorting from branch to branch as is to mock her in her misery.

She moved to sit on a broken log in the shade where she stayed for a long time, trying to evaluate her thoughts, assess her life, everything interspersed with a fresh flow of tears.

After all these years, Marjorie had finally found someone who loved her for who she was and with whom she too had discovered so much happiness. Now it had all been snatched away from her, smashed at her feet like some precious priceless china. Everything had all seemed so tangible, so right at the time. She could feel the years stretching away, waiting for her. The enormity of it both frightened and frustrated her – because the future lay completely outside of her grasp.

She had come out to West Africa as a Nursing Sister and was greatly satisfied in that, wanting nothing else. Now she had met Alan, got involved with him and she knew that she loved him dearly. Her eyes were red and damp, her heart heavy as she got up and dragged her feet back to the bungalow.

Alan was still there, and he held out his arms to her. "Oh, Marjorie, my darling Marjorie! What have I done?" he beseeched her, his eyes begging her to supply an answer she could not give.

At first she could not trust herself to speak. Tears were still close to the surface and she stayed silent trying to control her breathing

"Marjorie, come here, let's have a cuddle while we think what to do."

Now her reply came at once, violently spilling out of her. "How could you hurt me like that by letting me to fall in love with you? Nobody has ever made me happy like you." She ended with a sob and turned away, not wanting him to see her cry again.

"Please," he implored her, coming to stand in front of her, then began to pace the room. As Alan began to stride up and down, Marjorie watched him silently, noticing the exact shade of bronze on his tanned skin, the way his long fingers flexed, the shadow cast by the collar on his open-necked shirt, and the fine fair hair curling on his forearms. She listened to the silence between them.

"Alan, oh, I've been such a fool!" wailed Marjorie, fists to her forehead.

"Marjorie, I didn't mean ..."

"Yes you did. Don't lie to me. Don't lie to yourself. What's more, don't lie to your wife and your family." She spat the words out, and knew she was hurting him, but could not stop herself.

He looked at her, his face full of anguish. "I love you and want you so much, but I'm not free, and I can't offer you the things you deserve."

Marjorie looked away, not wanting him to see the tears she could not prevent glistening in her eyes and spilling onto her cheeks.

"Look, while you were away, I've come to a decision. I'm going to write to Gwen and ask her for a divorce. Then..." He hesitated and fixed her with a penetrating stare. "Will you marry me?"

"Supposing she refuses?"

"Our marriage has been in name only for years now. I wish now I had started proceedings when I was last home. Being home last time was lousy."

"I'm sorry."

They turned into each other then. She buried her face into his shirtfront and he held her firmly, yet tenderly. Then he lifted her face between his hands and kissed her swollen eyelids, then her mouth.

Marjorie looked up at him. She had no reason to doubt him. She would always remember him like this, the way his hair flopped onto his forehead, the concern and love in his eyes, but she could not give him an answer – not yet.

Chapter Eleven

The music filled the four-corners of a large room where a small jazz band played in the Ikoye club. Lapping around them was a sea of dancers as on a roller coaster under a blaze of lights. The noise of people talking, shouting and laughing all blended together with the rhythm of the music. Looking through the door leading into an adjacent room the bright colours of the ladies' dresses blurred together like a flock of exotic birds. The conga line snaked around the building, both inside and out, then back onto the dance floor, with Marjorie being swept along with them. However it didn't suppress the twinge of loneliness she suddenly felt in the midst of all these people.

Someone shouted, "It's nearly midnight!"

The band finished their number and everyone waited in anticipation. Exhilaration of the moment suspended in the air. The atmosphere suddenly reverberated with chimes and then the local clock began to boom out the hour. Marjorie imagined them all echoing all around like ripples on a pond. At the twelfth peal, everyone erupted into cheers, clapping and kissing each other. It was 1941.

Philippe, with whom she had recently danced a quickstep, turned Marjorie's face to his and planted a chaste kiss on her cheek.

"Don't look so sad. Happy New Year!" His English was good, but still held traces of a Dutch accent.

"Thank you. I was reminiscing about the last one."

He ran his finger down her cheek. "I'm sure this year will be much better."

Together they joined the huge circle to sing 'Auld Lang Syne'. Marjorie sang along with everyone else, but her heart was heavy. How she missed Alan. He was touring hospitals in northern Nigeria.

Philippe nudged her. "Come on, cheer up. Let's dance."

Marjorie smiled and stepped gratefully into his arms.

The party began to break up shortly after one in the

morning. Most people were going home with somebody. Suddenly, desperately, Marjorie longed for friendship – just simple, uncomplicated ordinary friendship. The effort of tonight after weeks of being alone felt too much, an almost insurmountable wall. She didn't want to leave this party alone. Philippe had shared the latter part of the evening with her. She knew it was shameful of her to ask him to walk her home for her own comfort's sake, but she was so lonely and tired, and she knew Philippe was kind.

She smiled at him. "Please, would you mind taking me home?"

He kissed her awkwardly, and held out his arm for her to link hers with him.

"Let's go," he said gently.

European Hospital
Lagos
Nigeria
Christmas Day 1940

My dear Bettie and Bill

I have just written to Mother and Father and cannot think of much else to say to you!

You can tell your friend the local scout leader that I am constantly reminded of him these days as a Sergeant Burrow, who used to be in the scouts is here - he was in hospital and went out on Monday. He asked me to his place to tea on Monday and again yesterday, and again tomorrow! I went yesterday and Monday, but can't tomorrow as I'm booked up. He also wants me to go to the pictures with him and all sorts, but he said he supposed the whole population in Lagos had invited me out and so felt there wasn't much chance of seeing me often. He has been to France and all over the place since the war started. He is only twenty-two years old and is terribly quiet. I think he's rather lonely here – he has only been here for two months. I think I will invite him to a party one evening when all the Christmas festivities are over. He sent a taxi to fetch me for tea yesterday and Monday, so I went all in state!

I seem to be thoroughly spoilt here socially and to my surprise, have heard from various quarters that people have been enquiring who the pretty sister is at the European Hospital as they would like to know her! That's me!

Please thank Mother and Father for sending the Telegraphs. I have received two bundles and am religiously doing the crosswords, and then pass them on to Moira who exchanges them for the Bournemouth Evening Echo newspapers she receives – then I pass the Echo on to Burrow afterwards.

I had a lovely time at a dance last night. The dinner was held at the Medical Director's house – then the dance at the Ikoye Club. I got booked up three or four times for the dances – of course there are far more men than women out here.

I have also become quite friendly with a Pilot Officer in the RAF. He is a Methodist and comes to sing-songs with me on Sunday evenings. He was a schoolteacher in private life. Sometimes he comes to tea with me here.

It has been terribly hot here this Christmas and dancing last night the heat was terrific. I was in a bath of perspiration the whole time, although we sat out of doors. It was a fancy-dress affair and I went as a little girl with a white slate and a toy clockwork elephant. However I lost the elephant, as everyone wanted to play with it as it caused a lot of amusement!

2.1.1941

I have made several attempts to finish this letter and now today I have a wretched cold, eyes nose and mouth all running! People say it's because I wore my dress above my knees to the Fancy Dress!

I don't know if you have heard that the **Apapa** *has been* *sunk. It was bombed and we heard that as people were getting away in lifeboats, they were machine-gunned. I believe only about twenty-two were killed though. One of our nursing sisters was among them.*

I have had three lots of perfume given me for Christmas, so I should at least smell nice in the coming year.

I am going to Dorothy's to tea presently. I am waiting for her to call for me – then we will go to the beach with her dog for a run. Maybe it will do my cold good.

No more news now,

*Lots of love,
Marjorie*

Even though she was seeing a lot of Philippe, Marjorie still received letters from Alan. He was currently touring the whole of Nigeria in one go, instead of his usual method of making individual visits to various hospitals. His letters were always interesting as they described what he had been doing, often including some quite amusing incidents. He did not appear to accept that Marjorie had ended their relationship. After several such letters she herself began to wonder if she had too. She did not reply to any of his letters; apart from not wishing to encourage him, she could not be sure of anything reaching him now that he was on tour. He obviously knew about Philippe and even referred to him occasionally. Marjorie wondered if, reading between the lines, she could detect a note of jealousy in some of his correspondence.

Philippe's company was certainly enjoyable. He seemed to be good at everything and was now trying to pass those skills on to Marjorie. Their outings would be packed full of instructions about the correct way to swing a golf club, or making her follow through and name various strokes in tennis to improve her game. He took her horse riding, which was a painful process, as she had never 'fore. Philippe had a car and was teaching ɔ drive and fathom the mysteries of how to ..-clutch.

All in all there was no time now to mourn Alan. Life was too full of so many other things. Yet in the quiet times of the day when it was peaceful and she was on her own, Marjorie knew that she missed him badly.

The European section of Lagos Hospital had about thirty beds. Muriel Henley was the Matron while Barbara Glover together with Marjorie supervised the African nurses. An extension was being built on out of necessity as more accidents occurred, most of them being plane crashes.

Marjorie never forgot that time when she was called back on duty to assist with seven badly burned servicemen. There was not the modern equipment to hand as there would have been back home in England. However even if it had been to hand, these lads were probably too badly injured to survive anyway. They were a pitiful sight, each had so much skin scorched away, and the smell was dreadful. Two Army Sisters were sent for, together with Evelyn Bailey, and an English nurse who was living in Lagos with her husband at that time.

Two of the men died very soon after they had been admitted, but Marjorie, along with the other nurses, helped the others to fight for their lives. Dr Wilkes examined each one in turn as best he could, but it was difficult. All five men were unconscious. Where any face was visible under the burns their pallor was waxy looking. One man had no hair and not only had that burnt away but so had the skin on his scalp. Clothes had to be cut away from their bodies, and even the merest touch would bring a large amount of charred skin away.

Despite the tropical heat the men needed blankets to assist their bodies to recover from such a shock and the nursing sisters were busy giving injections of Adrenaline. They set about giving drips of saline solution, but before each of the five remaining men had been properly seen to, another one died.

Coating the men in Gentian Violet to harden their remaining skin was the only other thing they could do. Each man now looked as though he was wearing some kind of purple pantomime outfit.

Marjorie was busy and often felt like an automaton these days. Nursing was not so rewarding when it was like this, knowing that nothing further could be done to relieve those airmen's pain and suffering. Two weeks after they had been admitted, each man had died. It had been a depressing fortnight witnessing real life war work amidst the comparatively carefree life in Nigeria.

As if to add insult to injury, having made friends with the two Army Sisters whilst they had fought for their comrades' lives together, Marjorie heard later that they had both been drowned on their way home to England a few weeks later following a torpedo. War stretched its ugly talons into this beautiful country to spoil the lives of the people here as well as in Europe. No one could escape it.

The extension was completed and opened in in April 1941. The hospital now housed a further fifty beds. More beds meant more patients to fill them, so Marjorie was continually busy, and often spent more time at the hospital that she should.

European Hospital
Lagos
20.4.1941

My dear Bettie and Bill

I think you owe me a letter but I thought I would be kind and write to you this afternoon. I haven't very much time as I'm on duty and will have to start bathing the patients soon, but while they are having their afternoon nap I have a few minutes.

You seem to have had a fair number of air raids lately

– I hope you are all safe and sound. You will send me a cable at any time if necessary, won't you?

29.4.1941

I suppose you are beginning to get warmer weather now and so are not so envious of us. Our rainy season has started now and every night we have terrific thunderstorms with almost continuous lightning and one gets soaked through in a second.

I am learning to do all sorts of things out here. Philippe is a Dutchman and a friend of mine. He is teaching me to ride a horse, swim better and dive, play good tennis and drive a car – so I ought to be perfect by the time I'm finished! I had my first riding lesson last Friday and we did a bit of trotting which I thought was quite brave of me. My seat was very sore the next day, though!

I went to a birthday party on Saturday – there were sixteen people there – we went to dinner at the Ikoye Club. It was very enjoyable.

Last Wednesday a Methodist missionary took two of us out in his yacht. He has a lovely big boat and we were out for two hours and got very sunburnt.

Our new hospital wing is open now and so we are still very busy. We are expecting two Army Sisters to come out and help but they haven't arrived yet.

I don't think there is any more news. I am longing to hear from you again and hear all your news. Has Grace's baby arrived yet?

With lots of love from
Marjorie

The day turned from light to dark. The lamps were lit and their light attracted large moths and other insects to come drifting in out of the darkness, first tapping their wings against the glass of the window, and eventually gaining entry to fly round the light itself.

They sat facing one another across the candlelit table, talking quietly, leaning on the table to study one another. The steward boy silently waited on them, seeming to understand the atmosphere between them. From the darkness outside moths and other nocturnal insects continued to flutter against the glass. As the meal came to an end, it was obvious that there was romance in the air.

Philippe left the table and put a record on the gramophone. He wound it up vigorously.

Holding out his hands, he said, "Come, let's dance."

He held her close as together they twirled and bumped around the small room, laughing at themselves. Philippe spoke to the pieces of furniture as if they were other dancing couples. Marjorie giggled until she was almost helpless.

Then the music slowed and their movements matched it. That particular moment seemed to be when time stood still as it appeared to freeze and stretch itself out of normal time zones. Philippe kissed her briefly and studied her face before pressing his lips hard on hers. Marjorie closed her eyes. Was she ready to love again?

Eventually it was time to part. Philippe instructed the house-boy to call a taxi. Marjorie thanked him for a wonderful evening and left unwillingly.

The black night outside seemed thick enough to make her feel that she could reach out and touch it, pressing the velvety folds of it to her. The fact that she would probably disturb the unimaginable creatures that rustled in the even blacker shapes of the trees made her shudder. Just listening to the sound of them made her shiver involuntarily.

Stepping into the car she sat on the back seat and watched the road intently as it unwound ahead of them. There were familiar landmarks to be greeted secretly as they passed by.

Flashing lights ahead interrupted her thoughts.

It was a police car. A policeman flagged them down. The taxi slowed and stopped.

The police sergeant stuck his head in the rear window

of the car to address Marjorie.

"Your name please."

"Marjorie Heath." Her heart lurched with fear as she told him.

"And is that your full name?"

"My full name is Marjorie Louisa Heath."

"Would you get out of the car please, as we have some questions to ask you?"

Asking the taxi driver to wait she followed the policeman, afraid of what was to come. Although she was innocent of any crime she felt her knees go weak. The policeman was Nigerian and only being able to see the whites of his eyes and teeth in the darkness did nothing to incite calm.

"What is your date of birth please?"

"Second of December nineteen hundred and eight."

"Where were you born?"

"In England, in the village of Charlton Musgrove, in Somerset."

"What is your occupation?"

"I'm a Nursing Sister at the Lagos European Hospital."

"May I see your passport please?"

Marjorie dug around in her handbag, relieved she had it with her. It often got left in the drawer at the bungalow. She gave it to him.

The policeman took it and examined it closely by the light of his torch. He shut it with a snap.

"What have been your movements today?"

Marjorie recounted her time at the hospital and the hours she had been on duty, remembering to add the extra hour she had stayed there to help out.

"And this evening?"

"I've just been having a meal with a friend."

"And who is that please?"

"Philippe. Philippe Hauser."

"Have you known him long?"

"Not long. I met him at the last New Years Eve party."

"Do you see this friend often?"

Marjorie was about to protest that this was none of his business when she realised that this was wartime and it might well be.

"A fair bit, but being a nurse, I don't get much time to be sociable."

"What time did you go to see your friend tonight?"

Marjorie took a while to answer as she had to think when she came off duty and work from then on. She told the policeman what he wanted to know, then added "And I've just come from there now."

"How many other people were there?"

"It was just him and me for dinner. There was nobody else apart from the steward-boy."

"What did you do whilst you were there?"

"We were simply enjoying a nice meal. Afterwards we danced a little. Now I'm on my way home. That's all."

There was a break in the conversation while the police sergeant scribbled notes in his little book.

"Please," she asked. "What is all this about?" I haven't done anything wrong, have I?"

The policeman handed Marjorie her passport. "On your way now," he said, ignoring her last remark. "And be careful."

Marjorie trembled as she climbed back into the taxi. All kinds of thoughts chased through her head. The taxi driver turned round as he drove off.

"You all right lady?" he asked.

"Yes, yes thank you. Just get me home quickly, that's all."

As she left the taxi, the driver extended his right hand to her, clasping hers warmly.

"Am sorry you have upset. I pray for your good sleep tonight."

He inclined his head slightly and smiled, his brilliant white teeth gleaming in his dark face vaguely outlined in the darkness.

As she flopped into bed that night, Marjorie was worried. What was that all about? Then realisation dawned. *Could Philippe be a spy, a fifth columnist?* The thought repelled her, but all the pieces seemed to fit into the jigsaw; the way he only ever saw her during daylight hours unless he was in his flat. She would certainly ensure that she never contacted him again. She shuddered at the thought that the police had tailed her. How long had she been under suspicion?

Why was life never straightforward? Almost everyone with whom she had enjoyed a relationship seemed to be wrong for her in one way or another, and neither was it the normal cooling of emotion. She seemed to have a knack of attracting all the wrong people.

Trying to put her so-called love life on hold and leave her concerns behind her, next day, despite the heat, Marjorie went for a walk by herself along the beach during her lunch break. There wasn't a sound except sucking water and shingle crunching beneath her shoes as she walked. As she trudged along she thought about the quality of her own life so far and how much she wanted to do. In the future, she wanted to marry and bear children of her own. However, she believed there were still unrecognised opportunities that were slipping by. She must discover and reach out for them with both hands.

In July 1941, Marjorie was due to have three weeks local leave. She decided to spend it in Accra looking up old friends there. It would be quicker to fly there. Despite having some reservations about this form of travel; she boarded the small aircraft. Accelerating bumpily down the runway it left the ground and floated noisily in the sky she was enthralled by this new sensation. The whole of Lagos came into view with its islands and sandspits bursting with buildings to the water's edge, then the glassy blue lagoons flashing in the sunshine dotted with the shipping population in one form or another. The scene spun away as they headed in the direction of Accra, climbing yet higher into the blue sky.

The patterns below changed to a series of abstract

paintings, then forests dappled with changing shades of green, dwindling into a plateau.

Seeing the trees and savannah from so high up reduced it to dolls' house size and Marjorie felt no fear at being so far above the ground because it was more like being Alice in Wonderland. Perhaps she would soon wake up and, like Alice, find all this had been a dream! But no, here they were taxiing along Yumdum airstrip, and there was the familiar hospital jeep with its white cross painted on the sides.

Her letters to Bettie and Bill were read avidly as they described these three weeks so accurately. Now that she had the time to spare, Marjorie was enjoying writing to her stepsister and the rest of the family as she tried to describe her life in Africa.

European Hospital
Accra
Gold Coast
16.7.1941

My dear Bettie and Bill

Very many thanks for your letter just received dated 18.5.41. It has taken over two months to get here – of course it had to be forwarded from Lagos. Mother's arrived with yours dated 18.5.41.

It was nice to hear from you, but it was written before Grace's baby arrived. Thank you for the cable about her. I like the name Marion. I'm afraid lots of your mail and lots of mine has been lost as we hear from this end the names of the ships that have been sunk. One man from Lagos heard that his wife and children had been killed in an air raid at home. He went on the next ship but it was torpedoed and he was drowned – a tragedy – but perhaps it was a good thing for him really.

A nursing sister from here was on the way home and she was torpedoed. She and most of the others were in their lifeboats for six days and four of those without water. They were in a dreadful state when they were picked up. Several of them had died from exposure and exhaustion. She is not coming back here any more.

I am enjoying my stay here in Accra so much; it is nice to meet old friends again, and I seem to be booked up to go out to dinner several times in one evening! I'm sorry I can't accept all the invitations, but I've been able to go to tea or lunch if I haven't been able to manage dinner.

Miss O'Rourke, the matron, is giving a big party on Friday. She has invited all the Army Sisters and Army Officers and us. There will be about fifty of us altogether. We are having a buffet supper and dance and games. I said I will make some sausage rolls and cakes for it.

The other day I just happened to mention that I was in a cake making mood, so the others wouldn't let me rest until I'd got started, as they are so fond of cakes. I made orange cakes – one big one and sixteen small ones but all the small ones had gone by tea time and they only came out of the oven at four o'clock!

Colonel Shipman and Captain Wildman took me out to dinner and to the pictures last night. They are both army doctors and are very nice indeed. Patricia Burt (Nursing Sister) and I are going there for tea today and then we are going to the Ramages for drinks. (Mrs Ramage is acting Colonial Secretary as Mr Lonsdale is in South Africa on leave.) After that we are going to Mr Barnhill's to dinner and then play Mah Jong. I don't suppose you ever play with the set I left at home. I have bought a new one now – I think it's a marvellous game.

I am writing this sitting on the veranda in the sun trying to get a suntan – the sun is not very hot today though and keeps popping behind the clouds. I am leading a nice lazy life as I am local leave. I don't get up until nine o'clock or sometimes half past, then have breakfast in my dressing gown. I do needlework or something all morning, often go out to lunch, come back and rest, and frequently go out to tea, play tennis or golf or go for a walk with Patricia's dog or go swimming and often go out to dinner and the pictures or dance.

I have made a dress for Patricia since I've been here and have been darning some of the men's socks and sewing buttons on shirts for the Army Officers and other men whose wives are not out here.

I went surf riding with Captain Wildman the other day. It was lovely. However, I've bruised myself in several places with the surfboard because the waves were very strong.

I must remember to send a cable to you the day I leave here which will be the 21st July. I hope I won't forget in the excitement of getting on the plane. It's nice to feel I've been on a plane now. Actually I think it's a marvellous way of getting about. I wasn't airsick at all coming here from Lagos. I wrote to Mother and Father the other day and told them all about it.

Patricia is coming to Lagos for her local leave now, so will stay with me which will be very nice.

Two days before I left Lagos, Philippe rang me to say he couldn't collect me and take me to the pictures as arranged. Apparently the police had been and taken his car away and he had to be in his house by seven every evening, neither is he allowed to leave it before seven in the morning. He is not allowed to go to any club, cinema, hotel or bar – which means he can't ride, play tennis go to dances or anything. Apparently, all aliens are being treated in the same way just now. He has written to the Governor asking if he could be allowed to appear in Court to have a trial to prove he is not a suspicious character, and to be allowed to use his car for business purposes. At present he has to use a bicycle. Also he wants to go to the cinema, and asked if he could go under police escort if necessary! I don't know what the outcome of all that was, as of course I left Lagos just then. I can't believe he has done anything he shouldn't and don't think he has, but I suppose after the things that have happened here recently, the police can't be too careful, and all the innocent aliens have to suffer with the guilty. I had a letter from him yesterday, but he didn't say much except that his dog Spotty has had five little Spotties! His letter had been censored. He didn't seem upset about this restriction business – he said he realised that as there was a war on the police had to do their duty and he must put up with it, though it was rather annoying.

No more news now – please write again soon,

*Lots of love
Marjorie*

Chapter Twelve

They saw each other across the room and he threaded his way towards her. Steward boys, ladies in smart cocktail dresses, men in white tropical dinner jackets – all these were obstacles between them.

They were about three feet away from one another but they didn't speak, just stood mesmerised, gazing at one another. The buzz of conversation and the clink of glasses just faded into comparative silence as Alan slowly came towards Marjorie and kissed her tenderly on the cheek. It felt more intimate than any of the others had been.

He could see her face was more defined since they had last seen one another. Time had formed more noticeable shadowy hollows about her features, yet she was more attractive than ever. After their weeks apart Marjorie looked a little older, even more graceful and self-possessed.

They studied one other; there was no need to talk yet and silence was suspended between them.

At last he spoke. "It's good to see you again."

He stretched out both hands in a welcoming gesture. She took hold of them and did not let go of as she sat down.

"I couldn't believe it was you," she said simply.

A steward-boy hovered near them with a tray of drinks. Alan took two glasses and handed one to Marjorie.

He smiled as he raised his glass. "To you. To us!"

"To us," she echoed.

Now that they were together again, almost isolated in the social splendour as everyone else melted into the background, it was hard to know where to begin. The drink helped a little, loosening Marjorie's tongue and slowly they started to talk. Suddenly she seemed to understand everything with absolute clarity. She was here now, in the midst of her life with Alan.

When they next met, Alan handed Marjorie a small red box.

"For you," he said with a little bow.

Marjorie took it from him and removed the lid. Inside was a beautiful little porcelain figurine standing daintily in her crinoline with just a hint of white petticoat peeping out from beneath. She was leaning pertly on her parasol.

"Oh, Alan, she's exquisite. Thank you so much." She stood on tip-toe to kiss him.

"She reminded me of you, that's why I bought her, and, er ..." he looked at his feet, embarrassed. "I've got an identical one at home to remind me of you!"

Marjorie turned the piece over in her hand. It certainly wasn't cheap china by any means.

"She's called *Priscilla* according to the maker's name underneath. It sounds a bit prim. I prefer Marjorie. He kissed her and set the figurine on the mantelpiece.

Alan was a perfect companion. He was a romantic and Marjorie loved him for it, in fact she loved everything about him. His success at the hospital matured him. He talked about all sorts of things as well as hospital life, bridging the space of time, short though that was, that separated them. He listened intently to everything Marjorie contributed to the conversation. He made her laugh. She loved the fabric of happiness they wove, so desirable, yet as delicate as gossamer.

She knew how badly she wanted their future together and listened hard for any mention of it. She dreamed of being married to him and to bear his children. Yet to bring Gwen's name into any conversation would be unthinkable, even though the woman held the key to their future happiness together.

Their friendship had been strong and each had drawn their own strength from it, yet Marjorie realised she had a kind of wariness about her that almost frightened her. She was afraid of being hurt again.

She was first aware that Alan was truly serious in his quest to deepen their relationship when Frances Doyle gave birth to her baby. She was a mutual friend, and, being English, this created quite an event, as white women did not usually have their babies abroad. During the war the British Parliament ruled that children and pregnant women must not travel overseas.

Marjorie and Alan were both on duty when Frances was admitted with labour pains. Between them they delivered her of a perfect baby boy. Alan promptly went off and returned bearing a bottle of champagne to celebrate. Marjorie, having no idea about such things, trotted off and came faithfully back with corkscrew to open the bottle. Alan's face creased with laughter and a lock of his fair hair flopped onto his brow. She lifted her head, and for a moment their eyes met. An instinctive rapport flickered between them which Marjorie was convinced she had not imagined, as a sudden irrational surge of happiness overwhelmed her as she felt the warmth of colour grace her face.

For a long peculiar moment they could have been the only people in the ward, in the hospital even. As she watched, the quality of his smile changed a little to the professional appearance in which most people saw him. He turned to Frances, holding up the unopened champagne bottle in one hand and the corkscrew in the other.

"Any suggestions?" he asked wickedly.

Alan, together with Frances and her husband Derek, teased Marjorie for days about that.

As the baby was passed round for cuddles later on, Marjorie was holding him when Alan leaned forward and whispered in her ear, "Wouldn't it be lovely if we could have a little baby like this one day."

Marjorie caught her breath, lost for words. She and Alan stared at one another, volumes passing between them in total silence.

Knowing now that Alan had a wife, Marjorie was somewhat afraid of their relationship in a way that even she could not understand. Both of them were reluctant to advertise their love for one another. However, it was clear to even the most casual onlooker that they were deeply in love from the way they glanced at one another, tried not to monopolise one another in a crowd, almost to the point of avoiding the other's company at times. Yet Alan contrived to sit next to Marjorie at luncheon and dinner parties, searching for her hand under the tablecloth whilst holding a conversation with someone opposite or on his other side of him. They rarely left a social gathering at the same time, yet he would always catch her up, if she had left before him, or be waiting for her if he had been the first to leave. He always escorted her home.

Outwardly, their friendship was just that – two people sharing similar likes and dislikes, enjoying one another's company and naturally coming together a lot in the course of their work. Only they knew how much in love they were and how evasive they needed to be to try and conceal it from the public eye.

Marjorie was astonished at how furtive they had become. Yet it was nice having a secret. Nobody challenged them about their romance because their relationship was not supposed to exist. She felt warm and secure with their open secret --for open it was, as their love was too strong to deny for long.

Marjorie went practically of her way to evade Toby Wilkes. She felt he had deliberately tried to hurt her and sever the relationship between her and Alan when he had glibly referred to Gwen after lunch that day on the terrace. He surely should have had more tact than to blurt out something like that.

Those piercing blue eyes under his bushy eyebrows seemed to read her mind these days, and Marjorie began to avoid the thick-set man who posed such a threat to her happiness. She wasn't entirely sure what he would do, but having ensured that she knew Alan had a wife back in Wales there was no knowing what his tactics might be.

When she saw him approaching in a corridor, she would dive into a ward to elude him. Sometimes she couldn't escape and she would avert her eyes as he swept by her, his white coat flapping, emphasising his huge form. Her very silence seemed to pound her conscience into feeling pangs of guilt.

Alan had suggested a picnic, so he had brought along a hamper with him when he called for Marjorie. He chivalrously opened the car door for her whilst bowing from the waist.

"Your carriage, princess."

Marjorie stifled her giggles and replied in the same vein. "I am honoured, O prince."

He settled her comfortably and then climbed into the driver's seat. The car slid smoothly forward down the drive and Alan headed off towards the bush.

Suddenly he slowed and stopped. "I've got a better idea."

He turned the car round, creating a minor dust storm in the road as he did so, and headed back the way they had come.

"What's going on?"

"Wait and see!" Alan was full of surprises.

They headed towards the sea, and Alan parked the car as near he could. He helped Marjorie out of the passenger seat and leaned into the boot to pick up the hamper.

"Come on!" He took her hand and led her down to the jetty.

"This will be a cooler spot." Alan jumped into the motor boat and handed Marjorie down into it. The motor throbbed into life and they chugged away from the mainland towards the island owned by the Medical Department.

The sea was as blue as sapphires and sparkled like gems under the hot sun. Once on the island they headed for the bungalow and its sheltered garden where they laid out their picnic on the veranda. Their meal over, the heat became too intense and they moved into the shade.

Marjorie murmured her appreciation. "Mmmm, thank you. That was superb."

The shadows of the trees dappled her face and she shifted her head to a dark cooler place.

Soon it was too hot to be outside and the bungalow greeted them like a refuge. Alan and Marjorie shut its door behind them, laughing and surprised by what was happening as they had come creeping here to steal some time together.

There were some minutes of relaxed silence between them, then Alan spoke unexpectedly. "I've written to Gwen. In fact I've written twice now asking for a divorce, just in case my first letter was lost." He paused, then, "Marjorie, please marry me."

She glanced up at him uncertainly. How she loved him, yet she didn't want to be accused of being a marriage breaker and she loved him so much.

"I love you," she said simply in a tone that for some reason tore at his heartstrings.

"You didn't answer my question."

"I can't."

A smile played round the corners of his mouth as he tried to ask lightly, "You can't marry me, or can't answer my question."

Her eyes pleaded with him to understand as she shook her head and lamented,

"Oh Alan! If only you knew! I would love to marry you... but, but it's my family; your divorce ...they're staunch Methodists, they wouldn't understand ..." She hiccupped as she finished speaking and ended with a sob.

Alan was immediately contrite. "My love, I am so sorry. Please put all that out of your mind for the moment. Just know that I love you dearly and want the best for you."

He took hold of her chin and tilted her face to look at him. Taking his handkerchief from his pocket, he gently wiped her tears, kissing her eyelids, then the tip of her nose to make her smile again.

"I don't want to do anything to hurt you, you know that."

She nodded.

"Let's go for a walk along the beach." he suggested, immediately following it up with "Oh no, it's too hot out there now."

They clung to each other, desperately knowing that come what may the future must surely draw them ever closer so that they could declare their love to all and sundry, when everyone would rejoice with them. Alan kissed her meaningfully and Marjorie responded with similar passion.

They fondled and caressed one another intimately in the way lovers do with almost casual intensity. At a time such as this when they yearned for one another so much it would be only too easy to get away into their emotions with actions they might regret afterwards. The deep love they had for one another bound then together like gold ribbon and neither wanted to break apart.

"Sweetheart, how I love you, I love you so much."

"I love you too,"

"Say you'll marry me just as soon as we can?"

Marjorie was the first to wriggle free, breaking the spell.

She stood up, adjusting her clothing and wondering whether she should feel guilty or happy and carefree.

"Sorry, but I can't answer that just yet."

"I'm sorry too. I was letting my heart rule my head. We of all people should know all about the birds and the bees."

"Me a nursing sister and you a leading surgeon pleading ignorance wouldn't look very good." Marjorie smiled as she felt more cheerful.

The afternoon had cooled a little, so they took off their shoes to paddle in the sea.

Alan regarded Marjorie with deeper interest. He had seen her often, but only now did he see her with perfect comprehension. Her nursing may have tired her, but it had also softened her. Her tranquillity gave her an added dimension of sweetness, and her concern for her family was touching. As they walked on the sand with the sea lapping around their bare feet, Alan realised how much he liked Marjorie as well as loving her. He knew and liked her better than he had ever done before.

Marjorie had waded a little further out. She turned and came splashing out to him at a run, leaving deep footprints in the wet sand which the sea promptly swallowed up after her.

"Alan!" she called. "Just look at the time! I'm due back at the hospital in less than an hour!"

Her glance held his for just a second and then her eyes darted away as she ran up the beach to collect her things from the bungalow. Alan followed reluctantly and shortly afterwards, they clambered into the boat, he cast off and the motorboat left the little jetty, chugging towards the coastline of the mainland.

Alan had proposed to Marjorie at least twice before she said to him.

"Look, I'm very fond of you, and yes, I do love you. But you *are* married, and so far your wife doesn't seem keen to divorce you. I certainly enjoy our friendship, but can't you see, we can't take it any further or discuss marriage, at least until you are free?"

"Certainly, I'll drop the subject for now, but I'll still bring it up again at intervals to remind you of my love for you, and until you yield to my charms and agree to marry me." His tone was bantering and he appeared to have stopped taking her seriously in order to conceal his desperation to have her agree to marry him.

Alan was well liked amongst all the people who knew him. Often, when asked to a meal of any sort, he would generously take along a bottle of drink, or even a ham or joint of meat with him. It was always good quality. The better Marjorie knew him, the more she came in for a large slice of his benevolence as he rarely visited her empty handed. When they went to Lagos to look around, Marjorie only had to admire an item on display and Alan would dash in the shop and buy it for her. At his insistence he helped with a lot of the incidental furniture in her bungalow, such as a lamp-stand, cushions, a coffee table and even a small bookcase. She became rather embarrassed after a while and tried not to call attention to objects she liked the look of.

Alan was so well brought up and had such a placid nature that it was hard to believe whether he suffered as a result of Marjorie's apparent rejection to his proposals of marriage. Yet as time went on, he treated the situation as if it were some kind of game, assuming that one day they would be wed, pressing her with promises of a divorce along with lavish gifts and bouquets of flowers as if to prove his point. Although Marjorie was sometimes rather disturbed by it Alan never appeared to be discouraged. It seemed impossible to ruffle his composure or good humour, which Marjorie supposed was the reason why he had become the eminent surgeon that he was. Occasionally she wondered if it might be better all round if she ended their romantic relationship. Then she remembered how they had both felt when they had separated before, realising it would be like cutting off her nose to spite her face, because she had become very fond of him and he was such good company. She now admitted that she loved him. Should they separate now this would cause pain and embarrassment as their working lives were so entwined. The friendship didn't appear to be causing any harm, so it may as well stay as it was. It was comfortable.

For all his success, Alan was a homely man, and was able to spread an aura of comfort to all those around him, especially Marjorie. She appreciated that he was good for her, but this sometimes led to her being confused and afraid of making a mistake. He was always honest with her, and she was honest in return; the difference was that he still viewed her as his future wife, whereas she could only see him as her best friend.

When she perceived the situation against her family background and her strict chapel upbringing, Marjorie knew they would be shocked to say the least. She desperately wanted to marry Alan in her heart of hearts (and he had no doubt realised this, hence his persistence), but she knew that although she was sure Alan would be well accepted by her family initially, as soon as they discovered his marital history, he would be regarded as a social outcast. She could not bear to think about it, and consequently tried to avoid such thoughts and live purely in the present.

Every so often a bundle of newspapers would arrive for Marjorie from home. Usually they were old copies of *The Daily Telegraph*. The news would be several weeks old, but it was good to hear how England was surviving the war and to have rumours either confirmed or quashed. The cryptic crossword became a challenge too, and Alan and Marjorie rose to it as they pored over them in the evenings while darkness crept silently and swiftly from under the bushes and branches of trees. Her fascination for crosswords never left her.

Moira Woolmer occasionally received old copies of the local *Bournemouth Echo*, so they would read one another's and then pass them on to the hospital where patients read them avidly, so they soon became very tatty.

One day Marjorie burst into the staff common room and slumped wearily into a chair. She'd had a tiring day, with many sickly patients needing care and attention, so had been on her feet all day. She had not even had time to eat lunch. Now, at almost three in the afternoon, she needed some sort of respite. Too late she spied Toby Wilkes behind a newspaper in the corner.

"Ahah! Just the just the girl I want to see." He oozed charm.

Marjorie swallowed uneasily. "Really?"

"Yes, I believe it's your family who donate the *Telegraph* to us so regularly. Such a good dependable read. Do pass on our gratitude when you are next in touch." His honeyed tones betrayed something other than gratitude.

"Oh, yes, yes indeed." Marjorie relaxed. "It certainly gives more reliable war news than a lot of other sources, even if it is somewhat out of date."

"Hmmm." Toby continued reading an article, then looked up.

"Actually I really wanted to speak to you about another matter?"

"Yes?"

"Your relationship with Alan McKenzie. You two are still going around with one another?"

Marjorie bridled. "I don't see ..."

Toby interrupted her.

"If you are going to tell me that it is none of my business then I can tell you that it is. How do you think it looks to others when one of my nurses carries on with a doctor – a senior surgeon – a married one at that?"

Marjorie almost burst with indignation.

"I am not one of *your* nurses as you so quaintly put it. I am answerable to Muriel Henley, the Matron. I don't think it's good policy for you to make comments on my personal life!"

"I think it *is* my business," he responded calmly. "After all you do work in the hospital here and we do have a reputation to keep up."

"As long as Matron is satisfied with my work I really don't see what my personal life has to do with anything!"

"Oh, but I think it does." Toby sounded like a venomous snake.

"I'll not stay here to be insulted any longer!"

"I advise you to think about it, and your position here," he advised quietly in a derisory tone.

Marjorie, still with her hand on the door-knob, whirled round, her mind made up. "For your information, we are just good friends," she said, breathing deeply to keep her composure.

He leered at her. "They all say that!"

Marjorie gulped and decided to come clean.

Reluctantly she played her somewhat weak trump card. "Alan has asked for a divorce. He has also asked me to marry him, but up until now I have refused."

Toby sneered. "Then my dear, why do you lead him on by continuing your friendship? You have us all on tenterhooks you know."

Marjorie slammed out of the room and dashed out of the hospital and over to her bungalow where she collapsed into a heap on her bed. There she allowed herself the luxury of a good sob before sitting up and drying her eyes.

"Damn Toby Wilkes!" She was not going to let him spoil her relationship with Alan.

The altercation with Toby Wilkes niggled at Marjorie from time to time, but she suppressed it, assuring herself that if he raised the issue again, she now had a good base for quelling any further argument.

A few days after this incident, Marjorie wondered just how it might practically affect her relationship with Alan. Surely Dr Wilkes couldn't really harm them? After all, Alan was his senior by far. In reality Toby would surely honour his boss. No, it was probably herself that he was trying to unsettle in his malicious way.

She wondered whether she should tell Alan. Then she decided against it for it might sound like telling tales out of school. Toby may well want her to do just that in the hope of Alan confronting him, and a possible blazing row erupting and leading to – what? It wasn't worth getting het up about a man like that. Marjorie herself hated scenes, yet just look how soon Toby had managed to wind her up! She would avoid trouble and pretend that the drama had never occurred.

A barbecue was being organised on the beach. Over thirty people were present, all in very casual dress and wearing swimming costumes underneath. The evening swiftly turned to black night the sky a black velvet cloth scattered with shining sequin stars. The sea was black as ink and shimmered as it reflected the moonlight sending small lacy waves frothing onto the sand.

Steward-boys were left in charge of the cooking while everyone flung off their outer clothes and ran into the sea. Alan and Marjorie splashed in with them, and together they all dived, swam and played like children on a Sunday school outing.

"Dinner is served!" called someone, and they all evacuated their watery playground, whooping and charging up the beach as if going into battle.

A lot of barbecued chicken and meat was consumed, accompanied by some cold dishes. People flopped onto the sand afterwards, naturally grouping themselves into conversation clusters. Talking and laughter echoed on the night air as Alan and Marjorie slipped away for a lone walk along the beach.

They rounded a corner and were out of sight when Alan slipped his arm around Marjorie's waist, squeezing her gently. She put her arm around him and they wandered up the beach along the water's edge, their steps matching with the sea swallowing up their footprints.

"Marjorie ..." he stopped.

"Yes?"

"I just wanted to say – to say that I love you so much."

"I love you too." She turned to him and smiled her appreciation of him.

"No, I really want to say more than that, but I'm afraid of frightening you away!"

He turned her towards him.

"You know what I'm about to say, don't you? I desperately want you to be my wife."

Marjorie swallowed, trying to ignore the old arguments that kept popping up inside her head. Yet if she were true to herself, she was surely living a lie in encouraging this relationship. Alan sensed her discomfiture.

Releasing her, he shouted, "Race you into the water!"

They spattered into the sea, breathless, as they became hip deep in it. Together they plunged in, swam, dived, often coming up for air at exactly the same time. They both gasped in the magic of the moment, then and there in the depths of the lagoon and for all to see. Alan clasped Marjorie to him and kissed her long and passionately under the night sky. The water lapped around them and their bodies tingled. Later they floated idly on their backs watching the night sky as the stars hung above them, lit by the luminous moon.

Words became unnecessary.

It was some while later before they emerged to wander lazily hand in hand up the beach. Once they reached the remains of the barbecue, it was deserted. Everyone had gone, everything had been tidied away except for two piles of clothing left neatly next to one another.

"They haven't even left us a sausage," said Alan.

"Nor a bread roll to put it in."

Had they been missed? Had they been too careless on this fantastic night?

As if to cover any concern he may have, Alan grabbed Marjorie and scooped her off her feet.

"Come on, let's have another dip!"

Being tall, he carried her easily and after a jolting ride they dived into the water together. This time they kept hold of one another and he often embraced her in the water as they dived and emerged together like a couple of porpoises.

They splashed out of the water again and continued their close togetherness in the dry sand on the beach. As their bodies rubbed upon each other the grittiness of the dry sand contrasted to the softness of the water they had just experienced.

Before their emotions reached a peak, Marjorie rolled away. "We shouldn't be doing this."

"I'm sorry, we should never have been so long down here on our own." Alan stood up and held his hand out for

Marjorie.

They brushed sand off before going down to the sea and rinsing their bodies.

"We could have another swim while we're here!"

They didn't stay in the sea for long, but neither of them wanted this fantastic evening to end. By the time they were dry enough to put their clothes on and walk home it was nearly two in the morning. Even when they got home it was hard to part.

It went without speaking that they were both concerned about how much people realised was going on between them now.

Was their beautiful romance now public knowledge? Only time would tell.

They were shopping together in Lagos. Marjorie had bought a mound of writing paper and envelopes, as letters from home were so welcome; yet she knew that in order to receive some she must write some. Now that the euphoria of being abroad had worn off she was finding it difficult to write so much to her many friends and relatives.

Alan had stopped by the window of a small jeweller's shop. "Just a moment, I want to look at the watches."

Marjorie was not really interested, but stood passively by, until he disappeared into the shop and she followed meekly after him.

A dark-skinned man emerged from the depths of the gloom, only a flash of his white teeth as evidence of his presence until her eyes accustomed to the murky interior.

"Yes boss?"

"Could I have a look at some ladies' watches please?"

"Yes boss." The man shuffled off and returned with a tray full of gleaming dials.

"For the missus sir?" He nodded at Marjorie.

Alan slid his arm round Marjorie's waist.

"But I've got my nurses watch," she protested.

"Yes, but not a nice dress watch. See here, do you like this one?"

"It is unusual."

"Mebbe the lady try it on?"

The dainty art deco style gold watch with its brown leather strap was duly placed on her wrist and they both admired it.

"I like it. I've never seen a watch with a pink face before."

"I agree. I like the rectangular shaped face."

"Thank you, we'll take it." Alan paid the required sum and they stepped out into the bright sunlight again, blinking.

Marjorie was delighted and said so. "But there was no need for you to spend all that money one me."

"I enjoy giving you things, and especially because you always appreciate them so much."

Marjorie enjoyed wearing her watch. She had not realised how often she had asked people the time when not on duty. Being different, it was eye-catching, and was admired by her friends.

Muriel Henley was hosting a party. The evening was drawing to a close after a wonderful time of games, dancing and a buffet supper. Marjorie was with a small gathering of ladies, all having connections with the hospital around which the conversation centred.

A house-boy appeared at their side with a tray of drinks.

People were mumbling. "Well, maybe one more before I leave."

Marjorie stretched out her hand towards the tray when Ida Wilkes grabbed her arm. "I say, what a distinctive watch. I do like that!"

Others looked and murmured their agreement.

"Very pretty."

"So dainty."

"Is it new?"

"Yes, quite new." Marjorie took a sip of her drink.

"Was it a present then?"

"Yes, Alan gave it to me."

She immediately realised her mistake, but made no attempt to cover it up; to do so would be folly indeed.

"Well, well, is it your birthday or something?"

She grabbed at the chance of retreating a little from possible trouble.

"It's a late birthday present."

The subject was changed.

When Marjorie next saw Alan she was contrite from the start of their meeting.

"I've done something awful," she confessed.

Alan would not take her seriously.

"You dropped a thermometer?"

"No."

"You dropped a bedpan?"

"No, worse."

"You mean you dropped a *full* bed pan?"

Marjorie had to smile as she shook her head. "No far worse."

"You haven't dropped a patient?" She giggled at his mock severity and loved him all the more for his cheerfulness.

"No, it's nothing to do with the hospital; well it is in a way, I suppose." She was thinking aloud now.

"Oh, Alan, it's that watch. Being so unusual it often gets admired and the other evening at Muriel Henley's party, Ida Wilkes asked who gave it to me. I fell straight into the trap and without thinking and said that you had."

"So, what about it?"

"Well, people aren't supposed to know about us are they? She asked if it was my birthday and I said it was a late birthday present: but I could have kicked myself, especially as I could have directed her to the shop where it came from!"

"Well, don't worry about it. What's said is said. Whatever they *think* about us, they can't *do* anything. They can't alter my love for *you,* or *yours* for me. Anyway, I'm more senior to them. After all we haven't actually done anything wrong have we?"

"No," she admitted.

"Well, there you are then. Don't fret. Let's enjoy life while we can."

Enjoy life they did.

Work was enjoyable and all the more so because Alan was often there to work with, that is when he was not touring other Nigerian hospitals.

Social life was enjoyable. Marjorie knew a lot of people now apart from just those at the hospital. She had got to know folk from the armed forces, plus one or two missionaries. She had started attending chapel again occasionally and met more individuals there. With or without Alan, her free time was always booked up playing tennis or golf, sometimes swimming or boating. It was a life of luxury that was taken for granted because of the heat.

Alan had at last received a letter from Gwen.

Sharing its contents with Marjorie, he said. "She won't give me a divorce easily, but has promised she will let me go after seven years separation."

"Alan, I feel awful coming between you and your wife."

My dearest, it wasn't a happy marriage anyway. She shunned me after the girls were born, and has always refused to travel with me. As I've pointed out to you before, ours is a marriage in name only and we should have officially parted years ago."

"Yes, I suppose it is a fairly common saying out here that anyone can look after your children, but only a wife can look after her husband," mused Marjorie.

Alan saw his chance and grabbed it.

"Marjorie, I'm going through with this divorce whatever happens now. Please say you'll wait for me and marry me at the end of it all."

She sighed as she studied his earnest face, loving her, pleading with her. She thought of the possible conflict with her family – yet; did they have to know? Couldn't she tell them about him when he was single again and forget that he had ever been married before? They surely need never know. After all, he was marrying her, not her family.

She turned into him and put her arms around his neck.

"Yes," she whispered. "I'll stand by you. I'll marry you. It's what I want most of all."

"Oh, my darling! This is the happiest day of my life! I love you so much. You'll never know how much I love you!"

"I love you too." She found herself enveloped in a bear hug.

They embraced passionately and found it hard to part.

"When we're married we can start our own family. I want to be a father to our children, Marjorie."

"I'm longing to have your children."

"I feel now that whatever I have to face in the future, I can do it with you." He reached for her hand and squeezed it as he smiled tenderly at her then clasped her hands against his chest.

Marjorie's heart lifted to see how elated she had made him, indeed she was exhilarated herself. Why had she not thought of such a solution before and just forget the whole truth of the matter when introducing him to her family? To think that both of them could have been much more exuberant so much sooner!

"Perhaps I should have told you about this before," Marjorie hesitated about the possibility of putting a damper on their joy.

"Go on." He inclined his head to listen.

"A few weeks ago Toby Wilkes challenged me about our relationship even before the situation with the watch."

"Tell me about it. I thought we shared everything."

Marjorie described the time when she had come upon Toby in the staff common room. Alan was outraged.

"But you should have told me, not carried it around, worrying about it on your own."

"I suppose I was afraid you would say something to him and everything would blow up into something horrid.

I hate scenes and atmospheres, so I hoped the least said the better."

"Well, my darling you were very brave, and it seems now as if we are both going to be very brave."

A further letter was written and sent to Gwen demanding that Alan be released from their marriage contract as soon as possible. In it Alan stated that he was prepared to wait for the maximum length of seven years, but made mention that he had not lived in the marital home for five years due to his work in West Africa. However, he pointed out that he was intent on divorce and as there had been nothing to their marriage for some years anyway, he was hoping she would make it easier for them both by taking the first legal procedure as he was the guilty party and had no intention of returning to the matrimonial home. Marjorie secretly prayed that Alan would be released earlier from his marriage, otherwise she would be past the age of forty before she could think of bearing her first child, which would be dangerously late. She bit her lip as she recalled her own mother giving birth to Jessie and the complications that had set in.

Life seemed wonderful. Marjorie felt happy and settled. Lagos was a beautiful place to work in, and most of all, she had Alan to love and care for her.

Then her peaceful regime was shattered when she was handed a letter at breakfast one morning by the house-boy. It was from Headquarters. She couldn't imagine what it was about and turned it over thoughtfully in her hand before opening it. She read it and re-read it several times before she was able to grasp its meaning.

The letter informed her that she was being posted to Calabar Hospital, nearly five hundred miles round the coastline. The message was contrived to make it look like promotion as there would be only Marjorie and one other nursing sister in charge of both the European and African Hospitals there. All Marjorie could think of was that she wouldn't see Alan again. She went to her bedroom for a private weep, then felt better and ready to face the day ahead. She must not break down in front of the patients.

Alan was away visiting other Nigerian hospitals, but she prayed that he would be back before she had to leave Lagos at the end of the month which was only ten days away. She struggled through her work mechanically that day.

Two days later during the evening, there was a knock at the door. Marjorie wasn't expecting anyone, so she let the steward-boy answer it. She was surprised and thrilled to see Alan walking into the room. She almost threw herself upon him.

"My, what a welcome!" he gasped, as he staggered backwards a little. "I've literally only just got back."

"Oh, Alan, how glad I am to see you!" she gasped. Pulling open a drawer, she dragged the letter out to show him. He read it and drew his brows together in concern.

"Well, it's promotion for you," he said at last.

"Do you *really* think that?" she asked, a frown creasing her forehead.

He grimaced. "To be honest, it seems they know about us and disapprove," he said at last, with a sigh. "And this is their tactful way of dealing with it."

"D-do you think... no surely not," ended Marjorie lamely.

"Go on, say what's on your mind," prompted Alan.

"Well, do you think Dr Wilkes had anything to do with this?" He's never really approved of our friendship, has he?"

Alan frowned. "He's my junior, but I suppose he could register a complaint, which was investigated, and this is HQ's solution. Who knows?"

They were in each other's arms, consoling one another's grief. How could they live without each other?

"At least it'll be the end of it all when we're married. I've written back to Gwen asking her to release me sooner, but even if she doesn't, divorce will be automatic after seven years separation. Oh, I have never loved anyone like

I love you. Our love will stand the test of seven years in a lifetime, won't it?"

She leaned against him. Tenderly he stroked her hair

Marjorie's guilty feeling gnawed at her again as she realised her decision to deceive her family, especially her father. They would all be horrified if they thought she was even thinking of marrying a divorced man. She might even be a family outcast, so high were their morals. Even though she had been keen to leave home, she would not want to have no home to return to. Now she loved Alan so much. She too felt she would never love anyone quite like this ever again. Suppose her family did find out? Would Alan's love for her and her love for him be enough for the rest of their lives? She was stumped for an honest reply, and just buried her face in his chest, crying tears of grief, guilt and yearning which stabbed at her heart like a sword. Alan' response was to hold her tighter.

Alan came to collect Marjorie in his car to take her to the quayside and see her on board ship. She had attended two parties so that people could say farewell to her. All her belongings were packed and she had a last look round the bungalow, not because she might have left something behind, but because she wanted to recall some happy memories and imprint them on her memory.

First she went to the kitchen and thanked the cook for all he had done, and the steward and steward boy. They bowed their appreciation of her as she left them and went to her bedroom, where she stood, looking round, before re-entering the lounge.

Alan was standing there, waiting patiently, with understanding written all over his face. He put his arm around her and they stood close together, each silent with their own memories.

He finally broke the quietness. "Come on, or you'll miss that boat!"

"That's a good idea," she said, and sat down, smiling up at him.

"What do you think HQ will do then?" At least this is a kind of promotion for you," reasoned Alan. "Come on, we ought to go now."

He stood back to let her pass in front of him before going through the door, then kissed her as she did so.

Outside there were some large plants dripping with scarlet zinnia blooms. Marjorie smiled and stared at them. Their very brightness seemed to leak into the atmosphere. The colour was hot and vivid as her own blood. An intensity of feeling swept over her which Alan noticed and felt it with her. He led her back inside and took her in his arms.

"The ship will wait," he murmured as he kissed her firmly on the lips.

Marjorie responded, loving the comfort of his arms and desperately wondering how she could manage on her own, without the comforting knowledge that he was always around when needed, that he cared for her and needed her as much as she needed him. They parted and he held the door of the car open for her to climb in. The steward-boy had already loaded the boot with luggage. Alan slid into the driver's seat, put the car into gear almost with the same movement as starting the engine, and the vehicle purred down the drive, over the little wooden bridge, leaving Creek Hospital behind them.

Once at the docks, Alan located the ship and escorted Marjorie to it, the massive hull looming high above them. He took her into his arms.

"I'll never forget you. I'll write," he declared. "We'll find a way of being together."

Marjorie nodded, too emotional to speak and their tears mingled as their cheeks touched, before evaporating in the tropical sunshine.

It was time to get on board. She plodded up the gangway, her heart heavy, sobbing quietly. Leaning over the rail she waved bravely, assuming Alan was somewhere below waving back, but she could not recognise anyone through her tears.

Chapter Thirteen

Marjorie went to Calabar Hospital prepared to hate it. It was a lot hotter and stickier than Lagos, being further south. An African met her off the ship and took her luggage, opening the rear door of a large car for her to climb into. He sat in the front looking smart in his khaki chauffeur's uniform and whisked her through the town at a frightening pace to the European Hospital which was on the top of a hill outside the town. Her living quarters were in a bungalow similar to the one she had occupied before.

She met Freda Kingston who was the other nursing sister there. Later that evening, Marjorie walked over the compound to Freda's bungalow where she had been invited for dinner. Tiny flickering lights in the lower branches of the trees showed the location of the fireflies, and all around she could hear the clicking of the crickets and the whizzing of tiny insects. Coping with flies at dinner was not so pleasant!

Miss Kingston was plain and severe looking. She was the same age as Marjorie but looked older. Being tall and slim she wore spectacles which added to her austere look. Marjorie was embarrassed to discover her on her knees praying one evening. Freda was a devout Christian. Now Marjorie's conscience began to trouble her as she realised that she had hardly ever attended church since she left home, but had enjoyed herself at parties and dances, and most of all, the company of a yet-to-be divorced man. She also recalled the way her father had kneeled down in the little kitchen at home to give thanks for keeping her safe when she arrived home after being torpedoed. He believed that she had been saved for some special purpose, which surely had not yet come about. She sighed; she really must stop thinking like this.

The African hospital, which was also under Freda and Marjorie's care, was about a mile away down town. Freda had a battered old car she would drive between the two if the weather became extremely hot. Marjorie sought out two willing Africans who were happy to carry her in a sedan chair for a modest sum. Calabar was really too hot sometimes to feel capable of doing anything.

On her first day in the African hospital, Marjorie was horrified by the overcrowding, with some people on either side of beds, even underneath them.

"Good gracious!" she said to Freda on her first morning. "How on earth can you nurse these people in such cramped conditions?"

"They're not actually all patients. Some are friends and relatives."

"Surely they get in the way?"

"Well, it can be awkward when making an examination, but they can be quite helpful to us. Africans are suspicious of our food, so their relatives come and keep them company. They make up what look to us like little messes of food and the patient will happily eat that rather than the food we serve."

"Don't you find you're always falling over them?"

"Not really, because they hold us in awe to a certain degree, and are adept at melting into the background if they need to."

"It all seems very strange to me."

"You'll get used to it. I think patients recover quicker because they have familiar faces around them, making them feel as if they're in a safer environment."

Marjorie soon got used to the relaxed, less clinical way of Calabar hospital. She was relieved of several of her more menial tasks by patients' relatives, and in this heat, the less she had to do, the better.

She also witnessed first hand some of the ignorant and superstitions these people had. Some had been helped by relatives over long distances through the forest to reach the hospital. Occasionally patients issued blood-curdling screams, not from pain, but because they had discovered chicken bones outside their huts. They were sure they were bewitched and were going to die. There were others with a wide variety of diseases, the most common being yaws, tuberculosis and malaria which was spread by the mosquito.

At least here there was a swimming pool to use in her leisure time, a luxury that other places had not had. Marjorie began to find it easier to write letters home. Not once had she mentioned Alan before, unless it had been by casual reference, so that latterly she had been hard put to write any news at all, because Alan had become her life. Here he wasn't.

Something Marjorie had never come across before in a hospital, was bribery. The Europeans in charge had to keep their eyes on some of the African nurses who wanted money out of all situations.

One afternoon Freda signalled urgently to her from the other side of the ward. As Marjorie approached, she grabbed her arm and pulled her aside.

"Look over there." She nodded instead of pointing. "Do you see that large African nurse with her back to us just about to administer a bedpan?"

"Yes."

"She is blackmailing the patient into paying her money before she gives it to her. Come and investigate with me."

Together they went to the scene. Freda spoke to the African nurse.

"Come along Nurse, you mustn't give a bedpan without screens."

Marjorie realised this was her cue and trundled screens round the bed. Grudgingly the patient was given the bedpan.

"Thank you, oh thank you," said the patient when the African nurse had bustled off. "I was so sure I would bust! I know you don't hold with that sort-a thing."

After that, Marjorie was able to detect and intervene some blackmailing deals. Life out here never ceased to amaze her.

Overall the hospital was free and easy with no regular

visiting hours; after all, so many relatives stayed most of the time. Marjorie discovered for herself that the Africans were suspicious of European food, although she herself thought she had never seen anything quite so revolting as the mish-mash the Nigerians served up. Consequently the local people would bring prepared food in bowls for their hospitalised relatives each mealtime. Sometimes the whole family would come too and sit on the floor round the bed having quite a party amidst the sterile situation surrounding them.

She had been in Calabar for little more than a week when a letter arrived for her in Alan's handwriting. She tore it open, hungry to know what he had to say. He was missing her, and asked her to write to him, which she did by return. Soon they were writing to one another on a daily basis.

Meanwhile, Marjorie tried to keep the social side of her life alive and began to get to know people here in Calabar, starting a fresh round of parties and dances. Describing these to Alan in her letters, he would often comment in his letters that he knew quite a few of the people with whom she was socialising.

After a particularly harrowing day, Marjorie came off duty over an hour late, with just one thought – that of a cold bath and bed. She was hot and exhausted. She trudged down the hospital steps as the heat of the sun suddenly beat down, its glare temporarily blinding her, then walked towards her bungalow.

A voice called after her. "Hey, Marjorie!"

She stopped in her tracks, not daring to look in case her ears were playing tricks on her.

Alan approached from behind, waving. "You walked straight past me!" He laughed, then hugged her closely to him.

Marjorie blinked in amazement. "What on earth are you doing here?" she asked incredulously.

"I worked out from your letter where you would be and what your duty times were. I'm staying with the Stockleys for a few days."

"Oh do you know them – Ian and Brenda?" I met them a couple of days ago."

"Know them? I've known them since I first came out to Nigeria!"

They hugged one another enthusiastically again, then studied each other's faces. There was no need to talk yet.

"You see, I said our love would find a way," said Alan as they wandered slowly over towards Marjorie's bungalow.

Once there she sought out the steward and ordered an evening meal for two. Neither felt like going out, but it was bliss just to be together again.

Marjorie excused herself.

"I really can't entertain you like this. Do you mind if I take a quick bath and change? Then I'll feel more civilised."

"You go ahead, sweetheart. I'll raid the drinks cabinet!"

She kissed him and indicated where it was. "Help yourself!" she called over her shoulder.

Her lethargy fell off her like a cloak as she stepped into the water, had a quick wash and towelled herself dry. Dressing speedily she put on a dress that she knew Alan liked.

She surprised him by being so swift with the task in hand, and on approaching the lounge, watched his profile from the doorway for some seconds before he realised she was there.

He looked tired, no doubt exhausted because of travelling in the heat. Yet here he was, having travelled all this way to see her. Her heart was jolted into another spurt of love for him.

Aware of being watched, he turned. "Hello, darling. You were quick. Come here."

She walked slowly towards him, still unable to believe he was real.

"You're wearing my favourite dress! You look beautiful!"

She sat on the sofa next to him and laid her head on his

shoulder.

"This is the perfect resting place for my head. "We're meant to be together." She sighed. "It's a perfect fit."

He smiled and stroked her hair.

During the first part of that evening it was just enough to be together again. They sipped their drinks in mutual silence, having so much to say that a starting point is difficult to find. After about half an hour the steward-boy came to announce that dinner was served.

The food seemed to loosen their tongues in more ways than one, as conversation began and it was difficult to being it to a halt as they recalled old times together, asking after mutual friends. Time sped by. All too soon the evening was over and Alan stood up to go.

"Can I see you again tomorrow?" he asked almost shyly.

"Of course. I'm off duty at the same time, although you've probably worked out my off duty times better than I have!"

He grinned. "I believe you have a day off the day after that?"

"I do," she smiled back.

"Let's go out somewhere, then."

"There's not really anywhere to go round here; it's a something and nothing kind of place."

"Never mind, I'll see you tomorrow, and we'll decide what we can do the following day."

He kissed her goodnight, and their bodies seemed glued together so reluctant were they to part.

"This is to make up for those goodnight kisses we've missed," he murmured.

She leaned into his chest and sighed. "I must try and tear myself away. I've got to work tomorrow!"

He took her by the shoulders and stepped backwards, leaving her at arm's length.

"'Bye, my darling. See you tomorrow!"

"'Night," she whispered after his retreating figure.

After that Alan often appeared most unexpectedly, staying with mutual friends and meeting Marjorie in her off-duty time. He seemed to have a great deal of time off, but being the 'Big White Chief' Marjorie supposed it was his prerogative. However some of his visits were under the umbrella of genuine routine visits to the hospital. Calabar hospital certainly came in for a good few of these whilst she was there.

Alan wrote to her regularly; lively and friendly letters to which she replied in kind. Sometimes flowers would be delivered for her, and before reading the card, Marjorie would know they were from him.

She was having more difficulty with her letters home, trying not to mention the one person she thought and dreamed most about. She was still afraid to think how her family would react if they found out about his background.

Calabar, being much nearer to the equator than anywhere else she had worked so far, had a scanty population of Europeans, probably no more than a couple of dozen, thirty at the most. She soon got to know everyone it was possible to be sociable with and longed for the halcyon days of Lagos.

Medical Hospital
Calabar
13.11.1941

My dear Bettie and Bill

It is your turn to write to me, but I thought I would start writing to you. I have just finished breakfast at half past seven and it's not quite time to go on duty so I have a few minutes to spare. I expect you think it's unusual for me to get up before I need to be. I often am out here. One can get up easier in the hot weather I think. It is beginning to stoke up now – by Christmas it will be very hot. They tell me that Calabar is a lot hotter than Lagos.

This evening I am being taken to the cemetery to see the grave of Mary Slessor – everyone talks about her out here. I wished I had read the book Father has about her – 'Mary Slessor of Calabar' *– but I expect it will be in the library here somewhere. I believe she died in 1915. A chap here apparently went to her funeral. Our cook who has been here since 1903 says that she died in this hospital, but she didn't!*

<u>Later</u>

I had my first game of golf here yesterday. Tennis played quite a lot here too, but it's getting rather too hot for that now. It has been terribly hot here today. I went for a walk and was absolutely soaked in perspiration this evening.

There are very few white people in Calabar – only twenty-five, possibly thirty altogether, and I think I've met them all now.

We went to the pictures last night and saw the Ice Follies of 1939. It was very good – it's a funny little picture house here. The Africans get in for one penny on Friday nights – we can too if we want to. Other nights it is 1/6 and 2/- seats.

I don't think there is any more I can tell you as I wrote to Mother only the other day and I expect you will read her letter. I am going to bed now – it's only half past eight in the evening – unusual for me, but there are thousands of insects buzzing around and it's better to get under the mosquito net out of the way of them.

I hope you have a Happy Christmas and New Year.

Lots of love,
Marjorie

Medical Department
Calabar
22.1.1942

My dear Bettie and Bill

Very many thanks for your interesting letter received at Christmas time. You wrote it on 27.9.41.

Fancy your local Scout Master being in the RAF. There are lots of RAF out here now – wouldn't it be funny if he came out? There are hosts of Pan American Airways chaps too – not in Calabar though – this is a very dead-alive place here.

13.2.42

I'm afraid I put this aside for sometime – sorry about that. I have now received another letter from you the day before last dated 12.12.41. I wonder if you have got your skirt knitted yet? You seem to be feeding Bill well if he has gained 1 1\2 stones since you got married!

Yes it would be lovely to go to London when I come home again, though if you are having this baby that you speak about (suppose it's no longer a secret) you may not be able to come, but of course he or she may be at school by then!

We have all worked out that the war will be over by March 1943 – another year to so.

Now I will turn to your letter – you said you hadn't written for ages but it was fairly quick compared to the length of time I had to wait for the last one, ages and ages it seemed – of course one or two might have been lost.

It must be nice to have Ronald at home again, I expect. I can't imagine him as a Civil Servant in Whitehall. Your letter seems to be full of births, deaths and marriages – or forthcoming births!! I feel quite excited about yours, I wish I could send you some baby clothes. However I sent two to

Grace for Marion and Morgan, but they were opened by the censor and returned to me, so I am hoping that someone out here will have a baby and I can give them away.

You also tell me about Felicia. She sounds very nice – I'm glad she and Ronald are engaged. Do send me a snap, will you – that is if Ronald will allow you to have one! Better still, Ronald can send me one and write at the same time as I haven't had a letter from him in answer to my two.

I have only just finished writing to Mother, so cannot really think of anything more to say; I wrote reams to her last night and was rather later getting up in consequence. Will have to be up betimes in the morning as a female patient we have in the female ward at the European Hospital is having at operation at half past seven in the morning and I have to give the anaesthetic. (I expect you think you are glad it's not you having the op. with me giving the dope!) However we have to do all sorts of things like that out here which only a qualified person at home is allowed to do. I shall have to see about sterilising the instruments and preparing the theatre too. One is a 'Jack of all Trades' out here —there is a doctor to operate, I will say that, but I wouldn't let him do anything to me, though. I would go to Lagos or South Africa. It is very difficult to get to South Africa now as everyone is going there and there are so few ships left. I have been asked to wait until June if my health permits

I played golf alone last night, just to see how many strokes I took to get round. It was seventy for nine holes – not very good I fear. As I was playing the last hole, Bertie Frith and Raymond Taylor came along and 'acted the goat', trying to stop the ball and goading Winston (Bertie's dog) to run after it, etc. Raymond has asked to play with me tomorrow. There are four young lads altogether, Raymond, Bertie, Len and Harry who are all friends. We call them 'The Yams' and if they are not doing anything in the evenings they ring us up and ask if they can come up or else for us to go to the pictures sometimes. I am going tomorrow to see The Great Waltz. *I saw it in Lagos several months ago. All the pictures go to Lagos first and I have seen lots of them before. Have you seen* Goodbye Mr Chips? *If not, you should do – it's by far the best picture I have ever seen. Of course they are all pretty ancient by the time they get out here.*

It is dreadfully hot here at present – we have to have the fan on all the time. Every house has an electric fan fixed in the ceiling in most rooms, if not a punkha.

I am liking Calabar much better now, though I will always prefer Lagos.

I had a letter from Patricia in Accra the other day, saying she had been invalided home and is not being allowed out again. She is heartbroken as she loves it here. She has had Malaria twice and Dysentry twice this tour and she came out after me this time. Do you remember I spent the last night in London with her? She hopes to be able to go to East Africa or somewhere but that will be decided when she gets home.

We get awful looking diseases amongst the Africans here. They always take anaesthetics very well and seldom vomit – though to look at their food would make you sick – chiefly rice and messy looking meat, and they usually eat it with their fingers out of an enamel basin. They have two meals a day at eleven in the morning and five in the afternoon, or thereabouts. They can be terribly annoying – my boys try me to the utmost sometimes. I sent my small boy to the Post Office and the Bank and he was away for three and a half hours. I expect he had been playing with his friends. Then last week I told my steward boy and the small boy that I wanted the skirting board of my sitting room washed. The small boy should have done it really, and the steward boy should have seen that it was done. I came back from the hospital at noon to find only half of it was done. The small boy had done half and refused to do any more. I have always said that the small boy must do the floor and the steward boy the dusting and polishing of the furniture, but as the skirting is neither, they went bolshy about it!

15.2.42

I don't think there is anything else to answer. The rainy season seems to be starting here – we are getting terrific thunderstorms. Last night was a really big one and there are lots of branches of trees down this morning. I am on duty at mid-day today until nine this evening so will not be able to go to church. I haven't been up very long – got up at half past nine and had breakfast. I was latish last night. I went to see The Great Waltz *with five others. After the pictures at half past eleven we all went back to a neighbouring house for a cup of tea (a Calabar habit these days) and got home half past midnight. I don't have many late nights in Calabar, very seldom have dances here, except the ones 'The Yams' and ourselves make.*

Hope you are both well – love to all,

Lots of love,
Marjorie

Alan still appeared unexpectedly, staying with different sets of mutual friends and meeting Marjorie in her off-duty time.

When she had been at Calabar for nine months, she was due for three weeks local leave.

She was beginning to have second thoughts about marrying Alan. She certainly loved him, yet her family ties and their outlook still held her. She therefore pleaded with Alan to please leave her alone so that she could spend her leave in peace and make up her own mind about their situation. Freda was also due for local leave, so they decided to take it together.

Freda had heard of a leper colony at Itu which welcomed visitors, so deciding to investigate, they planned to visit it.

Chapter Fourteen

They left Calabar at eight o'clock in the morning on the only launch of the week, travelling up the Cross River, passing all the places that Mary Slessor, the famous missionary used to visit years before.

Monkeys swung across the branches above them, while logs of crocodiles lurked in the waters beneath.

(The following is taken from my mother's journal, with her permission).

Dr and Mrs MacDonald of the Scottish Mission met them off the launch. They were medical missionaries and had founded the leper colony in 1928 with only one patient who was a leper and had suddenly appeared asked for help. Dr MacDonald had told him to come back in three month's time when he may be able to help by providing a cure.

The Colony was situated on an island centred in the Cross River in the heart of tropical forest. It stretched for three square miles and was entirely self-supporting. Originally a passage had to be cleared through with scythes and very primitive equipment.

By 1931 there were one thousand and one hundred patients and when Marjorie and Freda arrived in 1941 this number had increased to three thousand. They reared their own goats, sheep, pigs, cows and chicken, along with vegetables and fruit such as yams, guava, plantains, paw-paw, cassava, rice, oranges, lemons and limes. Castor oil trees and palm nuts were also grown. The palm oil and castor oil were both extracted and then refined from their own workshops.

The Colony was divided into small villages which consisted of rows of streets, all named after the apostles. There were small red and white mud houses, with two lepers living in each. The houses were kept very clean and neat, all being inspected by Mrs MacDonald every week. All the lepers who were able to work did so in order to make a little pocket money. They were taught how to make furniture, how to mill rice, also to refine palm oil and castor oil. There were farmers, sanitary men and women, cooks, laundrymen, nurses and teachers. The children kept the Colony grounds clean whilst women looked after the church.

Dr and Mrs MacDonald's own house, also built by lepers, was quite unlike anything that Marjorie had seen in Nigeria. It reminded her of a cottage and cottage garden in England, having a roof thatched with palm leaves which was apt to leak during thunderstorms and tornadoes.

Mrs MacDonald had been a Nursing Sister before her marriage and she and her husband both worked unaided for several years. Now at least they had two British helpers, namely Mr Wills from Devonshire and Mr Faulkes from Lincolnshire.

The church on the island had also been constructed by the lepers out of red mud and stone (including the seats, pulpit and choir stalls). There was a church band, in which almost twenty people played, all trained by Dr MacDonald. To begin with, out of five hundred and sixty-three lepers there were only ten with a Bible. By the time Marjorie and Freda visited many had been converted to Christianity and a great work was being done as many of the lepers went out to their own towns once they were cured. They had become different people in body, mind and spirit, so they all had great testimonies to share.

Every Sunday there was a congregation of over two thousand. Many of the lepers did not want to leave the Colony when the time came for them to go, although of course they were compensated for this in the pleasure of seeing their families again and living useful lives. For the duration of the church meeting, Freda and Marjorie were given seats on the platform by the pulpit. The lepers sat in sections according to the severity of their disease. There were two hymns and a prayer led by one of the lepers given in the Ibo language and translated into Efik language. The sermon, given by Mr Wills was also translated into both languages. Marjorie found the whole ceremony very moving.

There was a hospital with eighty-four beds, staffed by thirty-eight female and ten male nurses, all of whom were lepers themselves. They would work three weeks on duty and one week off. For this work they were paid one shilling (five pence in today's money) a week. Those admitted to the hospital were the real medical cases with large leprous ulcers, for instance. The surgical cases would be operated on free of charge. However, for minor surgery, such as a hernia, a small fee would be charged for the operation.

The nurses all slept in a dormitory, all together near the hospital, but they had their food in the women's quarters of the town, as is the African custom.

Mrs MacDonald would inspect all the dressings, of which there were hundreds, twice weekly. Hypersonic saline was injected into the leprous ulcer and bone if it was affected, and this was found to be very beneficial and effective. Injections of Hydnocarpus oil, extracted from the fruit of the trees grown in the Colony were given twice weekly in some cases, but only the female species of the tree bore the fruit from which the oil could be obtained, and there were three hundred of these in the Colony.

The lepers had a back rubbing parade on Wednesday mornings, when they rubbed the oil into each other's back – all in one long row. About a hundred of the very infectious cases were attended to in their own homes – within the Colony of course. All the two thousand or so helpers who were on injections had their temperatures taken morning and evening, and there were eighty-eight temperature clerks to deal with this.

The leper children went to school and were taught in the mornings starting at half past seven. They were taught up to Standard VI free of charge. School was compulsory for them.

Mrs MacDonald was sorry for the girls outside the Colony, so had them in her house to do a little housework and a little domestic science in between school hours. In return she paid for their books and taught them to read and do arithmetic. There were twenty-four of these girls aged from six to sixteen years. Eight would be on duty in the morning, eight in the afternoon and eight in the evening. Marjorie was very touched when there was a knock on her bedroom door at seven o'clock one morning and in walked two little girls with a tray of tea for her. They looked so sweet in their little blue dresses and white aprons.

The adult patients who could not read had to attend school in the evenings from half past four until six o'clock. They were taught to read the Bible in Efik and Ibo languages. Of the adult patients, only one or two in every hundred would have had any schooling.

Every patient paid three pounds on admission to the Colony, which covered food, education and treatment for three or more years that he or she would be there. Each patient was kept there for at least three years, even if they had been symptom free for some time.

Mr Faulkes who was a keen missionary, and who also organised the mid-weekly prayer meeting ran the office.

In the centre of the Colony was a market where patients could buy food and all kinds of things that had been grown or reared on the premises.

In the hospital there were twenty-four cooks; twelve working alternate weeks. They not only cooked for all the hospitalised patients, but for all those unable to work or cook for themselves and the children. Everyone was given the kind of food he or she asked for as far as possible. Those who could, formed a queue and collected their own.

There was a library and reading room were patients went to read. It was well stocked with books and magazines for those who could read English. Picture books were the main attraction.

The cinema had been donated by Nessbrook Bible Class together with miscellaneous films bought second-hand by a Glasgow shop. Mr Wills and Mr Faulkes ran this project. It was an open-air cinema with seats made out of stones and clay, sloping from the back to the front. It would be pandemonium at the opening show as people were all so excited! There were shows about once a fortnight and these were popular and well attended, especially by the children who talked about it for days afterwards. The European staff would have headaches for days afterwards! When Marjorie was there, a simple silent machine was in use and all the discarded films from home were shown, such as *Popeye*, *Mickey Mouse*, all of which fascinated the children.

There was even a Court with its own Judge and Jury to settle any palavers and disputes. The Colony's own police force looked after the island and would also ring bells at intervals so that everyone knew the time for meals, treatment etc, as there were very few clocks about.

Marjorie heard that once, whilst on leave in South Africa, Dr and Mrs MacDonald were offered a very good practice down there which they seriously considered taking up. However, they received very pathetic letters from many of the lepers begging them to come back. The Colony even held its own special prayer meetings to pray for their return. When they did eventually come back to Itu they were given an unforgettable welcome: the band played; flags were flying and everyone turned out to shout and cheer!

The Colony was to have a remarkable effect on Marjorie for the rest of her life. Never had she seen so many people, all dependant on each other and working together in such harmony. Despite their illness, they were all obviously very happy. She decided she herself could learn a thing or two from their example and maybe a lot of other people could too, as its atmosphere was so full of love and caring.

NB *(Marjorie was thrilled to see Dr and Mrs MacDonald on television in the 1960s when Eamonn Andrews sprang a surprise on them of* This Is Your Life)

At the end of their three weeks stay, Marjorie realised

that she had not given a serious thought about what she and Alan ought to do. She had been so engrossed in the lepers and their lives that the world beyond went on unnoticed. Being a self-sufficient island had cut her off from her problems as well. So it was that she returned to Calabar, still unable to offer Alan any proper decision to his proposal of marriage.

When the time eventually became due to take her three months' leave home, Marjorie was advised that it would be safer to holiday in South Africa, as ships were not being torpedoed so much in the southern part of the Atlantic. That seemed likely to be a safer journey. She duly booked her passage in June 1942.

The day before she was due to leave, a cable arrived from Bettie and Bill announcing that Bettie had given birth to a baby girl who was to be called Heather. Knowing that she was about to set sail on *SS Awgum* for Lagos prior to heading south, Marjorie decided to send her congratulatory cable from there to surprise them. The ship was not due to stay long in Lagos, just long enough for more passengers to board and for Marjorie and Alan to meet furtively on the dockside. She was able to give him the message she wanted to send to Bettie and Bill, her heart thumping as she realised that this might probably be the nearest her family would get to know Alan, for the time being, at least.

After the passengers had been on board waiting to sail for some three hours it was discovered that there was something wrong with the ship's engines and they would not work. Everyone was allowed ashore, but had to return to the ship to sleep. Alan and Marjorie were thrilled to have this unexpected bonus of time together.

They had four days of this before Marjorie awoke to find they were moving. She rushed up on deck to wave 'Goodbye' to Lagos and also Alan, should he be anywhere in sight.

Then to everyone's dismay, the engines stopped again

when they were only one hundred yards offshore. A launch chugged out to them, coming alongside at around midday, and the ship's Captain said that anyone, who wanted to, could go ashore on the launch and return on it at half past eight next morning. Marjorie had been staying with friends, Gilbert and Hilary Milbourne when she wasn't seeing Alan, so she took the opportunity of staying overnight with them again. Next morning she was ready to return to the *Awgum* when a phone call was received by Gilbert, saying that its engines were still not working, so Marjorie would have to stay ashore until she was contacted again. There she was, stuck with only one change of clothing to hand as everything else was on board ship. At least she had some good friends to stay with, which was more than some passengers, who were running up expensive hotel bills. Alan had heard the news and called round at the Milbournes that evening. It was unfortunate he wasn't able to see her next day as he was off to visit a hospital in another part of Nigeria.

As the days went by, Marjorie began to wonder if she would ever reach South Africa. All this waiting about seemed such a waste of time when there was a new country down there just waiting to be explored! Eventually she was informed that a passage had been booked for her on another ship, the SS *Bonny*. When it docked, she went to the quayside and supervised her luggage being transferred from one ship to the other. By this time the *Awgum* had been towed ashore again for what appeared to be extensive repairs. At last, she left Nigeria, over a week late, and extremely grateful to the Milbournes for their cheerful hospitality.

Medical Department
Lagos
22.6.1942

My dear Bettie and Bill

I received your cable on Thursday saying that Heather had arrived, and that was the day I was to be on board ship, so I decided to send you a cable from here just to surprise you, adding that I was just leaving for South Africa. However, I am still here because the ship's engines wouldn't work, so we are still stuck! Fortunately the Captain has allowed us ashore each day as long as we go back on board ship to sleep. Yesterday morning I woke up and we were moving, but we only got about one hundred yards when the engines stopped again. We have been stuck here ever since. To start with, the Captain said we could go ashore in a launch, which I did, to return next morning, but the ship is still not repaired, so here I am with only one change of clothes to my name! If and when the engines ever work, she is doing a trial run, then coming back to Lagos again, so the Milbournes are kindly hosting me. I always seem to be unfortunate when I'm travelling, don't I? In cars the engine often gives out or there is a puncture, or the petrol runs out or something! The people on board who know no one in Lagos are getting desperate – having all this delay.

I can't remember what I said to you in the letter I started writing on board ship, but I will send this now instead.

I'm so glad that you and Heather are both well – quite a nice normal weight, too. I suppose you will have to stay in hospital for a fortnight or so? I hope you didn't have too bad a time. I can't imagine you with a baby somehow. People always seem to be getting engaged, married or having babies or something while I'm away, so that I miss all the fun – except your wedding, of course. Grace got married while I was away, then she had Marion and then Morgan, and now you've got Heather, and Ronald got engaged to Felicia. They will no doubt be married before I get home again.

I started knitting a matinee coat on board and apparently have unknowingly broken the law of the land in doing so, as one is not allowed to take knitting-wool on board! I didn't know that. Another passenger wanted to make a jumper but the Customs would not allow her to bring the wool on board so I've given her two ounces of mine and she is knitting some baby bootees. Perhaps she will give them to me for you afterwards. It's terribly boring not having anything like knitting or sewing to do on board, so I'm lucky. One can play Draughts, or Ludo, or Patience, or Bridge, or read, or play the piano, or radiogram, and eat and sleep and that's all!

I expect your hands are full now looking after Heather – babies take up a lot of one's time don't they, what with bathing, feeding them and yourself, washing nappies etc.

Has Bill been called up yet? And I wonder if Jessie has started anything yet? It was a good thing I came ashore on Saturday as there was a letter from Mother and Father and another from Grace. I fancy I shall have done nearly two years by the time I get to South Africa and I feel just as fit as when I came out. I was at the same dining table as Dr Hedley (the ship's doctor). He was on the Adde when I came out on her, and he was on her when I was torpedoed and is now on this ship. He asked the dining room steward to put me at his table. There are two women on board who are going to have babies and going to South Africa to have them. If we don't get away soon, I shall have to assist with things on board – I hope not!

Let me know if there is anything you especially want and I will try to send it from South Africa. I hear things are getting rather scarce for you now in England. It's very expensive down in South Africa I believe, so will probably be bankrupt when I return – the hotels are very expensive. At this time of year it's very cold I believe, so I may cable you asking you to send my winter clothes to me. Apparently it starts to warm up down there in September as that is their spring. As clothes and everything down there is likely to be so expensive it would be stupid to buy a lot of winter things which I would not wear again for ages.

There seems no more news. Hope you are all well. I

hear there have been lots of air raids on the south coast – hope you are all right.

Lots of love to you, Bettie and Bill.
Marjorie

Marjorie was thrilled by the Kei Apple Hotel in which she stayed, which was in Cape Town itself at the foot of the huge Table Mountain. Every morning she awoke to the view of the mountain covered with a white cloth of cloud. The hotel was in a residential part of the city and from its upper floors, cornflower blue skies could be seen to stretch out over the sea where brightly coloured fishing boats bobbed about on the water, disturbed only by the occasional large ship bringing produce as well as passengers like herself.

Walking the streets she saw there was a mixture of Dutch architecture, noisy African markets and cobbled streets. This concoction of European and African gave the city a unique exuberance.

Most evenings the sun flung a vibrant palette of reds and golds across Table Mountain. Marjorie decided that South Africa was showing her the most magnificent sunsets.

A golf course was near the hotel. Marjorie enjoyed exploring her new surroundings, discovering some pretty walks nearby.

She was surprised to meet a lot of people she knew. So many Europeans were coming to South Africa for so-called home leave. At least she had no cause to be lonely. Overall she was thrilled by the place, yet each morning she knew that far and away the best sight was that of Table Mountain as it stood forming a backdrop to Cape Town. The sea was so blue, yet the space impressed her as she saw mile after mile of beaches stretching so far as the eye could see.

Often she would watch the sun set over the sea. It was

dramatic as the sky deepened to purple and a huge furnace blazed as it sank beyond the horizon amidst ribbons and reflections of hot reds through to a range of pinks. In Lagos it was either day or night as the sun slid quickly from view.

She wrote to Alan, describing all the scenery to him, and they kept in regular contact for the whole of her long stay there.

Cape Town was a thriving metropolis. It seemed to have so many new and exciting things in the shops. Marjorie spent far more than she meant to, as so many things were not only expensive, but beautiful too. Her spending spree started when she fell in love with an attractive pale green tea set displayed in the window of a china shop. It caught her eye as it must have been almost exactly the colour of her first ball gown that she had made for herself all those years ago. The pretty green was offset by a white interior to the cups. As she stood there reminiscing, she caught sight of two dainty pink flowers blooming just under the rim inside one of the cups and she had to go inside for a further inspection. The china looked delicate. She might buy it so that she could always remember Cape Town. The set was a large one with nine unusual and beautifully shaped tea plates, tea cups and saucers, with a large cake plate to match. She then spotted a milk jug, sugar bowl and teapot all in the same design. Taking a deep breath she made her decision.

As they were being wrapped, the salesman remarked, "Very pretty, it's a shame to leave the coffee set behind."

Marjorie asked to see it, and on being shown the tiny cups, saucers with the tall, serviceable, but attractive coffee-pot, agreed to buy that as well. It was all delivered to her hotel the following day and she looked forward to using it when she entertained guests in the future.

[Author's note; despite its fragile looks, the set was to actually outlive its owner!]

Another time she visited an African market and

wandered happily among the richly patterned fabrics, beaded jewellery and wooden carvings.

Each morning, the brick red sun rose in a clear sky. It was winter time, yet by ten o'clock the heat of the sun had warmed the earth, releasing the scent of damp grass as Marjorie walked around the golf course. As she tramped round it one day, thinking of nothing in particular, a familiar figure came towards her. Shading her eyes she saw that it was Olive Benson. Marjorie had trained with her at Middlesex. Olive introduced her husband, Dr Stephen Waincote, and they fell into step together. It was wonderful to be able to recall old times. The Wainscotes explained that they intended to move on sixty miles down the coast in a couple of days' time.

"Oh, what a shame! I'll miss you," said Marjorie. Especially as we've only just met after all this time."

The following day when they met, Olive was beaming. "How would you like to join us when we go to Hermanas?"

"Oh no, I couldn't do that. After all you will have booked up ages ago."

Stephen interrupted. "Not at all. I phoned ahead and there'll be plenty of room as we booked a large apartment."

"Well, that sounds wonderful. It's very kind of you to include me. I'd love to come as I'm keen to see as much of this country as I can."

The next day they set off. Dr Wainscote drove their large car along the route towards Hermanas.

Marjorie sat, transfixed as they drove through the passing scenery. They arrived at what turned out to be a luxury hotel. It was here that she shared their luxury hotel suite for a whole week in absolute bliss.

Out of town everywhere seemed so lush and green. Everywhere was extravagant with colour and perfume. She occasionally sat in the hotel garden, breathing in the scent of freshly cut grass bordered by borders of brightly coloured flowers including lavender and roses. Amongst them, gaudy little birds busied themselves as they darted about. It was such a contrast to hot dry and dusty West Africa.

Olive ensured Marjorie tried typical South African food, such as Bobotie and Koeksisters.

"I like the Bobotie. It's spiced with curry but isn't too hot. As for the Koeksisters, well they are rather like sweet sticky doughnuts, and I've probably piled on pounds!"

She would sit on the balcony in the evenings, drinking in the beauty of it all. The nights had a special magical wonder of their own, as frogs croaked to one another, crickets chirped shrilly and urgently while the huge moon hung low over the black hills.

On her last day there, the weather changed overnight and the morning brought low clouds and mist. By half past nine it was drizzling miserably. The Wainscotes had business to attend to in Cape Town, so they all returned by car together. Despite the weather, Marjorie was cheered to see some baboons playing in the bush just beyond the roadside.

They said their farewells outside Marjorie's hotel. She had been in South Africa a month already and still had two months to go. During that time she was to meet several friends from Accra and Lagos also taking their leave in Cape Town, so she was never short of companionship.

She continued to write long newsy letters to Alan. There was so much to tell him. His letters to her were eagerly received.

Chapter Fifteen

When Marjorie returned from South Africa in October, she was posted to Warri Hospital. She was in sole charge there over the European and African nurses. It consisted of a small European hospital and a small African hospital with her own living quarters, a bungalow similar to before, situated between the two.

Dr Richard Milne was the presiding doctor there. He was a tubby, jovial man with a receding hairline and a ready smile lurking beneath his moustache. He and his wife Peggy lived in the bungalow situated nearest to Warri hospital itself. Both were cheerful outgoing people and Richard was a caring conscientious fellow, well suited to the medical profession. His wife Peggy was also plump, but seemed able to cope with any emergencies welcoming many people to their door, often appearing to cater for dinner parties at a minute's notice. They took their work seriously, and were just as concerned for the welfare of the staff as for the patients. Any problem, however large or small, once shared with them, became important to them until it was resolved. Thus it was, life at Warri was more about being part of a family than a work situation, and a homely welcome to everyone who visited their quarters.

There was also an isolation hospital, which resembled a bungalow, and Marjorie frequently used this to host houseguests. It was a short drive to the hospital buildings, and as all the others had been, this too was built on brick pillars.

Her first day back was a Saturday, the day when most Europeans gathered in the Club. There they would play Whist, American Charades and enjoy a convivial party atmosphere.

Starved of all these amenities for so long, Marjorie headed for the club as soon as she could. She was surprised to discover that the atmosphere was not what she expected, as people were concerned for just one man.

* * *

John Anderson enjoyed his work as a Shipping Agent for *Elder Dempster Shipping Lines*. It was extremely varied and interesting as he had a lot of dealings with different people. The Africans sometimes annoyed him when they did not carry out the tasks they were supposed to and acted irresponsibly, but others more than made up for this in their loyalty to him. Besides, it all made for a good story to tell on social gatherings in the club and in letters home to his wife and family. His son Warren was about to come of age and had recently enlisted in the army, whilst daughter Daphne was at present studying for her school leaving matriculation exams. He wished they could join him out here, but families were forbidden to travel abroad during wartime. John's wife, Elsie had never enjoyed travel, anyway, so had been content to stay at home with the children. It was a life they both enjoyed now they had got used to it. John and Elsie were too much of their own people to want to bow to one another's wishes for long. They each had their own friends and social circles, yet they were happy during the short concentrated times that they had together.

Today was a busy day. He had to oversee a ship being unloaded and then it had to be re-loaded with groundnut oil, ready for a quick turn round. Normally he liked to supervise this personally to ensure efficiency, but his desk held a mound of paperwork, and he had a hospital visit to make. One of the dock labourers had lost his footing from a crane the previous day and had been admitted to hospital with a fractured femur and a cracked rib. He was fortunate to have got off so lightly. Richard Milne had been very good and set the leg promptly. Good chap Richard. He and Peggy always made him welcome; but then they were courteous and cordial to everyone.

John ensured that work had started on the unloading of the ship and left orders with the foreman about starting to re-load should he not get back in time. He checked that nothing urgent had appeared on his desk since he last looked, then drove off to the hospital.

The employee was grateful for all that had been done for him, but he was anxious about his family. John promised to visit them straightaway. Sighing, he climbed into his car; his schedule put back yet again.

The man's wife was almost hysterical when she realised where her husband was. She was terrified of the white man's hospital and reacted as if John had told her that her husband was in the mortuary. He couldn't leave her in that state, so he transported her to the hospital himself to try and reassure her of the man's comparative wellbeing. His patience was wearing thin and by now it was lunchtime.

He called at his bungalow for a drink and a bite to eat. "Silly woman," he seethed, muttering to himself as he turned into the driveway. "Anybody would think her husband had *died*! What a job I landed myself with there!"

He was just leaving again for the docks when his steward-boy came in with a cablegram. John opened it, and it was almost a minute before he could absorb its contents.

ELSIE DIED SUDDENLY STOP WRITING SOON STOP LOVE DAPHNE

John had no way of knowing whether his wife had died because of an air raid and consequential bomb damage, which had certainly been heavy round the Liverpool area, but not, as far as he knew, in the area where they lived outside the city. Her death could have been from natural causes. If it was the former, was the house all right? Was Daphne all right? Had she been injured? If it was the latter, what disease had Elsie been suffering from? He had only been in Liverpool with her less than three months ago, and she had seemed well enough then.

Stunned, he sat down. Surely this wasn't true. This couldn't be happening to him. The cable must have been meant for someone else. He read it again. There it was, correctly addressed to him, John Anderson, mentioning Elsie and Daphne.

He felt like an onlooker in his own situation and returned to the office as if by automation. He supervised the start of the re-loading of the ship before going to his office to sort out some paperwork.

He was desperate to put his personal situation out of his mind. It was surreal, living out here, being in another world thousands of miles away from the everyday humdrum world of Formby, England, where their world had just been turned upside-down.

Looking out from his office window he could just see how the work was progressing on the dockside. John absorbed himself in work for a further two hours before deciding he'd had enough. It was Saturday, the night for frivolity. It was only when he reached the Club that the reality of his recent news suddenly hit him and he was shattered by it.

Richard Milne had been the first one on the scene. He and Peggy were both stalwarts; closely followed by that new nursing sister at the hospital. They were both so kind, but nobody could replace Elsie. He tried to pretend that nothing had happened, nothing had changed, nothing was different, but within himself he had to come to terms that nothing would ever be the same again.

Medical Department
Warri
Nigeria
17.11.1042

Dear Bettie and Bill

I am expecting letters from people in England any day now as I hear that several have been forwarded from South Africa and Lagos recently. I wish we had some of your cold weather – it is just blazing hot here, and I'm perspiring from every pore, even just sitting here writing!

I am playing golf today later on. It seems very strange living entirely on my own; I thought I should be a bit nervous but I am not at all. The Doctor here goes to Ugheli for two days twice a month, then I feel a teeny bit nervous when I realise that there is no other white person very near. In lots of ways it is very nice being on my own as I can do exactly what I like when I like. I have a cat and am having some Rhode Island chickens next month. Alan McKenzie is sending them round from Lagos for me, so I am getting the houses and runs made for them now. It's a job to get the wire-netting though.

My wireless is going very well, and my sitting room is looking very nice as I have made yellow curtains with dark brown tie-ups; also the green and brown and cream cushions which I had in Calabar go very well. I have a yellowy standard lamp too. Your wedding photo adorns my desk. Everyone who comes has a look at it and asks who the handsome couple are!!

I have two steward boys called Jeremiah and another called Motor (some of them really do have queer names! I remember we had one in Lagos called War Bonus, another in Calabar called Good Luck, and my first one in Accra was called Bicycle).

I have just come from playing golf with Mr Anderson. He is the agent for Elder Dempster's here. He had a cable the day before yesterday saying that his wife in England had suddenly died. He has no details, so does not know yet whether she was killed in an air raid or died a natural death.

Dr Menzies from Enugu is arriving tomorrow and staying until Saturday. He is doing a round of inspecting, so I have been rounding up the labourers getting the grass cut and the hedges trimmed as the 'big doctor man' as they call him is coming. I am making up a bed in the Isolation Hospital here for him to sleep in as the doctor here has no spare room in his house.

On the 2nd December (my birthday!) the Governor of

Nigeria is coming to do a round. How I hate all these dignitaries coming round! He is only staying in Warri for two days fortunately.

I think I shall like Warri. The people here are a friendly lot. Everyone here is at present busy making things for the 'Delta Do' which is a sort of fun fair to be held on 27th February in aid of 'The Win the War Fund'. We are always doing something here for 'Win the War'. The Warri people said they have heard that I am good at sewing, so have asked me to do something in that line. I am also making some lemon curd and chutney and pineapple jam. I've started to make some candied peel with orange, lemon and grapefruit peel, but I don't know how it will turn out as I've never made it before. I have one hundred citrus trees in the garden here, but they are a bit disappointing, as they are not bearing as much fruit as they should. They were planted six years ago in 1936 so perhaps they are not ready to fruit yet.

I got a letter from Ruth Saunders in Palestine the other day. She asked me to get a transfer and go there, as it is such a lovely place. She also said that there were a lot of Middlesex trained doctors and nurses there now, all doing war work, I suppose. She mentioned several people I knew, plus Beatrice Talbot together with her sister. I gather Ruth sees her once a month when she has her day off. Three Middlesex doctors are there, all of whom I know quite well.

We have some queer cases in hospital here. One woman is in a dreadful state after being tied to a tree by her husband for seven days without any food. The Africans here seem a very tough lot. They are always fighting and biting each other; we had one man up the other day who had had his lower lip bitten right off by another man. Yet another man came in who had had his hand bitten very badly so that his finger dropped right off! The patient wants to keep it for remembrance, he says. I wonder whether he wants it for evidence to bring a case against the other man.

Well, I am going to wash my hair and go to bed now as it is nine o'clock. I will finish this tomorrow and hope by them I have a letter from you to answer.

<u>*4.12.1942*</u>

I am so sorry I did not finish this before, but I have been very busy indeed; so much so that I have had to send to Burutu for Mrs Bailey to help me out. (She has helped me out before when she lived in Lagos). She is very nice, very vivacious and it's nice to have her for company. We are not quite so busy now the patient who we thought had typhoid fever is getting better, but still needs quite a lot of nursing.

Last night we both went to the Residency to the Governor's party. It only lasted an hour, but while we were there, a note was sent round to say that a case we had operated on about a fortnight ago had suddenly collapsed, but she died before we reached her.

Have just this minute received a letter from Ronald and Felicia – very nice letters too. Ronald had written his on the 15th October and Felicia on the 17th October. I will answer them as soon as I can.

I will finish now. I hope you have a very happy Christmas and New Year –

With lots of love to you both and Heather
Marjorie

John Anderson and Richard Milne played golf together. Peggy and Marjorie joined them sometimes.

Marjorie was with John soon after Daphne's letter arrived telling her father about Elsie's sudden heart attack. She had written bravely, but it must have been heart rending to write after such a dreadful shock, especially as she was only sixteen. Daphne had reassured John that Elsie's own mother had moved in to take care of her, and that she often spent weekends with her close friend from school, Ann Ambrose. His head was in such a whirl reading all this information, so he was glad of Marjorie's company when she arrived and they played golf together.

They arranged to play golf again. When she joined him at the golf club he said, "Do you mind if we don't play today?"

"Of course not. I'll go and leave you to your own devices."

"No, please stay. Come and sit down. Have a drink. I just need to talk, really." His speech was delivered jerkily.

Marjorie sat in a nearby chair.

"You see, it's this letter I've had a letter from my daughter."

Marjorie could see John's eyes were filling with tears.

"So you know the circumstances …"

"Yes, Elsie had a heart attack."

"Oh I am sorry! Still, at least Daphne is well and your home is all right."

"Yes, but she is so young to witness such tragedy, and on her own too, with her own mother." He shook his head. "I still can't take it all in."

"Well no, it's been a terrible shock for you."

He nodded.

"Was your daughter with her at the time then?"

"Yes, she was upstairs studying and heard this crash from downstairs. She found her mother on the floor and called the doctor, but she had died before she could be taken to hospital."

Marjorie shook her head. "How tragic."

"I think Daphne blames herself for not being quick enough, for not being immediately on hand."

"Probably most people would feel like that, but I'm sure there was nothing anyone could have done for her."

"Really?"

"Yes, really. You must assure her of that when you write."

John's story soon unfolded for Marjorie and she felt

deeply sorry for him in his distress. Richard and Peggy Milne often entertained him to dinner, and Richard would take him out for a game of golf when he could. Dr Milne confirmed John's circumstances to Marjorie suggesting that if she could, it might help him to have a round of golf occasionally; to try and help ease his grief.

A weekly game of golf soon became twice weekly, and eventually they played golf together often. John frequently used Marjorie as a sounding board and she tried to reassure him when she could.

Alongside all of this, Alan kept in regular contact. He wrote to Marjorie several times a week. He knew Dr and Mrs Milne well, so often he would come and stay with them, thus seeing a lot of Marjorie once again. Her life blossomed again as the hospital demanded a lot of her attention with only herself at the helm, and her social calendar was generally pretty full. She was soon on Christian name terms with Dr and Mrs Milne and they became Richard and Peggy and generously opened their home to her.

Marjorie was also aware that they knew about, and were sympathetic about the situation between her and Alan. It was good to be able to have their relationship out in the open, instead of constantly worrying about whether their friendship was approved of, as in Lagos, when Marjorie had often caught herself looking over her own shoulder in case she was being spied on.

The day of the Governor's Parade dawned. It was exceedingly hot. The brightness of bunting and flags seemed to add to the warmth and glare of the sun. The parade marched by the Governor's raised dais situated in the midst of about fifty other dignitaries under a temporary roof of thatched palm leaves. He looked so cool dressed all in white against the cubs, scouts, brownies and guides marching past in their dark uniforms, their chocolate brown bodies perspiring in the dusty heat. When the dancing started with its blaze of colours and urgent rhythms, the humidity became almost too much to bear;

this frenzied life-sized kaleidoscope of hues and tempos.

Music, especially drumming, was an important art form to the Nigerians. Singing and dancing was part of their culture. Therefore any excuse for a party or a celebration would mean that vibrant thrumming beat accompanied by whirling colourful twists of fabric as the bodies within twirled and stamped out the beat, apparently never tiring, and seemingly entertaining themselves as well as their European counterparts on the sidelines.

There was a natural break in the proceedings and Marjorie saw John wave and make his way towards her. They sat together in a comfortable silence for a while, Marjorie occasionally wondering what John was thinking. Ever since that first round of golf together, she would ponder on whether she was treading on dangerous ground. Was there anything there? Could there be something so embryonic, so fragile, that to try to name it, or even think of it, would be to destroy it and disperse it like delicate mist?

She didn't believe she felt anything more for him than sympathy.

He probably just needed a companion for reassurance in his grief. That was all she intended to be to him. She would not get involved. She was committed to Alan, yet at the same time, surely there was no harm in playing a few rounds of golf with John to cheer him out of the depression following his wife's death?

Marjorie was relieved when the vibrant performance recommenced and she could concentrate on that once more. The heat seemed to reverberate from the dancers to the audience. Anything was better that to try and sort out her feelings at present.

One day, Marjorie had not been on duty long when an African girl rushed into the hospital, holding her throat, from which came a steady flow of blood. Marjorie felt her face instantly drain of her own just to look at her.

"My goodness, what's happened to you?" she asked in

as calm a voice as she could manage.

"My man, my boyfriend – he get very angry with me."

"You mean he deliberately did this to you?"

"Yes." She looked down to avoid Marjorie's concerned gaze.

Marjorie helped the girl to climb onto the examination couch. "But why on earth would he want to do such a thing?"

"He see me with another man, see, so he drew his knife across my throat, so." She demonstrated with a dramatic gesture of her finger.

Marjorie cleaned her up and examined the girl's injury more closely. The wound was very deep but fortunately the slash had just missed the main arteries. Dr Milne had just departed for his two-day trip to Ugheli, just up river, and only he could deal with this type of emergency. This was the kind of thing Marjorie dreaded when she was left on her own. However, she did remember being fascinated by a man being fed by a tube when she was first training at Middlesex. Now she would have to do her own version! She oiled some rubber tubing and eased it into the gaping hole that was the girl's oesophagus, and fed the girl in the hospital on fluids until Dr Milne returned, when he praised Marjorie for her work and duly operated on the girl and closed the gaping hole.

Medical Department
Warri
Nigeria
19.1.1943

My dearest Bettie,

Very many thanks for your letters, one dated 15.8.42 and the other 13.12.42 which I received the other day, so that had not taken so long to get here. It seems a lot of letters have gone down with torpedoed ships though, as there are several ships that we have heard of and Sisters have been lost on them. Several people were also torpedoed on their way out here, but survived to tell the tale.

Your first letter is very stale now as it was sent to South Africa and then forwarded here! You had just received a birthday cable from me!

I suppose Heather takes up most of your time now that you have less time to write to me. She certainly seems to have got on very well, gaining all that weight. What a funny thing to remember that she smiled for the first time exactly a year after I was torpedoed! Tell her it is nothing to laugh about! I wonder if you have had her vaccinated yet. The younger the better, then she doesn't notice it so much. I hear that smallpox is very rife in Scotland just now.

I am making a smocked frock for Heather. Mrs Milne, the doctor's wife here, hopes to go home soon, and she said she will take it with her and post it to you from Aberdeen; but now there have been so many more sinkings, Dr Milne has put his foot down and says she is not to go. She hasn't been home for four years as they went to South Africa on their last home leave, and she is afraid her son of twelve years will have forgotten her as she hasn't seen him since he was eight. Anyhow, if she doesn't take it, I will get someone else who is going to England to post it. It is not allowed really, but perhaps they could smuggle it in before Heather gets too big for it! I do hope you have received the other parcels I sent from South Africa, especially the ones with the little dresses for Heather.

Yes, I received the cable you sent me for Christmas and New Year thank you very much.

What a pity that Bill was called up just before Ronald and Felicia's wedding. I expect you miss him a lot. You must be terribly busy too. Is Father able to help you at all while he is staying with you? I suppose he is still there? From your vivid description, I can imagine what a fluster it was trying to find a stud for Bill just before Ronald and Felicia's wedding. How funny! I haven't received the cake or card yet, but it may turn up some day.

Thank you for being the first to book me up to stay with you when I come home. I should love to. Heather's photo has not arrived yet either, but perhaps you have not sent it off yet?

<u>25.1.43</u>

I am so sorry this got put aside (as usual!) and since I have had another letter from you which was sent to South Africa and got forwarded, so it is even older than your last one! You had received a parcel with the chocolates etc. in but apparently the other ones hadn't arrived. However, Grace, Ronald and Mother had received some.

You had just had Heather christened. I am glad she behaved herself. It seems you were writing to me while I was on the high sea coming up from Cape Town. I also had a letter from Ronald yesterday which was forwarded from South Africa. He certainly seems to have written far more letters since he has been engaged and married. Has Felicia put him up to that? If so, good for her!

I had a very funny, but busy day yesterday. I was just having my breakfast when my steward-boy rushed along to say that I was wanted at the hospital immediately. I dashed over and there was a lorry outside with an African woman in it just about producing a baby; so I rushed her on to a stretcher and carried her into the hospital. I had no time to wash my hands or anything before the baby was born, though it was practically dead. I had to do artificial respiration for a long time, and get people rushing about getting hot and cold water to put it in etc. After about half an hour it started to breathe all right, thank goodness.

At the same time, we had another 'mother to be' on the go, so as soon as I had finished with this one I had to turn to the other one which was born all right after a time. I had almost forgotten that I hadn't had my breakfast, so eventually had it at about ten o'clock!

Just after that, a man came in with a huge spear stuck

in his loin. We thought it must have been through his kidney – it was in about eight inches and had been there for three days. He had come long distance. He was a burglar and was caught in the act and struck with a spear. We wondered whether it was a poisoned one, but he doesn't seem to have been poisoned. Dr Milne eventually got it out after a big struggle, as of course it had two barbs at the end and so flesh had to be torn to extract it. However, he seems to be getting on all right now, but is having seven years imprisonment when he gets out of hospital.

Then twelve people from Benin came to Warri yesterday to play Warri at cricket, so we were giving them a little party at the Club. Mrs Milne and I cycled down to watch the cricket. I came back to serve the patents' dinners, had just finished, when the nurse was sent over to say there was another maternity case in and did not seem at all normal; so I went over to the hospital and couldn't make it out either, so I sent for Dr Milne. We waited and waited for some time and nothing happened. Then Dr Milne said he thought it would be all right for us both to change into evening dress ready for the party and leave the African midwife with her for a time. I changed and went back to check, just in time to help with the birth of a twin baby weighing about two pounds. It was hardly breathing, so I had to do artificial respiration on her for ages. Then while waiting for the other one to arrive I went and changed back into uniform again. There was more waiting until we realised the other one would be quite a normal birth, so Dr Milne took himself and me on to the Club. The others had all started the dinners, but we soon caught up with them! When we got in at about two o'clock in the morning we called across to the hospital to see this case and the second baby was stillborn and the first one had died. The Africans hate having twins, and usually kill one of them. They always say the evil spirits have given it to them and always think it is a disgrace. Either one or both are often put out into the wood to die. I don't think this mother was very keen on me doing artificial respiration on the first child. It was a very wee thing anyway and would never have done very well.

Well, I don't think there is any more news. I hear on the wireless that there are several raids on the south coast these days, but I hope you are escaping them. The war news on the whole seems very good, doesn't it? I suppose Bill is still in England?

Hope you are well – my love to all and lots to yourself and Heather.

Marjorie

P.S. The enclosed letter is from my steward-boy whom I had in Calabar. I sent one from my small boy to Mother the other day. They really are amusing sometimes, but on the other hand, can be trying. It's like fan mail to the film stars!

c/o Miss F Kingston
European Hospital
Calabar
26.8.1942

Dear Sister Heath

This is my humble note to ask about condition over there. First of all I wish you safe arrival on your long journey to South Africa. I learnt ship disappointed you when you were at Lagos.

Please Maddam may you kindly tell me the time you will come back. I am still with Miss F Kingston waiting for your coming back. My living here with her is very troublesome.

I should have written to you, but my heart was not at rest. If you will come back to Calabar or to another station you let me know so that I may meet you up there.

Please Maddam kindly reply to me in time so that I may know what to do. I am waiting for you because you promised to take me back after your leave.

I am sending you my picture. Please remember me to your households.

I am
Your obedient servant
Tom

Marjorie was thoroughly enjoying her time at Warri. She felt fulfilled in her work. She was able to write long newsy letters home. At the same time she was also seeing Alan quite a lot too, so their ardour for one another was increasing. Both he and Richard Milne praised her for the way she handled quite difficult situations and she loved him even more for that.

Chapter Sixteen

Alan was still away, so when the invitation to the Club's dinner-dance arrived, Marjorie did not want to go. She couldn't imagine herself relaxing and enjoying herself without him at her side. However, she had no excuse for staying away as Dr Richard Milne had arranged the duty list to ensure that she could go to it.

"Don't mope," he consoled her. "Enjoy yourself while you can. That's what Alan would want you to do."

"I don't think I would really enjoy myself without him, especially knowing that he is so far away working in northern Nigeria. Don't alter the duties as it may be best to give someone else the chance to go."

"The duty list is already arranged and you are free that night." I'm not changing it all now. So come along and enjoy yourself."

The day arrived and Marjorie lingered at the hospital half-hoping that she would be needed to assist with some kind of emergency, but none arose. She went back to her bungalow, sat down and sighed.

How she wished Alan was here. He was still based at Lagos, which was relatively near to Warri, but he seemed to be away from it more than usual visiting other hospitals, some outside his usual circuit. It was certainly true that absence was making her heart grow fonder. She yearned to have him at her side, to feel his arms around her as they danced, and afterwards to enjoy those special moments alone when he took her home, to hear him whispering sweet nothings in her ear in that unique way that he had. Only that morning she had received another letter from him declaring his love for her and telling her that he was counting the months of the years until he could be free to marry her. He had told her again how he longed for the time when she could have his child.

Marjorie reflected on this. Having nursed so many babies and seen them come in all kinds of shapes and sizes, and having seen the look in the mother's eyes when she was first handed her child, she knew that she too wanted a child of her own. She wanted most of all to have Alan's child, but that could be dangerous. After all, she would be just turned forty by that time, and to have a first baby so late in life could be quite risky for both mother and child.

She spotted the time and shook herself out of her reverie. She would be late if she didn't hurry, and it might look as though she was rejecting Dr Milne's generous offer about the duty rota.

Quickly she bathed and pulled several dresses out of her wardrobe, wondering what to wear. She rejected two that she knew Alan admired her in and pulled on the third choice. Looking in the mirror, she brushed her hair and applied lipstick. Grabbing her little Dorothy-bag she headed for the door, thinking she had never got ready for any occasion so fast in her life. As she hurried towards the Club, she hoped that Alan wasn't there to surprise her with one of his unexpected visits, as she didn't feel she was looking her best.

She had not been at the Club long when John Anderson appeared. He was placed opposite her at the dinner table and frequently glanced in her direction, catching her eye with a little smile.

When the meal was over, the stewards pushed and pulled tables back against the walls to make room for dancing. Marjorie sipped her drink and danced with various people who asked her. She decided that perhaps this wasn't such a bad evening after all, but nevertheless would leave early and enjoy some much-needed rest.

Then John came over and asked her for the next dance. By this time the heat and general atmosphere combined to make Marjorie feel dreamy, yet strangely crucially alive at the same time. The shadows of the dancers flickered on the white walls. While watching the bold silhouettes, Marjorie almost believed herself to be in love with John – or was this Alan she was dancing with but in a different guise? *Oh lordy! Have I had too much to drink?*

At the end of the evening, John asked her to meet him at the Club sometime for a drink. She was not able to make immediate arrangements due to her duties at the hospital, but they parted on an agreement to see one another again sometime.

Even though they met casually occasionally, John was persistent and Marjorie eventually agreed to go out with him.

She agonised beforehand whether she was doing the right thing. Then she decided that this was only a casual meeting, mainly to console a grieving man whose wife had died. After all, he knew Alan, and he knew that Alan and Marjorie were involved in a long-standing relationship, so this couldn't lead to anything more. She wouldn't let it.

Marjorie was wondering what to wear after having taken a luxurious cool bath. She pulled out a pretty dress of dusky pink; no, that did not seem quite right. Fingering another, she decided it was too dressy for the occasion; another she cast aside because she kept it to wear especially for Alan, as he always admired her in it. Coming across another, she studied it for a few minutes before deciding it was too casual. She took several more items from her wardrobe and discarded them all for one reason or another. Then she became impatient with herself; she must not keep everything aside mainly, she had to admit, just for sentimental reasons because she last did this or that with Alan whilst wearing it. That was stupid. She grabbed the frock she had first pulled out and put it on.

John was already at the Club when Marjorie arrived. He was sitting at the bar, and ordered a drink for her before escorting her to a corner table.

He smiled. "We can be more cosy here."

Marjorie bit her lip as she returned his smile. She was not so sure now that she had done the right thing in accepting this invitation.

However, John was an interesting person to talk to, and they both relaxed in one another's company, especially by the second drink. Marjorie realised she was glad to be with John again. As he was quite a lot older than herself, she vaguely wondered if perhaps she was regarding him as a father figure, having not seen her own father for so long

John was looking at her. He took one of her hands, laced his fingers in hers and kissed the inside of her wrist.

"I love you," he said simply

Marjorie was so taken aback, she was unable to help herself. "I love you too," she answered softly, more to console him than anything else.

Reflecting on that moment Marjorie thought she was able to recognise the subtle and different kinds of love with their changeable variations; instead of one shining version that would supersede everything else. If only she could catch it and hold on to it.

Alan was a visitor with Richard and Peggy once again. Marjorie had not known that he was in Warri until she came off duty one afternoon, and stepping outside the hospital she saw him as he stood looking over the green hibiscus bushes studded with their large red trumpet blooms. Then he turned and came to Marjorie, standing close to her. She noticed the slight fading of his fair hair and the first few fine silver strands of it combed back over his ears. His eyes had a few more fine wrinkles at the corners and there were beginnings of darker hollows beneath.

She nodded as Alan put his hands on her shoulders, gazing deeply into her eyes, as if searching them for something. As her eyes met his, she knew that she still loved him, if anything she loved him more than when they had last seen one another. She hoped that she had learned enough not to let romance obscure her view any longer. This was some kind of achievement, albeit a very painful one. She must finally accept her loss and reassure Alan that his place must surely be with Gwen and the girls.

He took her arm, and steering her back to the bungalow, argued gently with her, persuading her that it was too late to mend his marriage.

"My darling girl," he stated. "Please, why don't you realise that my marriage was over before I even met you."

"If that's truly the case, why have you not divorced before now?"

"I'm sorry. That was laziness on my part, and also disbelief that I would ever meet someone as adorable and lovely as you."

"Tell me why you think Gwen's like she is."

Alan sat forward on the chair, his elbows on his knees with his head cupped in his hands.

"To be honest, I don't think we were ever right for one another. It was an arranged marriage by our parents. At the outset she seemed a really nice girl, and she's given me two lovely daughters. However she always seemed to get kind of het-up about such small things. Once the children were born she went into a kind of..." He hesitated. "...well, I don't know what it was really. I can only describe it as a kind of hysterical depression. However I tried to help, she just didn't want me involved in her life any more. When I first met you on board ship I had actually moved out of the house because living in the same place was so awful."

He hung his head as if in shame. "I'm sorry, I didn't want to burden you with all this muck from my past."

Marjorie rushed over to him and put her arms round him to console him. He was obviously upset remembering his past.

She tried to be encouraging.

"If you actually moved out of the marital home earlier than when you actually asked for a divorce, wouldn't that be part of the seven years desertion period she's making you wait?"

"I could try it, I suppose, it might make a bit of difference."

She kissed him to try and cheer him a little, especially as she realised she had been the guilty one in making him feel this way.

"I love you," she said, hugging him.

"All I want is you, my darling, he pleaded finally. He spoke volumes in those few words.

Marjorie's resistance broke again as she threw herself into his arms and wept. She did not know if her tears were for him, for herself, or for their situation. All she could think about was their great love for each other and the blind alleyway it seemed to be leading them down.

The steward-boys had long gone and they took the opportunity to physically demonstrate their love once again as they rode on a tide of emotions amidst a sea of desperation to be together.

"I couldn't live without you, so please don't even think of it again. You are not breaking up my marriage, you are helping to put back together the remains of my self-esteem."

Marjorie nodded, wriggling under his weight.

"I love you too much," she replied. "I just got to thinking too hard, and thought maybe my love for you ought to be true and sacrificial."

He laughed. "If that's the way you think, then stop thinking!"

He caressed her intimately and they fell asleep as darkness covered them like a blanket.

Marjorie was enjoying a quiet evening on her own when there was a knock at the door. She had sent the steward off earlier than usual so she went to answer it herself, and opened the door to John. He was wearing comfortable looking shorts and a shirt that was starting to fray round the collar. He was completely familiar and welcome to her as she stood and smiled up at him.

"Aren't you going to ask me in?"

"Oh, sorry. You just took me by surprise, that's all."

John was towering above Marjorie. He took her face between his large capable hands and looked deep into her eyes.

"I don't know how you feel about me, but I was just

nearby and I just had to come in and tell you that I love you."

Marjorie was surprised. Up until now they had just enjoyed a comfortable relationship. Now Alan was away again ... was this going to be the acid test? She must be careful that she wasn't tagged as a woman who wanted a man at any cost. Marjorie realised she wasn't being very hospitable and went towards the drinks cabinet.

"I'm sorry, I was deep in thought. It was very rude of me. What would you like to drink?"

"Whisky and soda please."

"Would you like to pour your own? You know how you like it." She indicated the bottles. "I'll join you with a gin and lime."

They sat down, enjoying the noises of the night outside. When Marjorie looked into John's face she felt another surge of fondness for him. She didn't think it was pity or sympathy. It consumed her and burned up any fears. She began to feel brave and sure. Their faces turned to one another and he leaned closer, then touched his mouth to hers.

When they next played golf together, John called for Marjorie in his car and drove towards the golf course. He put his hand over hers, covering it where it lay in her lap, but did not look at her. She did not attempt to hold his hand, but was overtaken by a sudden yearning to make him happy, to wipe away all the sadness of the past months. She glanced sideways as he studied the road ahead.

There were quite a few people whom they knew playing golf that day, and Marjorie felt comfortable with John in their midst. Later, when they were alone together, Marjorie sat with John's arms around her and with her head resting on his shoulder.

After that John and Marjorie began to go out together quite frequently. To be true to her conscience, she told him all about Alan. He was remarkably understanding. He knew Alan anyway, and even admired her choice, adding that it still did not prevent him from loving her.

Marjorie looked into John's face. The corners of his eyelids had started to droop, revealing little lines. His cheeks were hollowing and his hair was grey at the temples, waving in little ripples back from his forehead. He wasn't an old man. Most importantly, Marjorie felt that he was still young – that they both were – and she loved him, but in a completely different way to the way she loved Alan. She just wanted to give him happiness and to be able to put the sadness of the past behind him. She was able to do that –it was surely within the limits of her power, and she would do it to the best of her ability.

She turned to face John, her hands on his shoulders, feeling the roughness of his coarse cotton shirt while he stroked her hair comfortingly. She felt her own selfishness and stupidity, but she also knew that she truly loved Alan. Her heart seemed to flip at the very thought of him.

John was truly fond of Marjorie by this time and had asked her to marry him. She was attracted to him, although he was fifteen years her senior. Alan was still the central figure of her life, except that he was not yet free to marry. *Oh what turmoil my life is in!*

She forestalled John's marriage proposal.

"Don't you think you ought to wait at least a year after your wife's death? It may help you recover from the shock of it."

She herself wanted time to think. She began to wonder if he was being fair to her. After all, he was aware of her relationship with Alan.

Majorie heaved a deep sigh. She loved Alan so much, yet she knew her family would be devastated by the thought of her being married to a divorced man. She began to wonder whether if they could have a wedding here in Nigeria with none of her family present, then none of them would be any the wiser as to his family background. Guilt seemed to stab its ugly finger at her from all directions.

Alan was currently staying with Richard and Peggy Milne

in Warri until his ship was ready and loaded to sail to South Africa taking him with it for his three months leave. Marjorie looked forward to having a few precious days with him, as normally the ship's preparation would take about five days. They both anticipated some special moments together that this would afford them the last few days together before being thrust apart for three long months to endure their enforced separation.

However, they had not reckoned on John being in charge of the turn-round time of this particular ship, nor of his super efficiency. To everyone's surprise, the ship was ready to sail in three days. All the passengers had to hastily collect their belongings and say their farewells. It was May – three long months before they would see one another again.

"My darling, how I wish you were coming with me," said Alan as the two of them wandered in the hospital grounds during Marjorie's lunch break that day.

"The sun blazed down out of a cornflower blue sky and they sought shade near a Frangipani shrub which issued its heady perfume over both of them. Alan plucked a twig covered in white flowers and held it out to Marjorie. She sniffed it.

"Whenever I smell this scent, it will remind me of you," she looked up at him, trying to hold back her tears.

"How I wish I were free. Then you could come with me, and we would marry on board ship and honeymoon in South Africa!"

"Oh Alan, that sounds so romantic. It would be a dream come true." She shook her head.

"One day we will be together, I promise."

"I'll wait for you. I'll always wait for you," was her reply.

"Come here," motioned Alan, and led her towards the hospital building. Once in its shadow, he pulled Marjorie underneath it and they stood in almost darkness, leaning against one of its strong pillars.

Arms around one another he kissed her passionately,

and she responded in kind, unwilling to let him go.

He caressed her tenderly, arousing her passion for him.

She returned his kisses and they stood close together, almost as one, with their bodies almost moulded together relaxing in each other's arms for some while.

"Oh my little lady, how I love you," he sighed squeezing her gently around her waist.

"I love you too," she whispered as if her heart would break.

"I know you do. Our love will stand the test of time. What is three months in a lifetime, after all?"

She nodded, afraid that tears would come.

Aware of her emotion, he kissed her yet again and reassured her.

"One day we'll be married, then there'll be no more partings."

They stood with their arms encircling one another each studying the other's face as if to imprint it to memory.

Then he said, "I don't want to dampen your ardour by mentioning this, but while we're apart, just remember that my divorce is going through now. It might take a while – well, we already know it will, but we'll win through in the end."

He paused to kiss her again and hugged her more closely, so closely that Marjorie felt as though he would squeeze the very breath from her body. She felt as though her heart was being wrung out of her.

In the distance a bell rang.

"Oh goodness!" exclaimed Marjorie. "That's the end of my lunch-break. I must fly!"

"We will be married one day. I promise. Now one last kiss to keep me going," said Alan and held her tightly, kissing and caressing her as tears flowed freely down Marjorie's cheeks. She buried her face in his chest, loving the smell of him, the closeness of him and wishing she could halt time for ever.

Alan tipped her face up to look at him, running his thumb across her chin. Her heart buckled as she realised how she adored this man and they were to be parted.

She must go now. Duty called. With a heavy heart she dragged herself away from him, then turned back and kissed him lightly on the cheek. Quickly, before he could witness the emotions chasing across her face, she turned and ran away lightly up the steps leading into the hospital, unaware that her muslin head-square had dropped to the ground.

Dr Richard Milne was worried. He knew the predicament Marjorie was in, yet she must not be romantically involved with two men at once for any longer.

"What can I do, Peggy? He asked his wife one evening after a particularly stressful day. "Marjorie has a responsible post out here, and if the officials got to hear of her having romantic involvement with two men at the same time, god knows what will happen. She would probably lose her job. I don't like to interfere in her personal life, but I am her immediate superior."

Peggy passed him a whisky and soda.

"Thanks. This may well suffer repercussions for me too, you know."

"Don't be too bothered about that, dear. After all we have been discussing the possibility of early retirement anyway."

They were silent for a while.

Peggy was the first to speak. "To be honest, I'd love to live in Aberdeen again before our poor son forgets what we look like. I worry about him, especially with the war going on. We could take him out of boarding school and…"

Richard wasn't listening. His profile was hard as if were carved out of granite. "How best can I advise Marjorie, do you think, Peggy?"

"Would you like me to talk to her?"

"I'd love you to, but I'm her boss. Perhaps we could both have a talk with her?"

"Alan and Marjorie are obviously so much in love and

they are so right for one another."

"They are," he agreed. "Even I as a mere man can see that!"

"I'm sure, once they were married they would be extremely happy."

"It's just that there will be a year or two before they can marry, and that puts such pressure on them both."

"Such a shame!"

"It will be some time before he is free from Gwen. I wonder why she won't let him go, when it's obvious that she doesn't want him."

"Spite? Pride? Jealousy if she's heard about Marjorie? Who knows?"

"Gwen seemed such a brilliant match for him to start with, but she just went to pieces after the girls were born."

They were silent for a while, then he said. "John said he had heard from gossip-mongers that Gwen and Alan hadn't actually lived together when he last went home to Wales."

"How did he find that out?"

"I can't think! Alan is a very private person, so how that kind of information got out I don't know!"

Richard shook his head. "I feel so sorry for Alan. He has so much love to give."

"He and Marjorie are perfect for one another," said Peggy again.

"In a way, it's a pity she met him and fell in love before she realised his past. She had such high morals that she would no doubt have persuaded herself that he was not meant for her before she had fallen so deeply in love with love with him."

"Mmm, but that didn't happen," continued Peggy. "She discovered his marital situation after their love started to blossom. Now they are devoted to one another."

"It's certainly not just a passing passion."

"And now John's arrived on the scene."

"Yes, John."

"As I see it, Marjorie just played the odd game of golf

with him out of the kindness of her heart to help him come to terms with his grief."

"Yes, it probably helped her take her mind off Alan when he was away."

"Yet John seems to want to take things further."

"Did you know he's asked her to marry him?"

"No! Really?" exclaimed Peggy.

Richard nodded. "Yes. So how do we advise her? John is a fair bit older, but he's a widower and free to marry."

"But I thought that was just a platonic friendship?"

"That's what Marjorie was thinking too, but it now has romantic connotations and soon somebody's going to get hurt."

"Do you think he's jealous of Alan at all?"

"Well, he has known about their relationship right from when he first met her."

"It's just that he personally supervised the turn-round of Alan's ship and it was ready two days early; almost as if he wanted him out of the way."

They sat silently, deep in thought for a while.

Then Peggy said, "Marjorie's always been very fond of children, hasn't she?"

"Why yes, you only have to see her delivering babies! She seems to pour love into each one."

"No doubt she would want children of her own some day?"

"Yes, but she could be almost too old by the time she's married to Alan."

"Perhaps that may be a point in John's favour, much as I hate to spoil the path of true love."

"Do you think we ought to talk to her?"

"Somebody ought to, but I don't think it should be us."

"How about Evelyn? Evelyn Bailey?"

"She would be ideal as a comparative outsider, yet also a friend. Oh I do hope this works out well to Marjorie's good."

Marjorie had been asked round to Evelyn's for evening

cocktails.

"What will you have to drink, Marjorie?"

"Gin and lime please."

"Now then, I'm afraid this isn't such a social occasion as you may think."

"Oh?"

"You see, the Milnes are very concerned about you."

"Really?"

"Yes. They are aware at how deeply in love you are with Alan, and he with you. I might add that you have their sympathies there, too. They are right behind you, even though you'll have to wait so long before you can marry."

Marjorie nodded, believing she knew what was coming next.

"However, now that John's on the scene, it does rather appear that he's fallen for you as well, is that right?"

"Yes."

"Well, you see Richard and Peggy are concerned that although John was aware of your relationship with Alan when he first arrived he was obviously taken with you, mistook your friendship for love, and is now in love with you himself. Do you see where I'm heading?"

Marjorie nodded again.

"When Alan's ship was ready so quickly under John's personal supervision, the Milnes became aware that he may be jealous of you both."

She held up her hand.

"No, I'm not inferring anything, just suggesting it as a possibility."

"Just supposing John was jealous of Alan. You cannot marry for some years. Would your love be so strong as to stand the test of that?"

Tears started to course down Marjorie's face and she tried to stop the flow.

Evelyn noticed.

"I'm sorry. I didn't want to bring you here to put you through the mangle. I just wanted you to be aware of all possibilities in the situation. You must be aware that you cannot have two men in tow when you hold such a responsible position as yours. HQ would get to know and you could well lose your job over it. Richard, as your supervisor may even come in for something or other as well. Do you see what I'm getting at?"

"So I must end everything with Alan?" she asked miserably.

"I didn't say that at all. What I did say is that you must end your relationship with one of them. Carefully weigh up which will stand the test of time against the surrounding difficulties.

Marjorie couldn't stop the tears.

Now that Alan was away for a considerable time and John was so close, it meant that he was wearing her down and trying to break her resistance, when all the while she knew that her heart really lay with Alan. Yet still this guilt about his divorce kept rearing its ugly head. Was it really love she felt for John or was it concern growing out of pity for him when his wife died?

"I don't know, oh I don't know," she wailed.

Evelyn patted her hand kindly.

"There's no need for a snap decision," she said kindly. "You just need to be aware of the situation and the routes out of it. I think Richard is hoping you'll make a firm decision one way or the other before Alan gets back. Don't worry about it. We're all on your side, it's a terrible decision to make."

Marjorie certainly couldn't answer those questions yet. She would have to go away and think things out for herself. Yet as her friends were advising her, she must make up her mind very soon before Alan returned from South Africa, which by now would only be in a month's time.

How time passed. It didn't seem two months ago that they had wrenched themselves apart before he sailed away for three months. She had received many letters from him and had replied faithfully to each one. They still declared their love for one another. As she thought of him, a familiar warmth wrapped round her heart.

That night she went to bed with a heavy heart, awaking with the light of dawn, knowing she had not slept well and nor would she sleep any more. She dressed and wandered down to the river where she sat near a clump of bushes that offered her privacy overlooking it and plucking at the coarse grass.

As she sat staring out over the water, Marjorie tried to unravel the threads of her life here. They had been knotted together for so long that they were difficult to pick apart. She made herself do it, trying to analyse her life without emotion, attempting to stand back from her feelings resolutely following the strands.

She was beginning to realise it could be a lack of love in her childhood that had given her this craving to be loved, which in turn had often led to her attracting the wrong men. Now though, she and Alan had such a close relationship and Marjorie was sure that this love was the real thing.

Of course she loved Alan. She had done from their first date together. She had fallen in love with all his courteous manners, sparkle and romantic ideas; yet not just those bits of him, but the whole man. She had responded to him and offered all the weight of her love in that she gave the whole of herself to Alan. Now it seemed too deep-rooted to dig up and transplant it elsewhere. How she missed him. She missed the smell of him, the tone of his voice and his throaty laugh. Everything about him.

As she gazed out over the water she felt guilty about the thought of even transferring that love; after all she had assured Alan that she would always stand by him. Her conscience struck her when she thought about her father and what his reaction would be when he eventually discovered that she was in love with a married man. Guilt crept in as she remembered Gwen in Wales. Would she really be able to deceive her family?

Marjorie pondered over the threads she had untangled thus far. It gave her no pleasure and she didn't like the picture that it had revealed.

She realised that people were hurting, her included, and it was because of her. Alan loved her, she was sure of that. She knew she loved him dearly too; or was it the romance he had about him? John needed her, and love had blossomed out of friendship. Would that be a better basis for marriage? Or was John about to marry on the rebound, needing to be loved. As she thought about it, she shook her head as she chased the thoughts of being able to give birth to her own child. Was that what was really driving a wedge between her and Alan? Her early forties would be dangerously late to start a family. Could she risk it? Supposing they did and the child was handicapped? Would their love overcome that? Would the child be a constant reminder that Alan should have returned to Gwen? If they didn't have children, would they always regret it? She hoped that she would never hold that against Alan, however much she wanted a child of her own. Oh, if only she could see into the future! Marjorie wrapped her arms around her knees as she tried to contain herself. The threads must be properly set so that they would never again get tangled.

However much she may want to, marriage to Alan was currently out of the question. He was already married. Marjorie's family would never allow it, and although she loved her life away from home, she still loved her father dearly, and would not be able to bear it if she upset him.

John was fifteen years her senior. He had been recently widowed and was free to marry. He had a son aged twenty and his daughter was near the end of her schooling. It would be a new, fresh start for both of them with no encumbrances.

She remembered Evelyn's advice. 'Don't be rash,' she had said. 'John will give you security. He is a good man and you will grow to love him dearly.'

The sun rose higher in the sky making her uncomfortable,

even in the shade of the bushes.

Marjorie made her way back to her bungalow wondering how long it had taken to grow up into herself. The thought both shamed and encouraged her.

It was at the end of June 1943 when Marjorie finally wrote to Alan whilst he was still in South Africa, before he was due to leave to return to Nigeria. It was written with a heavy heart as she told him of her decision to marry John. She knew it was cowardly of her to break the news to him that way, but on the other hand, having made her decision, she felt she had to get it off her chest and let him know as soon as possible.

When she next saw John, she shyly told him what she had done, and he smiled and took her into his arms. He held her head against his shoulder, stroking her hair, and she let it rest there. He held her differently from Alan.

"Well done!" he complimented her. "Now that you've made your decision, we can make our plans, eh?"

Marjorie nodded. "As long as you don't rush me. I must be sure of what I'm doing."

John was thrilled. He grabbed her in a bear-like hug and swept her off down to the Club to celebrate. He was slightly taller than Alan and his angular frame seemed quite gawky with boyish excitement. His piercing blue eyes twinkled down at Marjorie and she smiled up at him, her heart lurching within her. It was only seven months since they had first met, here in the Club when he had been the recipient of such tragic news. She noticed his hands for the first time; they were large and man-sized with long slender fingers, not unlike Alan's. She reined in her thoughts with a jolt. John was thrusting a drink at her and Richard Milne was proposing a toast.

"To John and Marjorie!" echoed around the room.

John smiled proudly down at her and she felt suddenly self-conscious and shy, but she laughed her feelings away.

Naturally people wanted to know when the happy day would take place. John and Marjorie had not really given themselves time to discuss these details, but they both felt it would be best if John were to go back to Liverpool on the next available passage, as he was due for leave any day now. He could then tell his son and daughter all about Marjorie before returning to Nigeria and marrying her the following October.

"As long as Alan doesn't grab her first!" jested someone.

Richard Milne foresaw what was to come and offered encouragement.

"Why wait? There's no time like the present!"

Everyone guffawed, but Richard had things all worked out in his mind.

"I'm sure we can release Marjorie from her duties. She could hand over temporarily to Evelyn Bailey, who, I'm sure would be pleased to stand in on such an auspicious occasion." He turned to Evelyn who nodded enthusiastically.

Her husband Charles chimed in. "They could use our house for their honeymoon, so we could move into Marjorie's!"

And so it was that John and Marjorie got swept along with their friends' enthusiasm.

PART THREE –

HOME AND FAMILY

Chapter Seventeen

John and Marjorie were engaged one Sunday in July 1943 and married the following Thursday on 15th July 1943.

Having such a short engagement meant that they were involved in a flurry of wedding plans, and this all came together so well that Marjorie decided she must have made the right decision.

Marjorie had a long white sleeveless evening dress that happened to have a one-buttoned long white lace coat to wear over the top, so her arms were covered in the traditional manner of a bride. A friend was able to lend her a veil of Brussels lace. The thirty or forty Europeans in Warri provided the reception between them. Normally there would be no vicar or priest to be had for miles around, but it just so happened that Canon Metcalfe was passing through on his way to East Africa, so he was approached, and was happy to perform the wedding ceremony. Even a wedding ring was provided. A mutual friend was happy to donate her own as a wedding gift then buy another when she could.

[NB: This explains why Marjorie had the names Tony & Elsie *inscribed inside her ring.]*

During the morning of 15th July, Marjorie was involved with a difficult birth at the hospital. Evelyn Bailey was taking over her post temporarily; therefore, because of a change of staff, an inventory also had to be taken that day. In addition to all that, Marjorie and Evelyn had to swap bungalows. There was really no time to think on this day of all days, her wedding day; the day she would remember for the rest of her life. Instead of eating lunch, Marjorie rushed out into the hospital garden and picked a large bunch of flowers and greenery, arranging them tastefully into her bridal bouquet.

Officially she wasn't due for leave, but Richard Milne had arranged for Marjorie to go to England with John as soon as a passage was found. He felt that the sooner the knot was tied, then the better things would be all round. Dr Milne had gone to a lot of trouble, going to Medical Headquarters in Lagos in order to obtain the necessary release papers. As he did so, he just hoped that Marjorie had made the right decision and that she would be happy. Certainly being in love with two men at the same time hadn't been helpful at all.

Eventually mid-afternoon arrived and Marjorie left the hospital exhausted, but free to get ready for her marriage. She bathed trying to soak away the rush of the day. As she put on her dress she mentally tried to prepare herself for her new life ahead. Adjusting her veil, she secured and decorated it with a real flower to match her bouquet.

She mustn't take long. She had asked Richard Milne to give her away. He had been a wonderful father figure to her since she had been here in Warri that he had been the obvious choice. He would be here soon, so she must make haste to be ready.

Richard arrived shortly before four o'clock. They climbed into the chauffeured car and it purred down the hospital drive towards the little church. This was a brick built place with white walls both inside and out, but topped by a corrugated iron roof, as were a lot of buildings in Nigeria.

As she entered the church on Richard Milne's arm, Marjorie caught her breath in wonder. The place had been transformed. The ladies had decorated the place beautifully with tubs of flowers from their own gardens. The perfume was quite intoxicating, and the cheerful, coloured blooms gave the incongruous little chapel the look of a cathedral.

John was waiting for her just a few short steps away.

After the vicar's blessing there came a triumphant burst of the wedding march from the harmonium. The congregation stood up and started to crowd into the aisle behind John and Marjorie as they strolled towards the church door, nodding and smiling to people on either side of them.

There were greetings and handshakes as everyone streamed out into the dreary day beyond as it released a shower of rain upon them.

"It's St Swithun's Day," said someone. "That means it'll rain for forty more days."

"Save on the confetti now it's wartime," joked someone else.

Someone else laughed. "And the rice!"

There were hugs and kisses and merry laughter as they grouped for the photographer. He was another friend, a good amateur photographer, who was standing in as a professional for the day. His gift to them was the numerous photographs.

The reception was held in the Club and was celebrated by anyone and everyone who happened to be there that evening.

By this time Evelyn and Charles Bailey had moved out of their Police House and into Marjorie's bungalow to enable John and Marjorie to have a few days' honeymoon in different surroundings. A lot of quips about their honeymoon hotel were flying about. Everyone was both jolly and relieved that day to think that Marjorie had settled down and they all hoped she had made the right decision.

John and Marjorie had been married only ten days before a liberty ship became available for them to sail home on. The one they had originally been booked on had been torpedoed before it had reached West Africa. There was no passenger accommodation, just the crew plus John and Marjorie who was the only woman on board. They had to manage in a tiny cabin with a single bunk that was normally supposed to be quarters for any of the crew who were taken ill. The journey was a slow and tedious one. It took six weeks and two days to reach England, when normally this would have taken twelve days. The ship seemed to plunge up every creek and river delivering and taking on cargo.

Surely this ship must be the most uncomfortable one afloat? Marjorie did not like to speak her thoughts out loud.

John had written a long letter to Daphne and Warren telling them about Marjorie. Before they set sail, he had followed this up with a cable informing them that they were on their way home. Marjorie had sent her family one too, and wondered what their reaction would be.

She discovered that she began to grieve for Alan as John had grieved for his first wife. She wanted to discuss things with John, to talk openly, for him to comfort her like she had comforted him when the news of Elsie's death came through. However, Alan hadn't died, he was her previous sweetheart, and she realised with dismay that deep down she still loved him. Marjorie yearned to be frank, to discuss things openly, but as she got to know John better, even in these early days, she knew she must keep her feelings to herself. They had been so open with one another before their marriage – at least John had with her, but Marjorie was aware that now she must keep her hurt and grief private absolutely secret and tuck any memories she had of Alan into the depths of her heart. John could be very loving, but also, she was coming to realise, a very volatile man at times.

She herself even began to wonder if she had made the right decision. There was a spark in the deepest corner of her heart that still smouldered for Alan. Would she be happy? Would she make John happy? As she asked herself that question, she determined to make her own happiness.

Upon reaching Liverpool, John took Marjorie to his home in Formby. When meeting his daughter, Daphne for the first time, Marjorie realised what an interloper she was to this family who were still wrapped up in their grief and needed to console one another and draw comfort from one another. After all, Daphne had not seen her father since her mother's death, and she obviously had a lot to share with him. John's son, Warren had enlisted in the Army, and was currently posted, (they were to learn later) in Scandinavia.

Marjorie found it extremely embarrassing to discover that Daphne had never received John's letter describing her and telling of their forthcoming marriage, so receiving a cable informing her that her father was on his way home with Marjorie had meant nothing to her. Daphne's maternal grandmother had also moved in to be with her and she was extremely annoyed by the news, with her hostilities being shot like machine-gunfire.

"How dare you treat me like this! I moved in to do the decent thing and look after my grand-daughter. Now here I am being turned out without a minute's notice."

"It's not like that at all, and you know it. There's plenty of room here for you to stay if you'd like to. In fact it will help you to get to know Marjorie..."

"I don't want to get to know your whore ..."

"Don't talk such rubbish, Marjorie is my wife!"

"You must have had a pretty close relationship to get married so quickly, and nowhere near a year gone by since poor Elsie passed away. How could you! You should be ashamed of yourself, John!"

John took a deep breath to try and rein in his true feelings. If he swore at her, which was his immediate reaction, his case for reasoning with the woman would be lost straight away.

"Look here, I first met Marjorie when I received the cable to tell me about Elsie. She was such a comfort to me, that's all, and I grew to love her."

"Huh! I don't believe you." She pointed her finger accusingly at John. "I believe you've been having an affair out there in West Africa, probably for years, behind Elsie's back, and now you've taken your chance to marry the woman. Or probably *she* took the chance to engineer you into it."

John was having trouble trying to keep his temper. If he lost it now he might even look to be as guilty as Mrs Lister was accusing him to be.

"Come on now, Marjorie's a sweet little lady. You'll

love her. Let me introduce you."

"I refuse to be introduced to that trollop! Out of my way this instant! I-I'll pack my things and leave this house now, this minute! Just you make sure that I don't meet her before I go, or I might do something I shouldn't!"

She elbowed her way out of the room, muttering about it being a disgrace getting married again so soon.

Not only was Marjorie mortified to hear the raised voices in the adjoining room, she was also upset on Daphne's behalf as she witnessed her face crumple with anguish in loyalty divided between her father and grandmother.

Daphne would come home from Merchant Taylors School in Crosby each evening. She was understandably very upset for many nights. John would go upstairs most evenings to try and console her. Marjorie, left on her own downstairs felt awkward. *Should I offer to move out for a while until things calm down a bit? Alternatively should I offer to try and comfort Daphne?* She decided it would be best not to push herself forward in any way. After all she was a stranger to this family and must remain on the edge of it until John felt it right to draw her in and include her in the heart of things. Trying to help now may be viewed as meddling in family politics. Daphne was desperate for her own mother's love at the moment, and the least Marjorie could do was let John try and comfort his daughter in the best way he could.

As she sat on her own downstairs, she looked around her and felt even more of an outsider in this house that had been decorated to another woman's tastes and design. There was a photograph of Elsie with Warren and Daphne as children. *I wonder what Elsie was like.*

Marjorie was still receiving letters from Alan. She never replied to them, although sometimes she found it hard not to, being in this marriage which somehow didn't include her at the moment. Now that she was married his letters were never more than basically friendly, reiterating all the Nigerian news as he was back in Lagos and working at the hospital there. It was almost as if he had acquired a habit he could not break. They offered her a kind of comfort in this strange cold world, where tempers were frequently frayed and stretched taut as their owners would circle one another, trying to gauge and assess.

Far away from her own relatives, Marjorie drew comfort from the letters she received from them, but especially those that came from Alan. Then came the awful day when John discovered these letters and his fury knew no bounds.

"What the hell are you doing, writing to him? You're married to *me* now!" he raged.

"But I haven't been writing to him."

"You must have done. How did he know where to send them?"

Marjorie shook her head. "Richard, perhaps?"

"Richard would have more bloody sense than that and you know it! How many more are there?"

Marjorie produced the fistful she had received whilst living in Formby.

John snatched them from her.

"What about the ones he wrote from South Africa and before that even? I trust you've got rid of those."

Marjorie felt a lump in her throat and tears starting to course down her cheeks.

"Well, have you?"

She shook her head, unable to speak.

"Where are they?"

"Upstairs."

"Show me."

Miserably she led him upstairs to their large bedroom with its old fashioned double bed, reflecting that this had probably been the marital bed of John and Elsie. There was a double relationship on both sides somewhere, but she couldn't get her head round these thoughts.

She opened her wardrobe. The letters were a huge pile of papers going back a long way and tied up with ribbon. Being short, Marjorie had to stand on a chair to reach for them, but John was tall and saw them instantly. He reached over her head and snatched them before she could take hold of them.

"I'll have those."

Marjorie was silent, terrified he would read them.

"And do you know what I'm going to do with them?"

She shook her head.

"I'm going to take great pleasure in burning them!"

With that he turned on his heel and slammed out of the door.

Marjorie sat on the bed and let the tears come.

Through the window she saw blue smoke snaking upwards and went over to lean on the sill. She saw that John had made a bonfire of garden rubbish and was scrunching up and throwing Alan's letters on it one by one, thus ensuring that each one was properly destroyed. She wept then, as the last vestige of Alan and his love for her was sacrificed to the sky.

After that she never received any more letters from Alan. John would examine the mail every day, and if any suspicious letters arrived for her, he would extract them and burn them before Marjorie had seen them.

She sighed. She often did these days. *Have I done the right thing? Will I be happy?* As she asked herself the question, Marjorie determined to make her own happiness.

At least Marjorie didn't have John's mother-in-law to cope with now. Mrs Lister had gone to live several roads away in rented accommodation. She still made her disapproval known, by deliberately avoiding Marjorie in the village. Having first ensured that Marjorie had spotted her, she would turn away from her by crossing the road or swerving to enter a shop she had just passed to ensure she made a deliberate snub.

Marjorie was beginning to feel desperately lonely until she realised that around her people were smiling, and that they were smiling for her. When she returned their smile, a conversation would begin.

"Excuse me, but are you the new Mrs Anderson?"

"Yes, that's right."

"How do you do. I'm Yvonne Durrant, the schoolmaster's wife. We've heard a lot about you."

"Oh?" Marjorie looked puzzled.

"Yes, from old Mrs Lister. She's making a lot of enemies hereabouts the way she's carrying on. Look, we only live just round the corner from you. Do drop in and have a coffee sometimes."

"Thank you, I'd like that."

And so it continued. Marjorie discovered that Mrs Lister's campaign was in fact having the opposite effect, and neighbours were curious to discover what John Anderson's new wife was really like, so they all befriended her, thus heaping more wrath from Mrs Lister upon themselves.

Of course, although Marjorie was now starting to enjoy life again it became far harder for Daphne to bear, as her grandmother relied on her loyalty even more. Both John and Marjorie became very concerned, but were helpless at that stage than to do any more than offer consolation and try to understand.

* * *

Daphne was sitting at the table in her bedroom. Trying to study, she was unable to concentrate. Resting her elbows on the table she cupped her face with her hands. Looking out of the window she saw sad drifts of leaves being blown down from the trees and across the lawn. The wind was bouncing the tree branches outside her window. She got up to draw the curtains and shut it out but she could still hear its noise as it whistled and whipped around the house. The tears ran down her face, mirroring the rain outside. She wiped her chin with the back of her hand, too tired to even reach for her handkerchief. The wind increased to a howl and seemed to mock her; all she wanted was her beloved daddy to enfold her in his arms and reassure her that everything was all right after all. She stared straight ahead, blue eyes wide with stricken grief.

Was this what life would be like from now on? I suppose Daddy's new wife probably isn't a bad sort; in fact she looks rather nice, if a bit on the shy side.

Getting used to a stepmother before she had rid herself of the grief she carried for the loss of her own mother was too hard for her. At least Marjorie hadn't insisted on being called mother. Daphne couldn't have borne that – she would have refused anyway. She reflected that Marjorie was quite a nice name.

Yet how could Daddy have done this? Hadn't he loved Mummy as much as he said he did? Crystal tears gathered again in her eyes, spilling over onto her cheeks. *If only he had given them all time to get used to the idea before getting married again. After all Mummy hasn't even been dead for anything like a year yet. No wonder Granny is so upset. She is such a stickler for tradition. Granny! She's another fly in the ointment. Couldn't she see how hard it is for me to have to live with her father and 'his woman' as she crudely refers to Marjorie, yet also be loyal to Granny by paying her visits two or three times each week?*

She was up here in her room and supposed to be studying. *Yet how can I do that with all this to cope with?*

She muttered miserably under her breath. "I'll fail my Matric and end up as a cleaner or something. It'll be all their fault then."

Realising the selfishness of her thoughts she became wrapped in guilt.

"Oh Daddy," she sighed. "Why couldn't life be simple and just have you and me in it with Warren?"

Christmas was approaching. Marjorie thought the festivities appeared likely to cause big problems all round, as whatever she and John did, and whoever they did it with would surely cause hard feelings elsewhere in the family. It was during their meal one evening that, as it happened, Daphne unwittingly solved everything by saying

"Daddy, you remember Ann at school?"
"Who?"
"Ann Ambrose."
"Yes dear," said John absent-mindedly, a forkful of food on its way to his mouth.
"Well she's asked if I could go and spend Christmas with them."
John and Marjorie looked at one another meaningfully.
"That's certainly a very kind thought, but don't you think her parents should have some say in this?" replied John, stabbing at a piece of carrot.
"They know. In fact I think the idea might even have come from them in the first place. Oh please, please can I go? It would be a real family Christmas..." She broke off suddenly, embarrassed.
"Oh, sorry, I didn't mean..." Daphne covered her confusion by staring at her plate and making patterns in the gravy with her fork.
"We'll see," was all John would say.
John and Marjorie were actually pleased by this turn of developments, but John was wise enough not to let his daughter realise this.

Their first Christmas together was a family one. Daphne had gone to stay with Ann and her family, thrilled with the idea. John also believed this was an excellent plan as it meant that she could visit her Grandmother whenever she liked without feeling disloyal to anyone.

Marjorie and John took the train and travelled south to Dorset and here he met her family for the first time. They stayed with Bettie and Bill, making their flat over the Bill's furniture shop crowded and festive as everyone helped, bumped into one another and laughed a lot. Marjorie was pleased that her family seemed to like John and that he seemed to fit in well.

Unfortunately she felt unwell on the morning of Boxing Day, and John was quite concerned about her. She had to dash out in the middle of breakfast and got to the bathroom just in time where she vomited in the lavatory. *Oh no! I*

don't want to ruin everybody's Christmas by being ill.
Later she felt a lot better, and was keen to join the party at Grace and Jack's for lunch.

Marjorie hadn't seen Marion and Morgan, Grace's children, for some while, and commented on how they had grown. She played with them and Heather for some while as John chatted with the adults, generally getting to know one another. Then Heather was whisked away for her nap. How she wished that some day in the future, she would have a child, or children of her own.

That Christmas was the first time that John had met her relatives *en masse*. Marjorie had felt a little nervous, wondering how he would fit in, how they would all get on together, although she told herself it was a bit too late to worry now, after they were married.

Bettie had confided to her that on receiving her cable, their father's first reaction was, "Oh no, what has Marjorie done now!"

However looking round, he seemed to accept John into the family. She looked about her, watching her family intermingle with one another, and felt happy and content as they laughed and joked, John relaxing among them, seemingly enjoying their company.

It was January and John was waiting to hear details of a passage out to Nigeria again. As it was wartime, he had been unable to travel home when his first wife had died, and therefore he had been allowed extra allowance of time as compassionate leave for the death of his wife, which had certainly helped him to cement a relationship with Daphne.

He and Marjorie would be travelling together.

However, Marjorie was having suspicions about her health and paid a secret visit to the doctor. She arrived home to find John engrossed in the newspaper.

"I wonder when this war is going to end?" he sighed as she came in. "Come here and give me a cuddle, and we'll shut the world out for a bit."

Marjorie smiled and went to sit beside him. "First, I've got some news for you. I'm afraid I won't be able to travel back to Nigeria with you."

John's concern was immediate.

"But why? What's happened? What's the matter?" He turned towards her, offering a protective arm, and Marjorie could hold out no longer.

"I'm pregnant."

"You're what?"

"I'm pregnant. I'm going to have a baby."

"You are?"

John's happy smile split his face in two.

Marjorie didn't waste her energy in contradiction or affirmation and they both sat grinning at one another for some seconds until John grabbed Marjorie around the waist and planted a huge kiss on her cheek.

"This calls for a celebration!"

"What with?"

"Oh damn, I forgot this is wartime Britain. Let's have a cup of tea then; anything to use as a toast!"

John broke the news to Daphne a couple of days later. He tried to point out the positive side of the situation that would be to her advantage.

"So now you will be able to get to know Marjorie on your own for a few weeks and have her look after you too, so you can concentrate on your studies."

"Congratulations," she said flatly, and turned away feeling worse than ever.

John had returned to Warri. Marjorie was getting larger as her baby grew within her. Daphne was studying for her matriculation examinations, and in between spent quite a lot of time visiting her grandmother as well as her school friend Ann. Marjorie, for the first time in her active life, began to feel lonely.

One day she was turning out when she came across a pile of Christmas cards from the previous year. Looking through them, she reminisced over people's names and greetings when she found one from Freda Thompson. The address was only a few miles away in Southport. She contacted her.

Four days later, Marjorie set out on a bus to visit Freda for tea. She arrived in Southport a little early, so decided to explore the area. She was surprised at how sedate and affluent it appeared with its large hotels, the wide esplanade, not to mention the exclusive and expensive shops in the two arcades. Surely nobody could afford to buy things here, especially on such a meagre ration of allotted coupons per person. Coming from the south of the country, she had always lumped the northern cities together in her mind as being full of factories, squalor and belching smoke. Only having seen Lime Street station and Liverpool docks on her journeys to and from West Africa had only served to reinforce this view.

As she approached the house, she realised it looked much as she imagined, small, neat and rather dull.

Freda was pleased to see her, and promptly made a pot of tea. They both enjoyed talking over the times they had together in Calabar and their local leave on the island with the leper colony. However, Freda still gave the impression of being an upright spinster, even having been so well travelled. Once more Marjorie began to feel her own conscience prick her as she sat in front of all Freda represented; things that she, Marjorie, should represent, coming from a devout Christian background herself.

Marjorie felt contrite after she left Freda, realising that she had used her in her loneliness, rather than seeking genuine friendship. In order to give herself something else to think about she concocted a special meal for Daphne that evening.

She was finding it hard being a stepmother, especially without John's support, as she wanted so much to do the right thing by the girl.

"Maybe I'm stepping aside a bit too much." Marjorie sighed. "I just don't know!" *Poor Daphne; she is certainly having trouble dividing her loyalties these days. After all she has no emotional ties to me and understandably, probably feels more like rejecting me.*

Marjorie did not want to be the one to upset what would be a precariously balanced apple cart. Mrs Lister seemed more than enough for Daphne to cope with, especially with exams looming on the horizon. She decided it would be best to keep a low profile, even if she did feel a bit like a housekeeper at times: so what?

She had married John, she had weighed up all the pros and cons. Maybe the present time was not so good but one couldn't go on enjoying life forever. There had to be some disappointments. If this were one of them, then things would surely improve. She had a baby to look forward to. That could never have happened if she had waited for Alan; he still had about some years before he could be free. Marjorie shook her head. She mustn't think of Alan. He was in her past life. She was married to John now, not long until her baby was born, and then John would return. She smiled as she mentally marked out the milestones ahead.

Chapter Eighteen

It was the first week of August. In Formby Nursing Home the nurse helped Marjorie to sit up and plumped up the pillows behind her head.

"Are you a bit uncomfortable?" she asked.

"A little," she said.

"See how you cope over the next half-hour or so and then maybe the doctor will give you something if it's really bad. But here's your little girl. Would you like to hold her?"

Marjorie held out her arms eagerly, as the nurse lifted a white bundle from the crib next to the bed. She placed it gently in Marjorie's arms as Marjorie had done to so many other new mothers. Now she herself knew the thrill of being a new mother. The swath of shawl felt surprisingly soft and warm; she turned down a corner of the cocoon and smiled. Her daughter sported the beginnings of a mass of blonde hair and was sleeping peacefully, despite being handled.

"Is she all right?" her first question had been, with the immediate concern of all mothers.

"Of course she is, she's perfect."

Marjorie went on staring at her baby; she was so tiny, being belittled by so many wrappings, yet she had a very definite presence about her, far more so than any of the babies she had delivered for other women. Something maternal struck deep inside her and she felt a lump rise in her throat as tears of joy threatened to overtake her. How she wished John could share this moment with her, together with their own child.

The nurse chuckled.

"You two get to know one another. Would you like a cup of tea?"

Marjorie nodded happily, pondering the thought that the English seemed to produce tea for celebrations and comforts alike before turning her attentions back to the sleeping baby in her arms.

A girl! Her own daughter! It seemed incredible to think of herself as a mother after all these years – and so much longing.

She leaned back against the pillows, cuddling the child and dreaming of the future.

The lady in the next bed leaned over.

"All right, chook?" she asked.

"Yes thanks, I'm fine."

"I'm Vera. Did you have a boy or a girl?"

"A little girl. Oh, and I'm Marjorie."

"Aw luvly. I had a little boy at five this morning."

"Well, I never, exactly twelve hours older!"

"You're quite new to this area aren't yer chook?"

"Well yes, fairly new. I've been married to John Anderson for just over a year."

"Eee, so you'll be living at that big house in Cropton Road?"

"Yes, *Linwood*."

"We live just at the back of it in Elbow Lane, number nineteen. You must come round so we can compare babies and things."

"Thank you, I'd like that."

"Have you thought of a name yet?"

"No we haven't. Somehow or other we thought the baby would be a boy and agreed on Barry!"

"Well, we're calling our baby Laurence. Laurence James after 'is Dad, my Jimmy."

The nurse arrived with a cup of tea for Marjorie.

"Eee, chook, can I have one as well?"

"Now Mrs Prenton, you had yours after lunch and at teatime when Mrs Anderson here was in labour."

"But there must be one in the pot now you've made some."

"Oh all right then, but don't tell. It's wartime with everything rationed." She bustled off, returning with a second cup.

"Don't tell anyone, or everyone will want a cup and I

only used a small pot. It'll be supper time soon, anyway."

Marjorie's first visitor was Daphne. She burst into the room eager to see her new half-sister. First she presented Marjorie with a small paper bag. Marjorie peeped inside and found an individual strawberry tart.

"I made it especially for you with the last of the crop," she explained.

Marjorie was touched by the home made gift. It was the first sign of affection Daphne had shown her. She reached up and pulled Daphne's head down so she could kiss her thanks. Daphne's arms enfolded Marjorie and the baby as she planted a kiss on the forehead of each.

"Please let me look at her."

Marjorie held out the baby and Daphne took the child into her arms. The baby slotted neatly into them and she laid a finger against each tiny cheek as she whispered to the infant.

"Hello, there little one." Then to Marjorie, "Isn't she beautiful!"

She glanced up at Marjorie from where she was perching on the bed.

"Have you decided what to call her?"

Marjorie shook her head.

"No, we tried to agree on some names before your father went back. We agreed on Barry for a boy, but couldn't really think of a girl's name. I quite liked Barbara, but he said he had a cousin of that name and didn't get on with her, so that's as far as we got! We've made some suggestions by letter, but so many have got lost the discussion petered out."

Daphne studied the contented child for some minutes before voicing her thoughts aloud. "I think she looks like a Diana. Do you like that name?"

Marjorie repeated it several times.

"Yes, I do like that, she agreed. "Shall we cable Daddy with the news and suggest it?"

From the beaming smile on her face, Daphne was obviously thrilled with the idea.

It seemed that John was too, as his cable of congratulations came back welcoming Diana Marjorie, which is what she remained, in honour of her mother.

* * *

Marjorie leaned over the crib again and breathed in deeply of that strange pungent new born smell. She remembered it from her midwifery days. As if sensing her presence, Diana moved and slowly wakened, her little fists waving in the air.

"You must be hungry little poppet," she said, gathering her into her arms.

With fumbling fingers, Marjorie unbuttoned the front of her night dress as Diana realised how hungry she was and started to cry. She turned her head, instinctively nuzzling, but although Marjorie had done this many times for other women, and shown them what to do, she felt herself go tense and awkward. Her baby's face distorted horribly as she opened her gummy mouth to yell even louder.

At last Marjorie managed to connect the nipple into the gaping mouth which immediately clamped round it as Diana began to suck strongly, creating a small satisfying tug deep in Marjorie's own belly. She looked fondly at the little face that had changed so quickly from fury to contentment.

As she fed Diana and held her close, Marjorie thought more about her own mother. She often wondered about her these days. She had heard what a gracious lady she had been. She believed her mother had a vivacious side to her character too. She knew that her father had been head over heels in love with her and Charlotte with him; yet knowing her father now, he seemed quite a different character. She cradled Diana and hugged her close until the child wriggled. Marjorie felt the link with Charlotte stretching backwards, yet drawing her closer as she gazed down at Charlotte's grandchild.

Marjorie had been home with Diana for about a week. She was enjoying her role as a mother. She leaned over the cot, looking down at the baby – her own baby! Leaning closer she breathed the familiar scent of her, listening to her little snuffles and snores as she slept. Love suddenly welled up inside her, as she caught the combination of baby powder and young baby's skin.

Later she walked slowly in the garden, feeling the sun on her face, smiling to herself as the warmth of it enfolded her. Diana was having her sleep, but she wished John were here to share the moment of contentment. A bird sang from a branch of a tree high above her, causing her to stop and listen in appreciation. The late summer sun was beating down out of a cloudless blue sky as she closed her eyes and sighed with pleasure in those few uplifting moments.

Marjorie was proudly pushing the pram homewards from her shopping trip. Her pace had slowed considerably due to the heat. She wondered how she managed to do so much whilst in the heat of Nigeria, then supposed that this was a different type of heat. Here it hung with humidity which made it exhausting.

It was the first week of September 1944, yet it seemed hotter than mid-summer had been, with reverberating heat being stored in the very slabs of the pavement. Diana was almost a month old. *I wonder if giving birth makes people feel things more keenly.*

The grass verge on the opposite side of the road was starred with wild flowers. Once a pretty patchwork of colour, they were now beginning to wilt. Although the days were still hot, the light was beginning to change as the shadows lengthened by tiny amounts. The fruit trees were already bowed with rosy apples and pale golden pears. Autumn was heralding its arrival and close on its heels would be the chill of winter. *I wonder what winter will be like up here in Lancashire. Will it be very much colder than winter down in the south of England?*

As she opened the front door, she spotted a letter on the doormat. It was addressed to her in John's neat handwriting. Quickly she manoeuvred the pram into the cool hallway. Diana continued to sleep peacefully, although it would soon be time for her next feed.

Excited, she ripped open the envelope and read its contents. Her enthusiasm waned as she reached the end of the letter. John wanted her to join him in Warri as soon as possible. Diana would not be allowed to travel with her of course, so he had suggested *leaving her in somebody else's capable and loving care.* Feeling the colour drain from her face, Marjorie sank into the comfort of the nearest chair. "Surely he can't mean that?" She read his letter again.

Only half an hour ago everything had seemed so perfect and now, with her baby hardly a month old, Marjorie was already facing the trauma of being parted from her child. She let her mind wander back over past events and she tormented herself with the thought of leaving Diana. She couldn't leave her with just anybody; not that she could bear to be parted from her at all. John wasn't due home for a year; Diana would have changed a lot in that time, all changes that she would miss. Could she bear to be separated from her baby for so long? Yet on the other hand, she must also try to see the situation from John's point of view. His first wife had never travelled with him regardless of whether it was war or peace time, so he must have led quite a lonely life. Yet surely, if he was used to Elsie staying at home, this shouldn't present him with too much of a problem. Then when the war was over they could all travel about as a family.

Marjorie went to the pram and saw that Diana was awake, so she scooped her up and cuddled her closely in her arms, being rewarded by a responsive gurgle. Tears filled her eyes, but she blinked them away, refusing to let them spill down her cheeks. As she fed Diana she talked soothingly to her, yet all the while asking questions of herself that she found difficult to answer.

She pondered these problems all through the day and

eventually put a trunk telephone call through to Bettie.

"Oh Bettie, what can I do?" wailed Marjorie. "John wants me to join him in Warri and I can't travel with a baby."

Bettie was sympathetic. "Oh dear, Marjorie, well I suppose you'll have to do what he wants."

"But what about Diana?"

"Oh dear, I don't know."

They exchanged news for a short while before Bettie said, "I've heard there's a very good children's home at Hinton Martell, about half way between here and Grace and Jack's farm. I could look up the details for you if you like."

"Right, thank you. Can I stay with you while I sort things out?" Even as she said it, she knew what she must do. She had been hoping that Bettie would take Diana temporarily, but she hadn't offered, neither had Marjorie felt it was right to ask it of her. It was not surprising really as Bettie was expecting their second child and her pregnancy had not been a particularly good one thus far, so she had her hands full with little Heather as well.

Once more she travelled south to Dorset in search of an answer.

It was dark when the train pulled into Poole station. The weather had changed suddenly over the past few days and the evening was shrouded in the wisps of a September evening mist as if to mirror her mood.

Marjorie stood beside the ticket barrier with her suitcase, squinting, because under the station buildings, fog seemed to thicken the air and her exhaled breath hung like a cloud in front of her. The wartime darkness exaggerated the misery of her own problem. She clasped Diana closely to her, somewhat fearful of the young baby being out of doors after dark on such a dank evening.

Pulling herself up to her full height she went out to the taxi rank. Stepping into the taxi she felt extravagant and they set off into the murky night.

Bettie greeted her with enthusiasm as she always did.

"I'm so sorry we couldn't meet you. Now that Bill's in the Fire Service and I've got Heather it makes things so much more difficult."

Once inside, Bettie admired Diana and hugged them both warmly. It was not long before both children were bedded safely down for the night and Marjorie could share John's suggestion with Bettie and ask her advice. She had been hoping once again that Bettie would offer to have Diana, but still no such offer was forthcoming and now she was here, Marjorie could understand why. With Bettie's own second pregnancy, coping with a third child would be too much to ask, however temporarily. She knew she couldn't be forward and ask outright.

Marjorie had been there a couple of days before Bettie showed her the details of the nursery she had in mind.

"Shall we go over and see it? I could take you this afternoon if you like."

They drove several miles down country lanes before arriving at the pretty little village. They all marched up to the front door of the house and Marjorie, feeling emotional, let Bettie do the talking, explaining that a place was needed for Diana and why.

The lady spoke in a friendly voice with a Dorset accent. Shaking hands she introduced herself.

"I be Missus Frampton," she said with an attractive Dorset drawl. Looking solemnly at Heather she held out her hand.

"Now who be yew?" she asked bending down to her level. Heather hid behind her mother's skirt, but Bettie encouraged her daughter to shake hands with the woman, explaining to Mrs Frampton that her daughter's name was Heather.

Bettie herself then held out her hand.

"I'm Bettie Tapper," she said, "and this is Marjorie Anderson, my sister."

"'Ow de do," said Mrs Frampton clasping Marjorie's hand as she cradled Diana in the crook of her left arm.

Marjorie spoke quietly. "It's my baby, Diana we've

come about."

"Oo aah, come on in then, and let's talk."

Mrs Frampton led the way into the dark hallway and they all sat down in her sitting room at the front of the house.

Marjorie explained the situation. "My husband works in Nigeria as a shipping agent. He wants me to join him as soon as I can. Of course I can't take Diana with me as the war on. We'll be back in England in a year's time. Hopefully the war will be over by then. After that we should be able to travel as a family."

"Aaarrgh. terrible thing this 'ere war," commented Mrs Frampton. "She'll be safe enough wi' me 'ere out in the countryside."

"Well, what exactly are your rates, and what sort of things would she need to bring with her?"

Mrs Frampton told her, adding that she did currently have a space available for a baby.

The nursery appeared to be all right and Mrs Frampton seemed very efficient. She gave Marjorie a list of things that would need to go into the nursery with her baby. She was pleased to see that she would have to take in all her named shawls, bonnets, clothes, vests and nappies as well as bottles. At least this meant that a good standard of hygiene was kept here with babies only using the equipment taken in with them.

Looking round after their initial chat, Marjorie and Bettie noted that the other babies and children appeared to be content. Marjorie promised to let Mrs Frampton know her decision within forty-eight hours.

Those two days were two of the most gruelling Marjorie ever went through as she agonised over what she would do. Alongside that, Bettie helped her to sew on named tapes to the tiny garments as if a decision had been assumed to be made.

In bed that night, Marjorie recalled past events in her life and examined each one before going on to the next, much as a child would examine coloured beads before stringing them together. She even mulled over her decision between marrying John or Alan. Recalling that, she remembered how desperately in love she had been with Alan, and he with her, all because he had no wife to turn to when he needed her. The phrase *anyone can look after your children, but only a wife can look after her husband* came rushing back to her.

Then a worrying thought came to her. *I loved Alan so much, but he wasn't free to marry me and give me children. If I married John just so that I could give birth to my own baby, then it's ironic that now, only a few weeks later I'm having to place that baby in the care of someone else so I can please John.*

Marjorie shook her head and held her breath. The final decision was made. Diana would go to the nursery under the care of Mrs Frampton as soon as it could be arranged.

On the appointed day, Bettie took Marjorie and Diana there with her named belongings. Marjorie was left on her own to say goodbye to her child. At the time she tried to pretend she was just settling her baby to sleep as she tucked her into the cot. She shook hands with Mrs Frampton who told her not to worry and assured her that Diana would be fine.

Bettie drove Marjorie back to the flat, and was deliberately making small talk about ration books and identity cards, anything to divert Marjorie from thinking about her baby. However, the tears could be held back no longer, and Marjorie gave way to her emotions as tears coursed down her face and her sobs echoed noisily around the car. Bettie slowed the car and steered it into a lay-by. She put her arms around her sister in an attempt to comfort her, yet the sadness of her plight caught hold of her too and she began to cry tears of sympathy for Marjorie. As they wept together, Heather gurgled happily from the back seat.

When they eventually reached Bill and Bettie's flat, Marjorie wanted to spend time on her own. She went straight to her room and thought of Diana in her cot. She imagined her little face turning up towards her with her arms outstretched, the chubby little fingers stretching out to hold her mother's finger. Marjorie folded her arms as if to hold in the longing which swept over her. How she wanted to cuddle her child, to keep her safe, to be able to bury her face in the sweet swelling pleats of her skin, cupping her little head in her hand. She knew that Diana would gurgle in response, and in that moment Marjorie missed her so much it was like an unbearable pain.

Soon she had to bear the physical pain of parting from her baby. Up until then, Marjorie had breast fed Diana. As the feeding time became overdue, her breasts would swell and overflow with milk that should have been nourishing her infant. The pain of her taut breasts became almost unbearable and she bound herself up as best she could to try and reduce the flow of milk as speedily as possible, yet the combination of physical pain as well as mental anguish was tormenting.

Marjorie was due to return to Liverpool by train the following day in order to wait for a passage to Nigeria to join John. That was another disadvantage of war – nothing could be booked in advance, one just applied and waited hopefully.

Just after Bettie had put Heather to bed that evening there was a distraught telephone call from Jack.

Grace had collapsed.

Bettie left Bill in charge of Heather and drove Marjorie out to the farm. Once there, Bettie took charge of Marion aged three years and Morgan, aged eighteen months.

Marjorie went upstairs to see Grace. Jack had got her to bed by that time and was sitting next to her, holding her hand, rubbing it as if trying to bring her back to consciousness. He stood up as Marjorie hovered on the landing and went to her. Jack told her that the doctor had been and diagnosed tuberculosis. An ambulance had been summoned.

Marjorie had been concerned when she first saw Grace

after such a long time abroad. Grace herself had suffered a difficult childbirth and had put her lack of energy down to that. As everybody was encouraged to do their bit towards the war effort, she was not going to let that plus a touch of flu stop her. She seemed to have lost a lot of that alertness and sparkle which had been an attractive part of her personality. Nobody else had noticed that she was particularly poorly. Now Marjorie was horrified to see her elder sister lying in bed really ill.

Marjorie rode in the ambulance with Grace to the hospital where she was diagnosed as having TB. She sat by her bedside constantly. Between them the family kept a constant vigil at her bedside, willing her to recover. She died four days later and the family was devastated. How could they have overlooked such a serious illness?

The funeral was a very sombre affair. Grace had been a well-liked and respected person so it was well attended. The service seemed to reverberate with the shock of her untimely death. In wartime such events were frequent, but for fate to creep in by the back door and deliver such an untimely blow in this manner seemed so unfair.

Marjorie stayed on with the family until after the funeral as they all needed one another at such a time.

Now that she had unexpected extra time in Dorset, Marjorie took advantage of it to visit Diana in the nursery. She arrived unannounced and took Mrs Frampton by surprise. Nevertheless, she was shown to the room where, to her horror, she found Diana propped up in her cot with a bottle of milk. That was bad policy. The child might have choked. *To think that Bettie had thought this nursery had such a good reputation!* Marjorie rushed to pick up her precious baby, cuddling her closely to her. After rocking her gently for a while she gave her the remainder of her feed, talking quietly to her. All the while, she felt as if her heart would break. She winded her and changed Diana's nappy afterwards. Even that duty seemed like a privilege when she realised that she would not see her offspring for another year. *She'll have changed a lot by then.*

Marjorie found it hard to drag herself away from her daughter at the nursery, all the while knowing that the longer she spent there, the harder it would be to leave. When she did leave she left part of herself there too.

She caught the bus back to Wimborne, but then stayed on it, travelling on to Poole, all the time concerned about Diana and the apparent lack of love and affection she was getting. Being a nurse, she knew how babies needed to be loved, cuddled and played with. Now she also had an additional worry as Diana could have choked to death on that bottle at such a young age.

Marjorie walked along the quayside at Poole, contemplating all that had happened over the last couple of weeks. She had left her baby in a nursery; her sister Grace had taken ill and died. Having stayed for the funeral, she had naturally wanted to visit Diana and was still shocked from discovering her alone, propped up in her cot with a bottle.

The cold wind bit her face as it blew in from the sea. The sea itself was a dull slate grey flecked occasionally with white and she could taste the salty spray on her lips. She walked quickly, trying to keep warm and trying not to think of Diana propped up in her cot like that just as if she were just a doll. She tried not to think of anything. The cold helped as it was distracting to a certain extent. There were one or two fishing boats tied to their moorings where they dipped and rode the playful waves.

Suddenly the reason for Diana being where she was and her own torpedo memories came flooding back to her. She looked away from the scene as nausea threatened to overcome her. The familiar chains of guilt, self-justification and a fierce protective love clanked around her. Having seen Diana supported by pillows in a semi-sitting position in her cot like that, Marjorie wondered if she was justified in leaving England.

She walked on a little further then sat on a bollard to watch the seagulls as they swooped and screamed overhead. She normally liked this place when it was deserted, yet now she wished she wasn't alone. The tide was out, revealing a small stretch of shiny mud before the shallow water began. Star like patterns of birds' feet were imprinted over one another in the mud and she glanced out to see the dark green blob of Brownsea Island at the edge of the bay.

Bettie will be wondering where I am. Marjorie turned her back on the quay and headed for a bus stop.

The following day, with a heavy heart Marjorie boarded the train to Liverpool. The engine chuffed loudly protesting as it pulled away, then it puffed a small series of steamy bursts as they began to increase speed. The wheels chattered occasionally as they went over the rails. They spoke a repetitive message to her. *You left her behind, going to see John. You left her behind, going to see John.*

Out of the carriage window the angle of the sun was declining as it filtered through tired looking trees that cast their long autumnal shadows across the fields. They stopped at some signals and she could see that some summer plants were twisted with bindweed. Spiders' webs stretched between the browning twigs that had once been colourful heads full of flower petals. Marjorie sighed. She was feeling like a dead flower head herself, leaving part of herself behind her in that nursery.

As the train re-commenced its journey northwards, spots of rain slanted against the carriage window.

"Oh John, please call me soon, so that I can come to you, love you, and put this awful episode behind me." Yet as her heart whispered it, she knew she would never forget her beloved baby.

Chapter Nineteen

Days passed. Weeks passed bringing November with a thick depressing fog. At times Marjorie was unable to see across the road. Occasionally she went out for coffee with new found friends in Formby and they visited her. She still yearned for her baby, but was at least comforted by the fact that Diana wouldn't be experiencing this awful atmosphere down in Dorset. She hoped that Bettie would be able to visit her and cuddle her sometimes.

Life at Formby had been grinding on for just over six weeks, such a long six weeks that it seemed like six months to Marjorie.

Then came the day when she received a cable from John.

CANCEL PASSAGE STOP HOME IN MARCH STOP LOVE JOHN

She twirled round with joy and promptly made a trunk telephone call to Bettie, asking her to accommodate her once again when she would come and collect Diana. Her delight knew no bounds. She was to be reunited with her baby very soon.

* * *

Spring was awakening. Snowdrops and crocus had heralded its coming and now daffodils provided carpets of yellow in the flowerbeds. The harsh skeletons of trees began to be softened by a froth of small green buds as they burst into leaf.

John is coming home! Marjorie could hardly wait to see him again and show him their little daughter. Cuddling her, she often told Diana, "Your Daddy is coming home soon!"

Diana was six months old now and had grown so much,

becoming responsive to different people and their actions. Daphne was also excited, longing to see her father again. Marjorie mused how difficult it must have been for the girl, as John had worked overseas for the majority of his working life. As Elsie had stayed at home with the children they could only ever been together as a family for three months out of every twenty or so.

Nobody was quite sure when to expect him, but Marjorie flung herself into his arms when she opened the door to John one sunny spring afternoon. They hugged one another enthusiastically before he asked to see Diana.

She was asleep, but he stood over her cot enthralled, just the same. They both stood looking down at her with such pride as if nobody had ever produced a baby before.

"No wonder you were so upset at leaving her in that nursery," said John with meaning. "She's a real poppet, isn't she!"

Then they went to see Daphne and Marjorie diplomatically left them together while she made tea. She was glad that Diana had been asleep so that Daphne could lay first claim to her father's attentions.

John was surprisingly keen to do things to help Marjorie with Diana. He explained that he missed so much of Warren and Daphne's early days that he was happy to try his hand at almost anything now. His older children had been born in the 1920s when men and babies just did not mix, as it was not the done thing in those days. Nappy changing was something John refused to do, but giving Diana a feed from a bottle and enticing her to play with a rattle seemed to amuse him as much as it did Diana. One thing he could not stand though was her crying. That was when he would make an immediate escape. Happily this was rare, as she was a good and contented baby.

It was after one of her rare bouts of bawling that John brought up the subject of returning to Nigeria.

"But I couldn't possibly leave Diana in the care of that awful nursery again." protested Marjorie.

"And I must have you with me – it really is hard to live

without you, my new wife. After all, is it too much for a man to ask his wife to come and live with him?" said John not without passion.

Marjorie's face crumpled with concern as she spread her hands and pleaded with her husband. "Oh please, this puts *me* in such an awkward situation. I feel torn in two as I find it hard to live without either of you," she pleaded, recalling yet again the saying that was bandied around the Europeans in West Africa – *anyone can look after your children, but only a wife can look after her husband.*

"If only you could have seen her in that cot! She was propped up like a doll and could have choked on that bottle! Can't you see *my* point of view?" she continued wildly. "Diana isn't just a toy to be shoved back in the toy cupboard when we've finished playing with her!"

She paused for breath, but she had touched on a sore point and John almost roared in reply throwing in some choice language for good measure.

Marjorie was too upset to properly hear the context of what he said laced with swear words that upset her. She just knew that he was angry; very angry. She sighed and swallowed the lump of emotion rising in her throat.

"Maybe some kind of solution will come up." She tried to brush the problem away, at least for the time being; then at least she could get on with the enjoyment of being a family for the short time they had together.

Jessie had been in the Land Army for most of the war. It was about this time that she was demobilised from these duties. She had scarcely been home in Broadstone for more than a couple of days before she was asked to stay with John and Marjorie in Formby for a while.

"Thank you," she said over the telephone. "Perhaps in the next couple of weeks or so. It will be lovely to see you again."

"No, actually, this is more urgent than that. Can you come up within the next couple of days? I've got something I must discuss with you."

"Gracious me! Well, all right then. As I haven't seen you for so long, I'll make you the first port of call the day after tomorrow."

"Thanks Jessie that would be wonderful."

As soon as her sister arrived, Marjorie answered the door to her and slipped outside.

"I'll get my coat and we'll go for a cuppa."

As they walked away from the house Jessie asked, "What about Diana?"

"You timed it perfectly. Daphne has just taken her out for a walk in her pram."

They neared the main street, "Oh, it's lovely to see you again," said Marjorie. "I expect you had to work hard?"

"The days were long but I've enjoyed my time on the land – made new friends – but I'm glad to be home."

They reached the small teashop and Marjorie ordered two cups of tea.

As they sat warming their hands round the cups of steaming liquid, Marjorie said, "Sorry about all this secrecy, but I didn't want you to feel pressured, so only you and I know of this idea of mine."

"Go on."

"Well, you probably heard about Diana being in that awful nursery for six weeks?"

"Yes, yes I did. That must have been awful for you."

"Well, John is due to go back to The Coast soon and he wants me to go with him this time. To be honest, he doesn't just want me to be with him, he is *demanding* that I go. He can't seem to understand that caring for Diana will be a problem. I feel torn apart."

"Oh dear. So what do you want me to do?"

"Jessie, this sounds a bit of a nerve, but have you got a job lined up yet?"

"Well no, not yet, but I want to do gardening and things when I do. I really love it now! I surprised myself when I found it fascinating."

Marjorie interrupted Jessie's musings.

"Jessie, would you be Diana's surrogate mother for the

time I am away in Nigeria with John?" There, she had said it.

"Oh my dear, do you think I could do that? After all I haven't had any training for that sort of thing."

"People like you don't need training to be a mother. It's a matter of common sense and doing what comes naturally."

"I've never really had any experience with children before, especially babies."

"Jessie, I wouldn't ask if I thought you couldn't manage. Bettie has her hands full with both Heather and baby Judith now, so I wouldn't dream of asking her."

"How long would this be for?"

"It could be a year, but more likely to be eighteen months."

"Oh goodness, can I think about it? It's a responsible job you know, looking after someone else's child."

"Jessie, I wouldn't be asking you if I didn't believe you were more than capable. Please give it some serious thought."

"All right, I'll think about it, and let you know my answer when I've done my rounds of the relatives to let them know I'm back in the land of the living."

They hugged one another affectionately and walked back to the house. John was just coming in through the back door, having tidied up some garden rubbish.

"Hello Jessie. Just arrived?" he said.

It was eventually agreed that Jessie would shadow Marjorie while she looked after Diana for a few weeks to give her the confidence she needed to be on her own with her niece.

John was summoned to Warri before Marjorie was ready to go, so she saw him sail from Liverpool and promised to join him as soon as Jessie was installed and felt confident to look after Diana.

Marjorie herself set sail about six weeks later, leaving her child in the capable hands of her younger sister. As Bettie now had Judith, aged six months, Jessie and Diana were to lodge with her for a short while to help one another with the children. Jessie was not very confident to begin with and was glad of Bettie's advice. In return she helped Bettie a little now that she had two daughters to cope with.

aboard t.s. Drottningholm
Sweden American Line
Liverpool
15.8.1945 1.30pm

My dear Bettie and Bill

I have just had a delicious lunch on board consisting of stewed mutton, carrots, potatoes and caper sauce followed by fresh fruit salad with pineapple, melon, peaches, apricots, cherries etc. with cream followed by coffee with cream. It was quite delicious. (Sorry to give you hunger pangs in a time of scarcities) We also had lashings of real butter – marvellous!

I hear rumours that we are not sailing until tomorrow morning.

So far I have met one passenger I know – a Mr Arguth – he was torpedoed with me – and has married since we last met and had left his wife and baby of ten weeks behind. However he hopes his wife will join him about next March if she can get the baby fixed up somewhere.

This is certainly a very nice ship – all newly painted and very well equipped. Most of the stewards and stewardesses seem to be Swedish. I had a bit of a job asking a stewardess where the lavatory was as she couldn't speak English and as you know, I speak nothing else but English! I shall probably get lost twenty times a day. I went to the wrong dining room to start with.

There are lots of babies and children on board – all shapes and sizes. One mother has two babies – one eighteen months and one seven months. I shall probably end up helping her with them – and I'll pretend it's Diana! All the children I believe are bound for South Africa for safety. There are five of them in the dining room and one about six months old (about Judith's size) was at the table next to me and yelled the whole time.

Quite a lot of relatives seem to be on board seeing their friends or relations off – don't know how they got on!

My cabin mate is Mrs Morris of Elder Demsters. She doesn't seem to have arrived yet. I don't know her. The first person I met at the Immigration Office was Mr Lowe of Elder Dempster. I knew him in Lagos. He works in Liverpool now. He said he fixed my cabin for me – Mrs Morris is the only other occupant. It's at the centre of the ship, not on the outside, but one isn't so likely to get seasick there.

The person I sat next to at lunch is going back to South Africa – Johannesburg, I think – to get married as she had an engagement ring on. She said this will be the first time she has left England. I believe our first stop is Freetown and then Cape Town. Everyone for the Gold Coast, Nigeria etc. has to get off at Freetown.

I have been thinking of you all since I left. In fact I can't seem to do anything else – especially Diana of course, bless her! I am ever so grateful to you for taking care of her Jessie. I am leaving with an easy mind knowing she will be well looked after. I expect you will be giving her lunch now and she is probably saying 'Mum mum mum' or making that funny face and singing in her way.

I am writing this in the music room. Seems to be no more now. I'll write a letter to Mother and Father –am not sure what time the mail has to be handed in, but will hand this in to be sure of it then you should get it in the morning.

With lots of love and kisses
Marjorie

PS Lots of love and kisses for Diana from Mummie.

John's house at Warri was long, low and grey, all on one level, but like a lot of European built buildings in West Africa, was resting on stone pillars. Not only did this impede any creepy-crawlies from illegal entry, but helped the air to circulate underneath and cool the building.

Inside, the rooms were large with high ceilings. Two electric fans hung down from the ceiling at each end of the main living area, continually turning slowly to refresh the air. The walls were white and housed tiny gecko lizards in the cracks. These creatures were nocturnal and would emerge at night to journey across the ceiling in their efforts to catch insects. Occasionally they would startle people beneath as they lost their grip and landed on whatever or whoever was directly beneath them.

The main lounge-dining room was huge. Its floor of polished wood gleamed and two large exotic rugs lay one at each end of the room. There was an oak dining table sporting a high gloss with matching high-backed chairs around it. Beyond it was a co-ordinating sideboard where silver candlesticks and a silver salver sparkled expensively. Cool looking comfortable chairs and settee were arranged at the other end of the room. Doors at its centre led outside to a large veranda where wicker chairs and table were grouped. From here were stone steps down to the driveway.

The house was set on a medium sized plot. It was mainly scrub land at the back, but the sides and front had a lot of grass, although this was only at its best in the rainy season. This was bordered by a seemingly endless low well clipped well-clipped box hedge, trained into an archway every so often, sweeping into a perfect circle at the front of the house.

Turkeys and chicken would roam together, scratching and pecking a living where they could, competing with Cheeky, the tabby cat that earned his keep catching rodents he found under the house.

It was to this house that John brought Marjorie, and it

was in this house where they were able to spend the first constructive months building up their marriage together after being wed for over two years. Their love and understanding for one another deepened, yet Marjorie often thought of Diana back home in England with Jessie.

Marjorie was just adjusting to life without her child when a cable arrived informing her that her father had suffered a severe stroke. She was desperate for more news, but this was hampered by the loss of several letters. She discussed with John the possibility of going home to nurse him.

"Marjorie, dear, after all this time, I've only just got you all to myself."

"But he *is* my father."

"He is also father to Bettie, Ronald and Jessie. Surely they can look after him between them? And what about your step-mother? Shouldn't she be the one to nurse him?"

"She isn't very good with medical things. Besides, I'm the only nurse in the family."

"Come on now, he's got his family around him."

"Well, Jessie's back in Formby looking after Diana, Bettie has two girls to look after now and Ronald and Felicia live too far away really because of him being in the Civil Service."

"Your step-mother will see to him."

"Like I said, she's so, so squeamish about illnesses and things."

"She'll just have to get used to the situation, after all she is married to him. Anyway, with so many letters being lost, we don't really know the true situation do we?"

"I would like to do something for him and help nurse him."

"And I don't mind losing a few letters, but I don't want to lose you."

John's kisses were persuasive, but Marjorie remained unsettled.

Ten weeks after receiving the original cable, Marjorie received a second one telling of her father's death. She wanted to grieve, but felt hollow inside. Being abroad and away from the situation for so long had made everything so unreal. It took a long time for her to come to terms with her father's death. Months, even years were to pass before she realised what a wonderful man her father had been, and although she had never been aware of it during his lifetime, she began to appreciate the long hard life he had lived, and the pure goodness of it. She wished they had made sufficient time to get to know one another better when she was adult and able to understand his motivations for doing things.

PART THREE –

MY STORY

Chapter Twenty

Apparently I never crawled, but got about on my bottom. I didn't walk either until my second birthday. Auntie Jessie had organised a small party, consisting of a few adults and their toddlers. She suddenly saw me with bottom pointing skywards as I stretched on all fours, and then uncertainly tried to stand. I tottered a few steps before losing my balance and sitting down heavily.

"Oh look! Diana's started to walk!" exclaimed Auntie Jessie, relieved.

Being August, the small party was a picnic in the garden of *Linwood* in Formby. Sandwiches and cake were spread out on a tablecloth next to a rug in the shade of a tree. Having thrilled everyone by my amazing achievement, I lost interest in my accomplishment and reverted to getting about on my bottom at an incredible rate, apparently keen to investigate the shady patterns of leaves as they danced on the fringe of the rug.

Understandably everyone had been quite concerned about the delay I had shown in walking, as I hadn't even made any attempt to do so. The doctor had examined me and declared I was just lazy.

Now that I had shown everyone I could walk, I was determined to get about speedily in the way I knew best. I set off at a fast rate on my bottom to inspect the colourful flowers in the herbaceous border, gathering grass stains on by best dress and with Auntie Jessie in hot pursuit.

She couldn't wait to write to Marjorie, to tell her the news, and in fact would always write regularly to tell my parents every little detail of my progress and the funny things I said and did.

Photographically there are hundreds of records of me in various poses and she sent a couple of each out to Nigeria at separate times just in case they went astray. Relatives were also given copies, as well as numerous *Polyphotos*. She used to take me to the photographic studios in

Southport and the result would be a foolscap sheet covered in inch square photos of my head and shoulders looking in different directions and with various expressions. There must be so many of these little photos around. I was blonde in all of them, the early ones showing my hair brushed up on top of my head, then into a fascinating sausage curl before developing a head of curly blonde hair. My mother had made and smocked lots of dresses for me, so Auntie Jessie tried to photograph me in each one so that my mother could see her handiwork being worn, even though it was only on black and white film. There are pictures of me standing with chubby legs splayed out on the lawn, bending to pick daisies, paddling at the local beach on Formby shore in a sagging knitted swimsuit, giving my teddy a tea party in the garden. Best of all, there were snapshots of me peeping out of the Wendy House that Warren had built for me out of packing cases. He had painted it too. I vividly remember that.

My mother was thrilled to bits with all the photos that Jessie sent her, and would show them to all their friends, no doubt boring them to death. She missed a lot of things that a normal mother would be thrilled by, such as my first tooth, the first proper words I spoke, and my first steps. However, Jessie faithfully described each incident in detail in her copious letters.

Jessie was also able to reassure John that Daphne had done well at school and passed her matriculation exams. She was about to go to secretarial college. Jessie felt that she and Daphne were developing a good relationship. After all, Jessie was not married to her father and posed no threats or strivings to gain his attention. She felt a compassionate empathy for Daphne, realising what a shock she must have had when her own mother died, never mind to then have her father turn up unexpectedly with a new wife. The war presumably had taken its toll and torpedoed the ship carrying his letter to her telling her all about Marjorie. It was not surprising that Daphne felt so threatened and vulnerable. Jessie fostered a kind of neutral relationship, encouraging Daphne to trust her. She didn't want Daphne to regard all the shocking upheaval in her life as destructive.

She hoped that none of her letters to Marjorie would get lost. They were full of sentimental value.

Jessie had also met Warren on the two occasions when he had been able to get home leave.

He arrived home unexpectedly looking smart in his soldier's uniform and flashed a brilliant smile at Jessie, which, she admitted years later made her feel weak at the knees.

He introduced himself. "Hello, I'm Warren."
"Hello, there, I'm Jessie Heath, Marjorie's sister."
"I believe I've got a new little sister?"
"Yes indeed, Diana's here, come along in."
"Can I see her?"
"Certainly, she's just through there."

So it was that the first time Warren saw me I understand I was on my potty, which was a most unceremonious way for a young lady to receive a gentleman. Nevertheless, apparently I endeared myself to him. Daphne was thrilled to have him home and Jessie was relieved that the pain she had been going through would no doubt start to heal.

I remember Auntie Jessie teaching me all kinds of songs. She used to sing,

The sun has got his hat on, Hip hip hip hooray!
The sun and got his hat on and he's coming out to play!

She could never remember any more, but made up for it by teaching me how to make a noise like a motorbike. I think now, it sounds more like a constipated moped.

Other music hall songs she taught me were

You are my sunshine, my only sunshine.

You make me happy when skies are grey.
You'll never know dear, how much I love you
Please don't take my sunshine away!

also

Daisy, Daisy, give me your answer do.
I'm half crazy all for the love of you!
It won't be a stylish marriage
For I can't afford a carriage
But you'll look sweet upon the seat
Of a bicycle made for two!

Apparently this was so ingrained in me that when I started nursery school, I burst into song whilst engrossed into doing something or other and disturbed to whole class. I never lived this down and it caused me embarrassment for years.

Then there were the nursery rhymes that have been handed down through the family and nobody knows quite where they came from.

Two little dogs sat by the fireside in a basket full of sawdust.
One ran away and the other wouldn't stay in a basket full of sawdust!

That song just consisted of those two lines!

Another was

Spotty and Dotty were two little dogs.
They went to sail on some floating logs.
The logs rolled over, the dogs rolled in!
They got very wet for their clothes were thin!
Bow wow, bow wow, bow wow, bow wow!
Oh dear lackaday, bow wow wow wow!

Spotty and Dotty got out again
They said the river was full of rain

The next two lines always got *la-la la-la'd* as they were never remembered, ending triumphantly with,

Bow wow, bow wow, bow wow, bow wow,
Oh dear lackaday, bow wow wow wow!

This last one had a definite moral to it.

1. As Tommy was walking one bright summer's day
Some rosy-cheeked apples he saw on his way
Saw on his way, saw on his way.
Some rosy cheeked apples he saw on his way.

2. He got on a bough that was ready to fall
And down came poor Tommy, bough, apples and all,
Apples and all, apples and all.
And down came poor Tommy, bough, apples and all.

3. When Tommy got up, he felt very sore
And promised that he would steal apples no more
Apples no more, apples no more.
And promised that he would steal apples no more.

This last song was one my mother also frequently sang to me in later years. She was never sure where she had heard it first. I don't think I'll ever forget any of those tunes.

My very first memory is of sitting in my wooden high chair in the kitchen and being fed mashed up stew by Auntie Jessie. I also recall seeing Warren in bed one morning. What fascinated me was his pillow. He had obviously tossed and turned in the night so that the pillow with its striped ticking cover was bulging out of the pillowcase. I had never seen that before.

Laurence Prenton (born on the same day as me) and I used to play together on our tricycles. I had a nice big blue one. He had one that was probably second hand and a bit of a rattle-trap. Sometimes we swapped toys, but I soon learned my lesson because once he got on my trike I never got him off it. I used to like playing round at his house best. Elbow Lane had lots of deep puddles so, wearing wellingtons we used to ride through them, fascinated by the trail of wash we made behind us. Sometimes, just jumping in them used to amuse us.

In the garden at *Linwood* was a large wooden wheelbarrow – at least I thought it large. Auntie Jessie enjoyed gardening and I enjoyed sitting in the wheelbarrow, especially when she pushed me around in it. She made me the first daisy chain I had ever seen. I couldn't do it for myself, but I picked copious daisies so that she could make necklaces for us both.

Then came the day after eighteen months when my parents came home. My mother especially was eager to see me, see how I'd grown and assess my progress. She and my aunt embraced fondly before I was hauled up to sit on my mother's lap. I was hugged tightly and my mother said, "Hello Diana, Mummy and Daddy are home!" but it seems all I wanted to do was to wriggle free and go to Auntie Jessie.

Eventually Jessie said, "I'll go and make some tea," and bustled off to the kitchen, calling over her shoulder, "While you all get to know one another again."

Apparently I tried to follow her, but the door was closed. My mother swooped down on me and gathered me up in her arms.

"Mummy's here now. Mummy's here now. Don't you remember Mummy?"

Apparently I writhed and struggled free from my mother, generally rejecting her overtures towards me.

John's face stiffened. He seemed to age in that instant.

He took me and held on to me for a few seconds whilst my screams and yells of rejection tore deeply into both my parents. He handed me back to my mother and strode off to find Jessie.

As soon as she came on the scene I held out my arms to her and buried my face in my aunt's neck as my mother let me go to her. Auntie Jessie hugged me in return.

Meanwhile, Marjorie rested her head against John and they thought out what to do next. It was an ugly picture. They had been away for so long that their own child was rejecting them. This reunion, which they had looked forward to and dreamed about for so long had turned out to be a nightmare.

Chapter Twenty-one

As time progressed it became obvious that I depended on Auntie Jessie for all my needs and related well to her. My father made enquiries, but although the war was over, there were still restrictions about children travelling abroad. The three months in England raced by as my parents tried to fit in visits to relations. Apparently Auntie Jessie and I often accompanied them. Marjorie was eternally grateful to her sister for having taken on such a momentous task, thus freeing her to travel back to Nigeria with John.

This time when my parents left Liverpool, Auntie Jessie also took me to the docks "to see Mummy and Daddy on the big ship". This must have been quite an outing for me, as I became increasingly excited at the prospect, although my mother must have had such a heavy heart.

The air was humid and appeared to slow the pace of everything. All around her, people seemed to be going about their business in slow motion. However, an afternoon shower of rain refreshed the air and the evening began to soften into night. As the sun set to the west of the silver stretch of Mersey, it silhouetted the cranes criss-crossing the sky and made cameos of the black funnels as their great ships rested at berth. One of these would take my parents away once again. Gulls gliding gracefully on currents of air above us completed the scene.

My father was the first to break the silence.

"Well, I'm afraid we must leave you now. By the time we actually set sail it will be far too late for this little lady." He chucked me under the chin and I held out my arms to him, grinning delightedly now I was more used to this couple who said they were Mummy and Daddy.

However this display of affection brought tears to my mother's eyes as she and my aunt hugged one another warmly.

"Don't worry about a thing. We'll be fine – and I'll write as much as I have time for, and send you lots of photos."

Marjorie nodded her thanks and reached out to me for a cuddle. She never thought she could do this; saying a prolonged goodbye to her own child, let alone more than once.

John patted her shoulder. "Come along my dear, we must go on board now."

Jessie took me and there were more hugs and kisses all round before my father finally led my mother away.

Apparently I pointed to their retreating figures saying in my childish tone, "Mummy going on big ship!"

Jessie thrilled to hear my voluntary use of the word *Mummy*, but it was too late for my mother to hear.

Yet again, Jessie was true to her word and sent Marjorie and John many snapshots of their daughter who was developing so rapidly she would spend much time in descriptive correspondence.

Auntie Jessie and I had a rapport between us. We loved one another. I depended on her for everything, and no doubt she had trouble trying to curb her true emotions towards me, knowing that I would be handed back to my parents in a year's time. Then she would have to relinquish her post of foster mother and become an aunt again.

By this time Daphne had a full time secretarial post away from home. This was at Heronwater, a boarding school for boys in north Wales. She seemed to be enjoying the life she was making for herself, just far enough away so that visits to Formby were not impossible if she wanted to look up old friends,

During Daphne's visits she would comment on how well Diana was faring. As she played with me, apparently Jessie mused that we seemed to get on well and that I appeared to be more secure with Daphne than with my own mother. She wondered how long it would take me to be truly safe in the love and knowledge of my own mother whom I knew so little about. Then she would shake her head, annoyed with herself for even thinking such things. Jessie herself had mixed feelings; she was thrilled to be able to witness the formative years of her niece, yet so sad for Marjorie because of all she was missing.

Jessie and Daphne were getting along well together too. Jessie imagined it must be because she didn't pose a threat or rival for her father's affections. This enabled Daphne to get to know Marjorie through the stories Jessie was able to relate.

Marjorie recited all the truths to herself yet again. It was good for Diana to be in England in the healthier climate. She could play in the shade under the large tree shading the lawn and pedal her tricycle round the house. Marjorie could picture so clearly how she would be, her blonde curls flopping low over the handlebars as she bent to put every effort into treading the pedals on her bright blue trike. It was good for her to be with Jessie – indeed it was very good of Jessie to look after her. She would give her time generously to her niece; certainly all the snapshots and letters reflected this. She had received so much literature about Diana now it would fit into a book already. Marjorie wondered how much had been lost at sea; it would be awful if *any* of Jessie's efforts had been wasted. At least now the war was over they were more likely to receive every report that Jessie sent.

After a couple of months, Marjorie found herself more drawn into the social life of Warri once again, and she mourned less for her daughter. There were often times on her own, when she would pore over the photographs and re-read Jessie's letters, pondering on what they might be doing at that particular moment in time. Then John would come home, or she would be distracted and the moment would pass until the next letter had arrived.

Towards the end of their stay in Warri, John heard that travel restrictions had been lifted. He and Marjorie clasped one another in glee.

"That means we can have Diana here with us next time!"

"Yes, it will be quite an experience for her – for me too, as it will be my last trip out here before I retire from the coast."

"Oh John, won't it be wonderful to be a family again, and to be able to celebrate your retirement by having our daughter to stay here with us. I must write and tell Jessie straight away!"

Marjorie duly wrote to Jessie and longed for the time when she and Diana could be reunited, now that they had a proper family future in view.

Time slipped by and John and Marjorie returned to Liverpool, eager to take over the responsibility of their child. However, the intervening year had apparently made me all the more convinced that Jessie was my rightful mother figure.

As time went on, I was still dependent on Auntie Jessie for everything and refused my mother's administrations. I would allow her to stay and play and do things that a visitor might do with a child, but Auntie Jessie was certainly the centre of my life.

My parents decided it was time to have a chat with Jessie, so after I had been put to bed one evening, they talked things over.

Marjorie tried to explain, but could not. "You tell her, John."

"Basically Jessie, we're finding it very hard to have our daughter reject us the way she is."

Jessie nodded her agreement.

"Now that travel restrictions have been lifted, we shall obviously want to travel back to Nigeria as a family, and Diana will need to realise that we are her parents."

Jessie bit her bottom lip.

"You have done an amazing job in looking after Diana and bringing her up so well."

"Thank you." It was one of Jessie's attractive traits, being grateful for the smallest things in life.

"I'm afraid we're going to have to ask you to leave so that Diana only has us to rely on and do things for her."

Jessie nodded again wordlessly.

"Oh Jessie," Marjorie went to her and knelt on the floor at her feet. "I'm so sorry it had to end like this." She shrugged. "It just goes to show what a good job you've done!"

Jessie patted the hand on her knee.

"I understand. It will be a wrench to leave the little mite, especially after the happy times we've had together. She is such a good child you know."

"We were dreading this moment, and how to put it into words."

Both Jessie and Marjorie shed a few tears, and then, for John's sake, they changed the topic of conversation.

A week later, Jessie saw an advertisement in the paper for a 'live-in housekeeper /gardener' in the Lake District. She applied for it and secured the post. She had a feel for the land and would enjoy this challenge. She returned to Formby looking very pleased with herself.

"You look like the cat that got the cream, Jessie. What's up?" asked Marjorie when she saw her.

"I've got a job, a living-in post in the Lake District."

"Doing what?"

"Well, it's just what I shall enjoy, being a housekeeper-cum-gardener. It will be in a large house overlooking Lake Coniston with a middle-aged couple who have adult children living away from home. They want a chauffeur as well and are prepared to pay for me to have driving lessons."

"Wonderful! It certainly sounds as though you've landed on your feet. You're sure this is something you *want* to do. I do rather feel we're pushing you out."

"I'm really going to enjoy it, Marjorie. They're such a nice couple and want me to consider myself as part of the family. To be honest, I think they want someone to mother now that their children have left home."

"When do you start?"

"At the beginning of next month, which is a Monday, and it's just over two weeks away."

"Do you think we could try grafting Diana a bit more on to me by then?"

"We can certainly try."

They tried. I certainly loved my aunt, so while I went shopping with my mother, I would be asking after Auntie Jessie all down the road, and was much reassured when she was at home when we returned. Each time we went out, the trips became longer, and the times that Auntie Jessie left the house without me were longer. However much they tried I would never go to sleep until Auntie Jessie had been up to kiss me goodnight. I must have made things quite hard for everybody all round.

The day eventually came when Jessie left Liverpool. John and Marjorie took me to the station to wave to her as the train left the station. They thought it would be best if I saw her actually physically go away and thus make a clean break of things. I was meant to realise that Marjorie was my mother and chief carer from that point on.

My mother said she found the first few days were heart-rending as I frequently cried out for "Anti Dessie! Anti Dessie!" then go searching for her in every nook and cranny. After the first couple of nights when, apparently, I cried myself to sleep, I began to realise that this couple who called themselves *Mummy* and *Daddy* would now dominate my life.

When she had her first spell of time off, Marjorie asked Jessie to tea, but they decided in advance that she wouldn't stay long in case her presence upset me all over again. Jessie, as always, was very understanding and made use of the rest of her time to visit other friends she had made in Formby as well.

Apparently I was overjoyed to see Auntie Jessie again. I took her by the hand and sat close to her all through tea, snuggling next to her on the settee for a cuddle afterwards.

When it was time for Jessie to leave, she and I engaged in a big long cuddle, which apparently satisfied me and I bravely waved her goodbye as she walked down the path. At last I seemed to have made a positive step towards accepting my parents.

Years later, my mother was to tell me that upon reflection of all this, she was amazed at herself. To think that she who loved babies almost to distraction when she was a child, trained as a children's nurse, doing midwifery, then marrying practically to ensure she had a child of her own. She wondered whether she should have waited and married the man she truly loved. She didn't deserve a baby. She had actually abandoned that child to the love of another woman, eventually dispensing with Jessie to force the young child to depend on her mother, to love her mother. When put baldly like that, Marjorie realised she must get a hold on herself as she was being silly now and must realise that from now on her responsibilities lay to her husband and child from hereon.

John was to retire from the Elder Dempster Shipping Company in 1949. This was to be his last tour there as he was due to be retired in October when he was 55, quite normal when serving abroad in those days. To ensure Diana was properly settled with Marjorie in her own home before removing her to foreign parts, she stayed behind, fiercely protective, attending to her every need, delighting in reading stories and generally gaining Diana's trust. Together they sailed aboard the *Aureol* from Liverpool bound for Lagos in July 1948. I celebrated my fourth birthday on board and had a cake made for me, so I felt quite special, although overawed.

Unfortunately one of the children on board was suffering from measles. Her mother didn't bother about keeping her in quarantine, so all the children on board caught the disease. I was confined to our cabin for what seemed like an eternity, once my mother realised I had measles too.

She came every so often and read to me from A.A.Milne's books of *Winnie the Pooh* and so it was that I became introduced to my favourite books of childhood. They continued to have special preference all my life. I did have my moments while thus confined though. My mother had bought some black and white postcards of the interior of the ship but I found a blue *Biro* pen and coloured in all the chairs and other bits of furniture. I can remember how annoyed she was. It was the first time she had actually been angry with me, and I can still remember how miserable I felt.

During the journey we docked at Las Palmas in the Canary Islands for a while. Passengers were allowed to go ashore and my mother took me to the market on the quayside where, amongst other things, dolls of every description were being sold. She said she would buy me one, encouraging me to have a plump black one, but I opted for a dainty one with European looks and dressed all in pink which was my favourite colour. I called her Sally. She had dark brown eyes and thick, curly shoulder-length brown hair. I loved her. The snag was that she was as delicate as she looked and her small pointed fingers eventually snapped off as I cuddled her too hard.

Chapter Twenty-two

My father met us at Lagos in his huge car – it certainly seemed so to me at the time! It was dark as we drove about fifty miles east to Warri and the tropical forest on either side looked very frightening to me, I remember from my curled up position on the back seat, Frequently I peeped out of the window. "Are there lions and tigers living in there?" My parents just laughed.

When we arrived at his house my father presented me with a huge doll that was almost as tall as I was. He was thrilled by my response, but I wasn't too sure of what to make of it. Added to this, I could see from the electric light that he had grown a moustache since I had last seen him and I wasn't too sure about him either. The doll could walk, and when laid down, would close her eyes and say 'Mama'. She was very big for a little one like me to manipulate, but I did enjoy her eventually.

It was late, so I was whisked straight into bed and didn't meet any of my father's staff until the next day.

They were called Richard and Sunday, the Africans often naming their babies after the day of the week on which they were born.

Richard, the first steward said, "Hello Diana," and held out his hand to shake mine.

I was so terrified by his dark appearance – the first time I had seen a black man close to that I ran away straight into the arms of Sunday, the second steward.

For the sake of politeness my mother made me stay and shake hands, then apologised and took me away to meet *Cheeky* the tabby cat.

It wasn't long before I conquered my shyness and became friendly with the African staff. I was a little hesitant about meeting Cook though, as he sometimes had quite a temper. I remember I liked Richard the best and he always made time for me, answering my many questions. I probably kept him from doing his work!

I still remember the sight of the little pink gecko lizards. They would creep out of the smallest cracks in the walls and ceiling after dark to hunt their prey of insects, darting jerkily over the walls and ceiling, clinging on with their little sucker feet. Sometimes they would fall and have to work their way back up again. My parents were quite enthralled by my fascination for these creatures, but I was really being wary, watching in case one lost its grip, to ensure I wouldn't be underneath it!

European mothers took their children to a local nursery school run by them so that at least their young enquiring minds would be kept active. My mother taught me to read herself and I remember surprising her by reading a simple book all the way through. It was about a little robin, including the phrase '...*and they were FLABERGASTED!*' in the centre of it. She was thrilled and so was my father when he came home that evening.

My mother sometimes took me to see the market displayed in the road that ran adjacent to our house. This market was quite different from those in England where everything would be neatly arranged on tables. In Warri the stall holders sat on the side of the road with their wares spread out before them. I remember seeing food in direct contact with the road, and even at that young age I realised that it should have been kept clean. There would be flies crawling all over the meat and my mother often remarked that she must make sure Cook never bought meat from the market! Sometimes the smells were so awful to our refined western noses so we tried to restrict our somewhat rare glimpses of the market, to the African pottery, brightly coloured fabrics, beaded jewellery, caged birds and chickens that would be wandering off all over the place.

All the colours were gaudy and garish and there were many interesting things to see. The women wore long draped dresses and they balanced and carried shopping and suchlike on their head which fascinated me. Most seemed to walk tall, and had good posture, so maybe that was why. The ladies used part of their dress fabric to secure their baby to their back from where it would view the world comfortably, or sleep unawares as the world passed it by.

Then came the night when I witnessed my first tropical thunderstorm. Everyone else was so used to them that they had not thought that I might be scared. The rolls and crashes of thunder were so loud it sounded to me as if all the trees around were tumbling down onto the house, or even that the house itself was falling down – or both. By contrast the lightning flashes were so bright and frequent, I was terrified, because I didn't know what was happening. Sobbing, I burst into my parents' bedroom, where I now believe I probably interrupted a bit of 'slap and tickle' as my mother's breasts were exposed to view. I had never seen either of my parents even partially undressed, and for a while I forgot my fear and became fascinated with my mother's torso.

By this time my father realised why I had rushed into them and started playing a game with me. He took me over to the window where we could see the rain lashing down outside. He told me that there was a crotchety old elephant in the sky who had lost his glasses so was looking for them. The lightning flashed again, its many forks lighting the whole sky.

"See! That was the elephant striking another match to look for his glasses." said my father.

Then the thunder crashed.

"He must have turned the wardrobe over that time to look for them." he said solemnly.

The lightning flashed again.

"He's struck another match," commented my father mildly.

The thunder roared overhead.

"That was a dressing table he turned over that time."

"How do you know which piece of furniture he turned over?" I asked.

"Oh, I just do. You try next time."

So I did.

"That was the elephant striking a match."

My father smiled and nodded in agreement.

The thunder boomed and rumbled loudly.

"I think that was a chest of drawers he turned over as I could hear all the drawers falling out!" I said, thrilled to join in the game.

"Very good, I think that's what it was too."

That's how the game of elephants in thunderstorms developed in our family. I have never had a fear of thunderstorms because of the game my father invented for me. Neither of us believed it, but we each tried to outdo the other as we made up the story! When we returned to the UK the thunderstorms seemed very tame by comparison.

Now that I had passed babyhood and was a little girl who could be communicated with, my father doted on me, and we related well to one another as we got to know one another better. I can remember him teaching me how to make boats out of paper that actually sailed on water, as well showing me how to make little purses out of empty cigarette packets. He smoked a lot, so I made many of them.

There are numerous incidents I remember about life in Nigeria. One was the fancy dress party for the European children when my mother dressed me as a fairy. There was a regatta to welcome the sloop. I was given a special seating arrangement for this because for some unknown reason I developed a huge swollen foot and ankle. Another time I developed a massive boil on my left knee. (I still bear the scar to this day!) My father was quite fascinated by its size, suggesting it could be a carbuncle, so despite the pain, I began to feel quite proud of it. Then there was the Governor's Day involving all kinds of parades in front of the Governor seated on a covered dais. I remember I was terrified of the *ju-ju* men dressed in black and purple and waving their black rods. (It wasn't until much later that I discovered the sticks to be made of blackthorn with macabre carvings of cow's skulls and a snake on them). These men had covered faces and were walking on tall stilts, looking such a terrifying sight, that I yelled and screamed in terror so had to be taken home.

I remember many of my parents' friends, many of whom when they retired, came to live near us in the south of England, enabling the friendship to continue. There was Reg and Hilda Handby and their adult daughter Joan. Reg had worked for the United Africa Company. Eva and Horrie Wood were another couple. The family who interested me was Dr Bruce Nicol, a dietician, and his wife Mary with their two children, Christopher, aged eight and Diana aged two (when we first met them in Warri). Knowing who was being spoken to became complicated, so we became Diana Major and Diana Minor. I thought Christopher was a fascinating boy to be with and made me aware of many things that interested him, such as philately and his Meccano set. When we were a little older, he also taught me how to play Canasta like the adults used to, and we eventually got quite good. He also tried to teach me how to play Mah Jong in a kind of way. My father and Warren later investigated the rules more fully, but none of us ever got the hang of this Chinese game. My father used to be amused by the sight of Christopher and I as we tucked into *Groundnut Chop* at lunch time. No matter how carefully we ate, we always ended up with orange stains round our mouths.

I used to enjoy playing with *Cheeky* the cat, but he wasn't used to people, so preferred his privacy and catching rodents from under the house.

There was a miniature box hedge growing and winding round paths that was really the front garden. I used to walk in and around it, pretending it was my own special town.

My father finally retired from what the Europeans called 'The Coast' at the age of fifty-five. He and my mother were given a tremendous send off by their many friends, and attended lots of parties given in their honour.

The three of us set sail on board the ship *'Sekondi'* in November 1949. I remember being fascinated by a little black kitten living on board which the sailors had rescued from a dustbin. I would search for it every afternoon while the adults were taking a nap. If a sailor saw it before I did, he would sometimes bring it to me. One of the crew members told me that in the previous century, sailors believed that having a black cat on board ship would mean that they would never drown. Having rescued this little animal from such a cruel fate, they felt their luck was in.

Perhaps the stormy weather that the ship passed through between Nigeria and Liverpool was a hint of things, which were in store for John and Marjorie.

Chapter Twenty-three

Bill Tapper had heard of a three-bedroom house to rent in Colehill about a mile away from where they lived over their furniture shop in Wimborne. Living in such a large house in Formby away from my mother's relatives seemed rather silly, when we could move south to be near family. The house was called *Pademba*. My father was reminded of a colleague in West Africa called Mr Biddle who used to live near the prison in Pademba Road when my father was working out in the Gold Coast. It transpired that it was this same man who intended to rent this property. We moved into it just before Christmas and I started my official schooling at the age of 5½ years in January 1950.

My mother had taught me well, as I was already ahead of my classmates. Just as I was enjoying myself and revelling in the teacher's praise, I was summoned to go up to the next class, where I found things more difficult, especially the sums.

I was not aware of this at the time, but apparently we were going to be short of money. My father needed to find a job, and these were scarce in those post war years. To begin with, he cycled to do office work in one of the many nissen huts on the Kingston Lacy estate, but this was only a temporary post as the army were soon to demolish them.

My mother discovered that a night nurse was needed at St Audrey's nursing home very near to us, so she applied and secured the part-time post of nurse there. She worked three nights one week and two the next, although in practice, she was often asked to do more. No doubt this helped with the family finances too. Consequently I had to be very quiet when I was at home during the day time as she would be sleeping. Her nights on duty were not always busy, so she began to make a lot of smocked dresses. Initially they were for me, but as they got admired, people would ask her to make little babies dresses or rompers. Latterly she was receiving orders from as far away as

Scotland and Cornwall. Her neat handiwork was delicate as she always took great pride in her work. She only charged twenty-five shillings (£1.25 pence in today's money) for each garment, which even I, at that young age, thought ridiculously low, especially as we needed the money and she had bought all the materials to work with.

Eventually my father found a job as a petrol pump attendant at Rodway's Garage in Wimborne. I don't suppose he gained a great deal of job satisfaction from it, but at least it meant that more money was coming in to the household.

Shortly after this, I had to go into Wimborne Cottage Hospital in order to have my tonsils removed in 1950. I had always been plagued with colds, having my chest and back regularly rubbed with *Vic* which I hated, as it used to feel all sticky. My father used to make me breathe in steam from basinfuls of hot *Friars Balsam* whilst underneath an old towel – another thing I hated doing, until he invented a game of crocodiles and I was roaring at him while he pretended to be another crocodile that was frightened of me. It all helped me take those take those deep breaths of the hated fumes.

I was admitted to the hospital, for a week's stay. In those days parents were not allowed to be with their children at all. Everything felt so strange, being taken away from my mother by a nurse who undressed me and put this funny gown on me. I recall my mother passing the window of our downstairs ward and waving to me in bed, having left a pile of comics for me. I screamed and cried so much, I had more of a sore throat before the operation than after it! The only good thing about that whole episode was being soothing fed jelly and ice cream.

By that time we had a beautiful semi long-haired grey cat called Smokey. She had been a stray, but we took her in and I loved her. However, she seemed to supply most of the neighbourhood with copious kittens. I would write long stories about each one. After a while I was told she had a new home to go to, but I would be allowed to keep one of her kittens. I chose a fluffy black one and called him Bundles. He was the first pet who had truly belonged to me and he would even follow me into bed, much to my mother's disgust. I was devastated when he got run over by an old lady driving her car. Our next-door neighbour witnessed the incident and came to tell my father. Together they dug a hole in the garden and buried him there. The driver obviously hadn't realised what she'd done. I was very upset.

After that I was allowed to have another kitten. We went to Uncle Jack's farm and I chose a sandy coloured boy, probably a cousin of Bundles. I unimaginatively called him Sandy. Even my father, who was a dog lover, became fond of him and discussed him with visitors in the same way people discuss their babies. However Sandy eventually got run over by the same lady and the same neighbour witnessed the event. History repeated itself.

About two years after having my tonsils removed I managed to fall off the back of a moving bus. Miss Irene Smart, one of our teachers lived in Colehill, was happy to see three or four of us on and off the bus to school each day. I remember the fare was one penny each way (that's in old money) and how vexed people were when the fare went up to 1½ pennies! I used to feel very grown up as I gave the conductor my penny in exchange for a green cardboard ticket.

On this particular occasion we got on the bus as usual, alighting at the stop near the bottom of St John's Hill, just opposite our school. I always used to hang back till last, being both small and timid. Then I would keep hold of the shiny pole at the back of the bus, sliding down it until my foot touched the ground before I let go. Unfortunately, the conductor did not see me hanging on so signalled to the driver that the passengers were clear. The bus jerked away while I still had hold of it and I was thrown into the road much to everyone's consternation. I remember being in pain, frightened by all the blood, crying a lot and sitting on a chair in the classroom being examined by the teacher and then the headmistress. Eventually my parents were summoned and I was taken to see our GP, Dr Hannay. I also had to visit the school's medical practitioner, and I hated this, because she was rough and I hurt so much. My mouth was cut about inside and out. My mother was told I had one cut the doctor could see daylight through. I had large scabs on my face and ear for ages. When my first tiny teeth came out they were replaced with huge tombstones by comparison, all growing crooked, mainly as a result of that fall. I must have cost the NHS a fortune in metalwork for all the various different orthodontic work I needed to re-align them.

My mother's step-mother (Hilda) died when I was six, so that must have been in early 1951. She refused to go into hospital. As the weeks passed, my mother believed she was suffering from cancer of the throat. Her former slim figure had now reduced to such an angular thinness that it was pitiful to see. Aunt Margaret came from Wincanton to stay with her and nursed her a bit during the daytime. My mother did all the night nursing when she wasn't on duty at the nursing home. As it had been with Grace, nobody realised just how ill Hilda was. Marjorie recalled how awful she had looked before people became aware that she was terminally ill. Once again, those closest to the sick person had not noticed anything untoward.

By this time, Bill Tapper had expanded his furniture shop in Wimborne so he, Bettie and family had moved to a house in Broadstone, fairly near to Bettie's mother. Uncle Bill would provide the transport for Marjorie to go to and from Broadstone thus enabling her to nurse her step-mother.

These journeys fitted in well with everyone's itinerary.

John, my father, was long-suffering through it all, as his wife was rarely at home.

I remember my mother coming up to me one Saturday morning, waking me and saying, "I'm sorry dear, but Nana died in the night."

In my childish way, all I could say was, "Never mind

Mummy, she'll soon be an angel," before turning over and going back to sleep.

Daphne moved south to live with us shortly after this and used her secretarial skills at *Poole Pottery* where her knowledge of foreign languages was often in demand.

In 1951 it was *Festival of Britain* year, a celebration meant to cheer up the country after the long dark war years. In Wimborne there was a pageant and procession which I was looking forward to. Daphne had made herself a beautiful mauve dress with a matching Juliet cap intending to enter as Juliet. I was desperate to go, but instead managed to contract chicken pox so badly that my spots almost joined together. I therefore had to stay at home and be dabbed with *Calamine* lotion. This was initially soothing, but as it dried, seemed to make the pustules itch even more.

Shortly after this I remember our teacher telling us all about the death of King George VI in February 1952, and we had a short silence in class to honour him. I went home from school and mentioned this to my parents, but they didn't believe me and told me that it was very naughty to say things that weren't true, especially in matters like that. I said nothing.

However, they apologised to me next day when *The Daily Telegraph* plopped through the letterbox carrying a full front page portrait of the king surrounded in a black print frame. He bore such a striking resemblance to my father and I was more fascinated by this, rather than the fact that my parents had apologised to me, when normally they would want an apology from me for something I'd done wrong.

Daphne married Leslie Young when I was eight years old. I was her only bridesmaid in a duck egg blue dress that my mother had made and smocked in burgundy red for the occasion. She had sewn some red silk anemones to match the smocking onto a piece of pale blue ribbon and finished off the circle with white elastic. I would have loved it, except Daphne wanted me in a short dress and not the long one I had longed for. Worse was to come; my mother insisted that I wore my hair in the two thick plaits just like I always did. I wanted my hair long and beautiful. Angrily I stomped up the aisle with white knicker-elastic showing at the base of my hairline. I was not a happy bridesmaid that day. I forgot my wrath at the reception, held at *Pademba* at the sight of all the food that was on display!

It was two months before my ninth birthday when the coronation of Queen Elizabeth II took place on 2nd June 1953. Mrs Phyll Bloomfield, the matron of *St Audrey's* nursing home where my mother worked had invested in a brand new television set for the occasion and invited many people to view the ceremony. There was a long tiled hall ending in shallow red carpeted stairs. The small screened, but bulky black and white television set was positioned with its back to the front door and people sat on chairs facing it all the way up the hallway, with us children sitting on the stairs where, although the screen was small, we had a good view if we stared hard enough.

After that I became friendly with one of the nurses' daughters called Rosemary. We used to re-enact the coronation in our play many times, but it always had to be on our stairs because she lived in a cottage where the stairs were dark, narrow and twisty, ending with a door. Warren had made me a crown out of old pink stiffened lampshade fabric. Wearing picnic rugs draped round our shoulders, we used to play the part where the Duke of Edinburgh, followed by all the other barons paid homage to Her Majesty. Singly, they climbed the few steps to her throne, then bowed and kissed her hand before backing reverently away. After a while, I got fed up with being the Duke of Edinburgh and was careless about how I reversed down the stairs and slipped. It caused great mirth, so I did it again. After that, we competed to see who make the other laugh the most, so I got to be the queen sometimes after all.

Pademba was a detached house that had a sloping roof on both sides. Off my bedroom was a little cupboard I could just stand up in at its highest point, and it ran the whole width of the house. It looked dark and creepy with its bare joists and woodwork. Christmas decorations and suchlike were stored here, but there was an old chest lodged just inside the door which served as a table, a shop counter or a serving hatch for me. I could just stretch my bedside light to stand on it. This transformed my bedroom into a shop, a café (using my dolls tea set) and all kinds of exciting things when I had a friend with me. However, if my mother were sleeping I would have to play downstairs. It was frustrating if I had a friend and we wanted a board game from the drawer at the bottom of my big heavy wardrobe. It made far too much noise to try and get something from it once my mother had gone to bed, so I would try and think of everything I might want and take it all downstairs beforehand.

We had a septic tank rather than main drainage. There would be a dreadful smell of sewage when the lorry came round to empty it. We could not afford to heat the water every day of the week. Another ritual of my childhood was bath nights. These were held twice a week. I would have first bath, then a little more hot water was added and my mother would bathe. Lastly it would be my father's turn, though I sometimes wondered whether the water was more like mud by the time he stepped into it. As I had long hair, I used to hate having my hair washed. It seemed more soap got in my eyes than on my hair. My mother used to use *Drene* shampoo which came in a little flat green bottle.

When I was young, I had to wear a vest, thin white cotton ones in summer and thick cream woollen ones with short sleeves in winter. On top of that would be a liberty bodice with lots of flat buttons. I must have looked much plumper than I really was.

My father then became the proud owner of a black and blue coloured Morris 8 car around this time. (I still remember the registration number – AJB 834.) He was often tinkering about under its bonnet as there was always something that wasn't quite right with it. Most frequently the indicators didn't flick out, or didn't light up when they did so. I remember Warren trying to help my father with this problem once.

He turned to me saying, "By the time we've finished with this car, both indicators will come out at once so we'll be able to take off and go anywhere we please!"

Something I had always wanted to do was to learn ballet dancing. In those days people only got to do this if they lived near London or were well off. We were neither.

I still wanted some ballet slippers. I have always enjoyed making things with my hands. My mother found some old white silky fabric that was a bit marked, but she gave it to me. I would make my own ballet shoes! Cheerfully I stood on an old cornflake packet and drew round my feet. I put a lot of time and energy creating those ballet shoes, but was so disappointed by the sloppy fit afterwards. I hadn't realised that ballet shoes have soles that are so much smaller than the feet! I wore them as slippers in the summer.

Another of my projects was tying up the curtains with string, so that with one pull on the correct string and the lounge curtains would sweep together. That was the plan. Although the idea was good, it was the string that was too rough as I only had thick garden twine to work with.

My mother made a few friends at the nursing home where she worked. One nurse, Kit Rummery, whose daughter was Rosemary lived out at Gaunts Common in a little cottage. Her father, Jack Rummery worked on a farm. Our fathers would take us to visit one another some Saturdays in the car. Mr Rummery had a Ford 8 car – a similar size and shape to ours.

It was raining heavily when my father took me to see Rosemary one Saturday. We travelled along a narrow country road that dipped and twisted. Rounding a bend we motored down a steep incline into a deep puddle. The car's engine flooded with water and we shuddered to halt. I shall never know why my father clambered out of the car, manoeuvred himself to sit on the roof to remove his shoes and socks rather than doing this in the car. He then set off on foot to get help, leaving me in the car, terrified that I would be swept away and drowned. As it was, it just needed another man to help push us out and eventually all was well again.

On washing days my mother would deal with a huge boiling pan of white washing of handkerchiefs, tea towels and towels on the stove, along with a 'bluebag' (a little cotton drawstring bag containing a cube of blue chalky substance), which, its makers claimed would enhance the brilliance of white washing. Apart from sheets and tablecloths that did get sent to the laundry, she used to do all our washing by hand in the stone sink with wooden draining boards on either side. Wash days were usually Mondays, unless my mother was working. I remember helping her sometimes, turning the handle of the mangle as she fed the wet washing through it to squeeze out as much moisture as possible before hanging it all outside on the line to blow in the wind to dry.

My father's shirt collars and cuffs had to be starched. To do this, some *Robin* starch powder was shaken from its packet into a basin and mixed with water. The clean items would be left in this to soak for a while before ironing.

Everyone dressed to look smart in those days. Jeans were clothes of the future and women wearing trousers were a rarity. Casual clothes such as t-shirts did not yet exist either. It seems strange to think of life without them now.

Miss Vaughan was an elderly lady who went to *St Audrey's* nursing home where my mother worked to recover from some kind of illness. She could not afford the fees to stay on, but did not have the confidence to live on her own again. Consequently she came to us and lived as our lodger. I remember clattering up and down stairs with meals on trays for her. Up until then Warren and his wife Iris, who lived in London, used to visit us during the school holidays. They both taught art, with Iris specialising in pottery. We didn't see much of them at all then, although from then on, when they came south they would stay with Daphne and Leslie who lived in Sturminster Marshall, a nearby village. Eventually they emigrated to Tasmania, and from there moved to Melbourne in Australia itself.

After lunch one day Warren said, "Diana, will you draw me something? Anything you like."

I drew an angular childish version of a cup and saucer.

He didn't criticise it, but asked, "When you saw that cup and saucer on that table did you really see that?"

I hadn't. I had just drawn a simple series of lines.

He patiently gave me a short lesson on how the cup had a curved handle and that the saucer was not a straight line underneath, continuing by adding light and shade so that his drawing looked just like the one on the table.

I was fascinated by it.

Sweets had been strictly rationed because of wartime shortages. My mother used to buy *Mars* bars and cut them into thin slices, thus making two last a week between us all. I was only allowed to have a slice if I finished all my lunch. I was somewhat finnicky over savoury food in those days. This was due mainly having to be almost force-fed some awful school dinners. However little I was given, I was keen to push it aside and leave a pudding-sized hole in my stomach, but that wasn't allowed either until I had eaten a certain amount of the *meat and two veg*. Happily I began to quite like lunch when it was home-cooked.

I enjoyed Saturdays when the delivery man from *Cowdry's* baker called to deliver loaves of bread from his huge oblong basket. He always wore a trilby hat, winter and summer and appeared to have just one tooth. I was never very keen on bread normally, but I would happily chew crusty chunks off the warm loaf.

It was around this time when I accidentally spilt sugar on my slice of bread and butter one tea time. Then sugar sandwiches became the treat of the day until my mother discovered Fry's chocolate spread and brought some home. I can still visualise it, sitting on the table in its waxed cardboard carton.

Fridays were the worst days as we often had fish which I hated. However, if my mother was sleeping, and my father was at home, he used to cook bacon and egg. He was an absolute whizz at making this just how I liked it, and would cut the rinds off the bacon, frying them separately to make little crispy curls which I relished. My mother always gave bacon rinds to the cat.

Tuesdays were ice cream days. The *Walls* ice cream van used to call about three o'clock on these afternoons, and when I was at school. My mother would buy me a choc ice, then wrap it well in layers of newspaper for me to eat when I arrived home. During the holidays I would meet with the ice cream man himself, a dark, good-looking man with an oval face and wavy hair.

I must have been ten years old when my mother took me to Montpeliar Row in Twickenham. She had always kept in touch with her nursing friends, especially Enid Saxton. Miss Saxton had been working as nurse / housekeeper for the poet Walter de la Mare for many years. I was surprised to see this frail old man in a wheelchair with a red plaid rug tucked round his legs. My mother knew his birthday was during the week in April when we were to visit, so we took him a fountain pen with his name inscribed on it. He was thrilled. Not only did he sign both of his poetry books my mother had bought to take with us, but he also gave me a copy of *Peacock Pie* which contained more poems by him. He wrote the first verse of the poem *Hide and Seek* on the title page and dedicated to it to me, signing it in his spidery writing.

His hobby was collecting miniatures of all kinds. I found them fascinating to look at in their glass cases. We had tea there before we left and headed for home. Afterwards I overheard my mother telling my father that Walter de la Mare had often asked Enid Saxton to marry him, but she had refused, partly because of the age difference and partly because she didn't want to upset his family.

My father was overjoyed when he secured a position at Witchampton Paper Mills in their Export Department doing similar work to that which he had done as a shipping agent. He became less irritable and easier to live with.

He was also thrilled when I passed my eleven plus scholarship to attend Queen Elizabeth I grammar school in Wimborne. He bought me a wristwatch to commemorate the occasion. I was the youngest in that school for a year, a, having an August birthday, the government decided that the school age should be determined by birthdays falling within the school year rather than the calendar year as it had previously been. Consequently my special friends with September and October birthdays were left behind at primary school for a further year while I started life at the grammar school on my own.

My mother's needlework projects were still going from strength to strength. In addition to home sewing she began to teach Smocking, Quilting and Dorset Stitchery at adult evening classes each Monday when she was not on night duty. This was something she enjoyed, and it gave her more friends, and I suppose brought in more money.

After Sandy's death, it was decided we could have a family dog. Naively I wanted a collie. Cross collie puppies were on sale near Gillingham on the other side of Dorset. We went to collect a young black and white female and called her Lyndy. She was a lovely dog, eager to please, with a lot of energy. Naturally she was bred to be a working dog, not a pet. My father decided to take her to dog training classes. These were not a success. Other dogs there were good, obedient to their owners. My father arrived with Lyndy in tow and all promptly became pandemonium. Lyndy wanted to play, and she somehow organised all the other dogs into playing with her so that obedience was out of the question. My father took her along many times and we witnessed a slight improvement although surprised she didn't get expelled. He took her for long walks, but instead of wearing her out, they seemed to make her more energetic. Letting her off the lead generally meant she would find some particularly pungent smelly mud to roll in and would need to be bathed.

The big news of 1958 was Daphne giving birth to their only daughter on 3rd October after being married some years. They called her Carolyn Daphne. In December of the same year, Warren announced that Iris had given birth to their only daughter, Elizabeth.

I was just starting the third year at the grammar school when I began to have serious *grand mal* epileptic fits with no warning. I wasn't told at the time what was wrong with me, but I just knew I felt awful when I woke up from – what? Adults seemed to be over protective of me whereas fellow pupils went out of their way to avoid me and I didn't know why. It was only soon after my father's death two months before my fourteenth birthday, when, whilst helping my mother turn out his things, I found my father's diaries with details of all my illnesses noted in them. At the time, I had simply been told that I had 'fainted again', or had 'not seemed well'. This was certainly a shock to me but I said nothing and kept my findings to myself.

* * *

The time came when Mr Biddle, the landlord wanted to sell *Pademba*. As tenants, we were given first refusal. I don't know what price he was asking for it, but it was certainly out of our price range, so we had to move. The four bedroomed house next door to *St Audrey's* nursing home was up for sale and Phyll Bloomfield made jokes about my mother buying it and setting up a nursing home in opposition. As things turned out, this is just what happened.

I wanted a day off school for the move, but this was not allowed, so I went home for lunch for the last time and ate my sandwiches on the stairs looking round forlornly at what had been my childhood home and which held so many happy memories. I hated leaving it.

We moved into our new home at the beginning June 1959, taking Miss Vaughan and Lyndy with us. We soon had a second patient. Both occupied the two large front downstairs rooms. At this time my father was due to retire in October at the age of 65, so he intended to do all the business side and keep the books. My parents had one front upstairs bedroom and I occupied the one opposite. Two patients would occupy the back bedrooms upstairs because they already had a washbasin plumbed in. This meant we just had the kitchen downstairs and the sitting room opposite it to ourselves.

I was about to study for my GCE exams when my father, who had always said he would never entertain the idea of having a television, decided to rent one. Of course we were all fascinated by it, including the patients, so it was suggested that they had their own installed in their room if they wanted one, but they suddenly seemed to prefer the radio after all.

As soon as we moved into our new house – or *Niger Lodge* as my parents had named it – my father wanted it dedicated. He was not a religious man, but still felt that as this home was going to be a business, then it ought to have God's blessing on it.

A number of family and close friends gathered one Sunday afternoon just three weeks after we had moved in. The vicar of St John's church, Rev R E Garrard came to say a few words of dedication and offered a few prayers. It was a short ceremony and everyone was soon chatting over the large tea my mother had provided.

Not long after that Rev Garrard approached my mother

and said he noticed that my father seemed to be listing to one side and perhaps he ought to be attended to. Together they went to him, and my mother realised he had suffered a stroke. The vicar helped my mother lift him onto the settee (out of my sight) and suddenly people started to leave.

Daphne and Leslie thought it best if I went to stay the night with them, so I was taken to their house in Sturminster Marshall. We were just about to drive off when Daphne said, "Oh, I haven't said goodbye to Daddy!" and rushed off to do so.

I realised I hadn't either, but I sank lazily back into my seat saying, "Never mind, I'll see him in the morning."

I settled to sleep all right but I woke with a start at six in the morning believing my father had died. Reassured by being in Daphne and Leslie's old-fashioned room with its iron bedstead, I soon went back to sleep again.

The next thing I knew was the Rev Garrard sitting heavily on my bed shortly after eight o'clock.

"I'm very sorry," he said, "but I've come to tell you that your daddy died early this morning."

Before even the tears came I asked, "What time?"

"Six o'clock," he said.

I wept.

Leslie took me home after breakfast as Daphne had 18 month old Carolyn to see to. It was to be the only time I ever saw my mother crying. I was whisked away while she put on a brave face for me and she never let me witness her emotions again.

I was not allowed to go to the funeral that was conducted by Rev Garrard. Nobody explained why, but as an afterthought perhaps they were afraid I might be shocked into having another seizure. My father's body was cremated at Bournemouth Crematorium following a short service at St John's Church in Wimborne. My mother didn't want his ashes buried either, or a rose bush planted in his memory, just scattered in the Garden of

Remembrance. Although his name was recorded in the Book of Remembrance there, she never went to see it and neither would she take me. As time went by I began to feel he was lost forever.

Chapter Twenty-four

My mother took me on holiday with her to Wedmore in Somerset soon after my father's death. A holiday had been booked there for the three of us during my school holidays. Happily the hotel had space for my mother and I immediately as it was out of season.

I was fascinated by Wookey Hole caves, which were nothing like as commercialised then as they are today. As my mother's family came from around that area we also looked round a couple of local cemeteries. We were intrigued to discover the graves of other family members going back a couple of hundred years. My mother was particularly keen to find her mother's grave in the churchyard of St Mary's church. We found others named Benjafield who must have been our family predecessors. Uncle Ronald was passionately interested in our forefathers so he had told my mother what to look out for.

Ronald had made a family tree, having discovered names going back to around 1700. Then a few years after our holiday he re-visited Wedmore himself and found an old bookshop where he discovered an old tome recounting many of the Benjafield families and even tracing our ancestry back to William the Conqueror. Uncle Ronald admitted that this was probably cheating somewhat, but I was thrilled think I could have some blue blood in me. It was not until I thought about it years later that I realised that due to the size of the country's population then and now, no doubt most of we English citizens are related to William the Conqueror or one of his knights who came over from France with him. Examining the facts more closely, it seems that on my maternal side of the family, we are actually descended from Sir John de Benville who came over from Normandy with William the Conqueror in 1066. Some decades later, after living around the north Dorset area, the name was anglicised to become Benjafield. One Sir John Benjafield was given the keys to the Dorset town of Shaftesbury in the thirteenth century.

Many years later I met my mother's cousin Ray Benjafield and his wife Joyce who lived at Wincanton. Ray was passionate about our family tree and had written it all out in his neat handwriting in a massive document which he stored in a brown leather suitcase. He gave me a sketchy copy, which I still treasure, even though computers could probably make a better transcription these days. Suffice to say that the name of Benjafield is rare and if anyone bears that surname, then we are probably related in some way.

After my father died, Uncle Bill Tapper kindly took over some of the business side of running Niger Lodge, as my mother admitted she was hopeless at it. She would have had the patients for free if she could afford to, even though most of them were extraordinarily rich. Extra aids had to be installed too, such as a second stair rail. A downstairs bathroom was added, plus a bath seat. The ground floor lavatory had to have a raised seat with handles to grasp all round. In addition to all this, a sun lounge was built to enable the patients to have their own joint sitting room away from their own room. They rarely used this though, and frequently came in to sit with us, giving us no privacy. My father certainly would not have stood for it and I became too embarrassed to ask friends back home.

Around this time, without my mother's knowledge, I made an appointment to see the family GP, Dr John Hannay. I told him that I had recently discovered that I suffered from epilepsy and wanted to know more about it. He was very understanding, explaining that, as with faces, we all have two eyes, a nose and a mouth, yet we all look different because these are slightly differently positioned or vary in size. In the same way, the brain has clusters of four cells. Each set of cells varies slightly from person to person making some more intelligent, others more likely to react to differing circumstances. He went on to tell me that he had been in the navy during the war. When it ended, they had all celebrated by making merry with booze, and generally got drunk. One sailor, however, ended up having an epileptic fit. Dr Hannay reassured me that he had never had one since, but this was how his brain had coped with too much alcohol. For other people, it would be different circumstances. In my case, it was deemed that I grew from a child to a woman too quickly for my brain to cope with it. I felt reassured, but this conversation also served to make me wary of alcohol!

The next thing I lost was Lyndy. She greeted everyone enthusiastically, jumping up when they came to visit. Often it was elderly people visiting elderly relatives, so she became something of a menace. She mourned my father as much as I did and we used to have reassuring cuddles down the bottom of the garden. I was upset to lose her, but I understood why.

Mr Barnaby, taught Geography and had a small-holding. After class one day I asked if he would be willing to take on our dog. He was. It was a sad day when he came to collect her although no doubt a relief for my mother.

He certainly trained her well. It was reported that she had been seen walking to heel in the midst of Wimborne's traffic. She was allowed to become pregnant and apparently made a good mother to her pups. Unfortunately, she was so pleased to see the family car after their short break away that she ran to greet them alongside the car, Mr Barnaby did not see her until it was too late and she'd been run over and had to be put to sleep. So sad.

Miss Grainger was one of the first patients. She was a grumpy old thing. My mother tried to cheer up the patients during our first Christmas without my father by taking them a tastefully decorated miniature Christmas tree to stand on their dresser.

I heard her yell, "Take that tawdry thing out of here!"

We had no pets by that time. When I asked, my mother said, "We can't have any animals now that we have the nursing home."

"Surely we can have a cat, though? A cat isn't bouncy like a dog."

"No Diana! When I say no, I mean no!"

However a stray black cat later adopted us and Miss Grainger wanted to keep it. She called it Toots and it was allowed to stay. Toots soon produced two little kittens, although one was stillborn. The living one was also kept. Once Miss Grainger died both cats disappeared.

I remember Mrs Kindersley was terrified of catching flu. She was perfectly able bodied, but just decided she didn't want to bother with life any longer and took to her bed, paying fees to stay in my mother's residential home. She was a great fan of Edmundo Ross.

Miss Bumstead was another patient – again somewhat grumpy. She would never call my mother by name as the others did, but insisted on calling her Rhoda. After she died, my mother was surprised to receive a small legacy from her. She used the money to demolish the wobbly wall round the paved front garden area. In its place a handyman built a low double rockery-type wall round the front of the house and filled it with soil. My mother planted white Allysum and purple Campanula there which spread and tumbled in a mass of colour.

Mrs Hibberd was a sweet old lady. She was the mother of Stuart Hibberd who used to broadcast on the radio during the war. However, she suffered from dementia and thought that my mother was her daughter, I was her grand-daughter and that Niger Lodge was her own family home. After one of my mother's regular days off every Thursday, she returned home to discover the hedge at the bottom of the garden had disappeared. After making enquiries it transpired that Mrs Hibberd, when asked earlier that day, had agreed that she was the owner of my mother's property and had given permission for the builders of the newly built house beyond it to get rid of our hedge. Fortunately a rhododendron hedge eventually replaced it.

Mrs Hibberd's GP said she would be better off with something to do. She became quite useful at shelling peas and preparing vegetables. However, she had to be watched as she made a start on the ironing one day, taking it up where someone had left off and burnt a big hole in my favourite nylon nightdress.

My mother had a dream of growing snowdrops and crocus dotted about the lawn under the large apple tree. She planted many bulbs there. Just as they came up and were about to bloom they would disappear, reappearing in tea-cups, individual tea-pots, or jam-jars of water as Mrs Hibberd picked them all and arranged them along the mantelpiece. She often asked the postman and delivery men to come in for a cup of coffee or tea. Fortunately they were either in a hurry or had got to know her, as we didn't need to entertain them at all. She would always sit in front of the television like the rock of ages refusing to go upstairs until my mother and I had gone to bed. Sometimes we would say goodnight and go up, then change into our nightwear and dressing gown before creeping downstairs once we heard her go up to bed. Her hearing was amazing as she always heard us and would down come to see what we were up to.

While Mrs Hibberd was with us Mr Locke was admitted. He was one of the few male patients my mother had. He and Mrs Hibberd used to go out for walks together. He used to get annoyed because she thought he was her husband. They often got lost and were returned either by someone who knew them or by having a ride in a police car.

One day when Mr Locke's bedroom door was wide open I saw him continually washing his hands over and over again in a plastic bowl as if they would never be clean again. I told my mother and she warned me that we had better watch him. I didn't know why at the time, but apparently this can be a sign of the onset of mental breakdown.

Next morning he climbed out of the sash window of his bedroom on the ground floor whilst still in his nightshirt, waving two brass candlesticks that had been adorning a shelf. He ran all down the road yelling that Mrs Anderson and Irish rebels were after him. Apparently it took three neighbours to control him and bring him back, by which time he had calmed down.

A couple of days later it was Thursday and my mother's day off. I came home to discover Mr Locke in a most peculiar mood. The nurse on duty had just restrained him from entering Miss Grainger's room by locking her in it and everyone else out. He was examining the clothes brushes on the monks' bench in the hall when I arrived on the scene and was talking strangely to Mrs Hibberd who was sweetly agreeing with everything he said like she always did.

I suddenly heard, "Get out of my way then!" I turned and ducked just in time to avoid a clothes brush flying through the air towards me. After a while, things went from bad to worse and the nurse on duty telephoned *St Audrey's* nursing home next door for someone to come and help. When Mrs Bloomfield, the matron came, she couldn't get in, as we had locked all the doors and hidden the keys from Mr Locke by then.

By the time my mother came home, it was agreed that Mr Locke should be certified under the Mental Health Act and admitted to Herrison Hospital near Dorchester. A couple of months later Mrs Hibberd joined him there, as she also became too much to cope with. My mother visited both of them in Herrison a couple of times and she was saddened to see how ill they both looked. Neither of them recognised her.

The only other male patient my mother was a cousin of Edward Shackleton, the man who had courageously attempted to reach the South Pole but had sadly died in the attempt during the early 1900s. He told some very interesting stories.

Miss Digby was a sweet old lady. She was a Christian and belonged to the Order of Grey Ladies. She lived with my mother for years until she died and was my mother's last patient until she herself finally retired.

My mother would often take her patients for rides in her car, and even to visit her own friends and relatives. Miss Digby came in for a lot of that as she became more of a friend than a patient. Every Sunday Miss Digby would be taken to church with us.

I remember I used to rush home from school on my bike for lunch each day so that I could take the patients' lunches round. Then I would gobble my own meal before retrieving the trays and starting the washing up. As we lived way up on a hill, it meant walking virtually all the way home, but at least I could freewheel back again. While I was still at school this did not matter too much as our morning classes ended at 12.40pm and afternoon classes would resume at 1.55pm. Once I started work in an office in Wimborne, I could only have exactly one hour for my midday break and this meant less time helping with lunches at home. My mother never seemed to understand this and would frequently say things like ...

"You never seem to help me as much as you used to."

"Come on, Diana, do help me."

"I'm doing all this for you, you know."

She may well have been, but she never understood how my life had changed when we moved from *Pademba*. My childhood had gone, my father had died, we had no family pets anymore and now I had to share the family home with old ladies.

In the end I got a job outside of Wimborne and stayed away all day.

One thing I had always wanted to do was drive a car. Against my mother's wishes, on my 17th birthday, I sent off an application form for a provisional driving licence. I had been free of fits for over three years by then. Nobody was more surprised than I was when it actually arrived, as I had declared my epilepsy on the form. My mother couldn't deny me lessons after that, so I had a wonderful time, and took to it easily. I passed my test first time, but when I made application for a full driving licence six months later, the DVLC saw their mistake, refused my application, and made their apologies. In those days, one had to wait ten years and be free of both fits and medication.

I always liked listening to *Family Favourites* on the radio, which often would be followed by the comedy show *Round the Horne.* Frequently I would record bits of these on my new reel to reel tape recorder. Equipment was not as good in those days, and "Diana, *will* you come and do the washing up *now* please" would frequently interrupt my recordings. My mother didn't appreciate my sense of humour and I didn't appreciate her sense of timing.

Various paid staff helped my mother. A trained nurse called Eileen (who incidentally was my friend Rosemary's sister-in-law) came most often and worked every Thursday to cover for my mother's days off. Mrs Pottle was not a trained nurse, but she would sit with the patients on a Monday evening. She was a widow and lived in a house on the far side of Colehill. My mother would always collect her and take her home and I recall many frustrating moments as Mrs Pottle took ages to get ready, smoothing down each finger on both gloves. I would have to stay with the patients during the few minutes she was away 'just in case'. Fortunately nothing ever happened during those times as I don't know what I would have done if it had.

I always enjoyed Monday evenings when we would mostly go to Broadstone and visit Auntie Bettie. I enjoyed meeting with her three daughters, Heather, Judith and Sarah. They were a happy family. We always had fun together.

It is said that one always remembers what you were doing when certain items of news come through. I remember the assassination of President John Kennedy whilst he was being driven through Dallas in 1963. I was helping Mrs Pottle take the suppers round to the patients when the news was announced on the radio. I leapt on my bike and cycled to the nearest newsagent near her house on the other side of Colehill. All I could find was a local *Bournemouth Evening Echo* and this just carried a small stop press item. We had to wait until the daily papers came out next day. I wanted to switch on our small black and white television on for detailed news, but Mrs Pottle wanted to watch *Coronation Street* which had not long been screened at the time.

Mrs Hoare used to come and clean. She and her husband lived in the house behind *Pademba*. I liked talking to her and would happily carry on a conversation under a table while she was dusting the skirting board. Not long after her old spaniel had died, we gave her the little black poodle that my mother accidentally won in a raffle. Poor little thing! My mother had only donated to the raffle, saying she didn't want a prize but he was delivered to us one evening. I called him Raffles. He was too young to leave his mother and howled in the night. Rather than let him wake the patients I brought him and his box into my bedroom, but he climbed up on my head, cuddling into my hair to sleep. A smelly mess trickling down my face woke me. He obviously had to go – and soon! Mrs Hoare was still grieving for her dog so we gave the puppy to her and she was thrilled with him. She called him Andy. We never did discover who put the poor little animal in a raffle. At least he ended up in a loving home.

Mrs X always mysteriously brought a shopping bag to work. My mother often used to go to the wholesalers, and frequently bought a box of *Golf* wrapped plain chocolate biscuits. She knew that I liked them and often accused me of eating a lot more than my fair share, not believing me when I denied this. Then all my first editions of A A Milne books went missing along with some other things and she began to suspect Mrs X was taking things. The next time she bought a box of *Golf* biscuits I wrote a tiny *NL* on the corner of each label. When the lady in question next came I looked in the nearly new box of biscuits and saw that a lot was missing. Just before she left, she put her shopping bag on the chair and I knocked it off onto the floor, apparently by accident. Of course many of these biscuits fell out and they were marked with *NL* for Niger Lodge.

I picked up a handful from the floor and showed my mother. "Look, someone else likes these," I said.

Mrs X tried to bluff her way out of the situation. "Yes, my family like them, so I buy them quite often."

My mother took one of the biscuits from me and looked at it closely. "How come this has *NL* for Niger Lodge written on it then?"

She had been caught out!

Mrs X said nothing, but grabbed her coat and her bag and disappeared as fast as her large body would allow and we never saw her again. The family moved away from the area soon after that.

Alongside all of this my GCE exams were looming. Having had a term and a half away from school because of my epilepsy I had lost a lot of ground, but a very nice schoolmaster, Mr Swinnerton used to take me back to his home for extra tuition in French and Maths on Tuesdays and Thursdays. His wife would always bring me a glass of orange squash. I still cannot fathom either as I had been absent for the basics of so much. Anyway I had been revising hard like everyone else.

I had hoped to take Biology separately, rather than lumped in with Physics and Chemistry which I never understood. I was allowed to sit the mock exam, but this happened to be on the same day that my mother was undergoing a mastectomy and I failed it, so was not able to take the exam for real in June. I was too shy to say anything, especially as I thought I would be told that I'd had too many privileges already. However, I managed to pass Art with 45% and English Language with 45%. I stayed on at school for an extra year so I could re-take the exams the following November. When exam time came I wasn't feeling at all well and could hardly lift my head from the pillow. It transpired I had contracted glandular fever. I did manage to sit the exam for Scripture, surprisingly getting a pass mark of 60%. Consequently I can only boast English Language, Religious Instruction and Art as my 'O' level GCE successes. I stayed on in the fifth year for a further two terms while I wondered what to do, as the class I was now in were studying a different set of everything. I left school on the 1st August 1961.

Another major event of 1961 was that the Russians put the first man into space. Major Yuri Gregarin orbited around the earth, returning safely after just over an hour and a half. It wasn't until July 1969 that the Americans sent three men to the moon and Neil Armstrong walked on the moon's surface for the first time.

I became very friendly with Ann Smeeth around the early sixties. We both used to sing in the church choir at St John's where I learned my first Christmas carol – the alternative version of *Whilst Shepherds watched their flocks by night* ...

While Shepherds washed their socks by night
All seated round the tub;
A bar of Sunlight soap came down
And they began to scrub!

Then there was also ...

Hark the Herald Angels sing!
Beecham's Pills are just the thing.
For headaches strong, or stomach mild
(Two for adults, one for child).
If you want to go to heaven,
Just take six or even seven!
If you want to go to Hell

Why not eat the box as well?
Hark the Herald Angels sing
Beecham's Pills are just the thing!

During the week prior to Christmas, the choir and the youth group would join together and go carol singing, collecting for the church. We used to ensure the area where we sang was pretty well-heeled, and always got a good reception, frequently being asked inside large houses for mulled wine and mince pies. Sometimes we might get a booking to call at a certain house on a particular evening. This generally meant the householders were having a party so everyone would be very benevolent towards us. Charlie Bullen, the church caretaker used to play a small accordion, and he would ensure that we all kept in tune.

Ann also taught me to dance the basic *Cha-Cha-Cha* steps in the vestry whilst waiting for other people to assemble for choir practice. I've never forgotten them, either.

We both attended St John's youth club, which immediately followed choir practise at 8pm on Thursday evenings. Ann owned a motor scooter and we would travel all over the place on it, often as far as Bournemouth where we would spend all day some Saturdays, shopping and having our hair done. Sometimes, we would just stay in Wimborne for an evening and frequent *The Courtyard,* its small coffee bar. This was made to appear even smaller than it was because of the huge skirts and bulky net petticoats we used to wear under them. Not having much money, I wore a cheaper, hooped petticoat instead. This, I discovered, was very effective in lassooing and dragging a table to the doorway. I never wore that again! We had nicknames for one another; she was Bubbles and I was Honey. Ann sometimes entered local beauty contests and at one time became Miss Dorset – so she was my first claim to fame!

Someone from the youth club challenged her about putting on a music hall type show and, always one to show her talent, and rise to a challenge, she did just that and it was much acclaimed. Linda Higgins was the accompanying pianist. As Ann was both the Director and Producer of it, there were several arguments from people who didn't want to do as she asked, so she just told them if they didn't like it they could drop out. If they did, she looked to me to be a stopgap, so I seemed to be continually in the wings changing costumes. It was great fun to do, though, and we raised a fair bit of money for church funds.

I went with Ann and some other girls on my first holiday away from my family to Butlins at Clacton. On Day Two I awoke with excruciating pain I had never experienced before. Everyone went to breakfast and I tried to get back to sleep. Ann made an appointment for me at the surgery. I was seen immediately and was rushed to hospital in an ambulance as its bell clanged through the town. I had to have emergency surgery to remove my appendix. That was scary. Once I had recovered somewhat I couldn't sleep because of all the snoring noises going on around me in the hospital ward. The girls visited me a couple of times, but then they went home at the end of the week.

Auntie Bettie brought my mother to see me once but I had to travel home by myself on the train in a seat in a compartment especially reserved for me. An ambulance took me from the hospital to the station and its driver settled me on the train. I was met in London by another ambulance that transported me to Waterloo where I was put in a compartment that was reserved for me. Before we left London, a crowd of people invaded my privacy and almost sat on my lap in order to seat themselves comfortably. I was too shy to pass comment.

Much later, Ann and I spent a memorable weekend in Torquay when we stayed at a women's hostel called the *Christian Alliance for Women and Girls*. It was a dreadful place where we had to attend morning and evening prayers, which were accompanied beforehand by a hymn on a tinny piano. We had to be in before the doors were locked at ten o'clock, so when we were five minutes late one night the door was locked and bolted. We rang the bell and were let in by an exasperated tall grey-haired woman in her dressing gown with her hair in curlers. Next day we saw some beautiful (well, we thought they were beautiful at the time!) cheap mauve dresses in a shop window, so we both bought identical ones, then went to a photo booth to have our pictures taken.

Ann got married shortly after that. I was one of her bridesmaids and she moved away and unfortunately we lost touch.

[NB Ann and I have re-discovered one another and have been in touch for the past 10 years.]

Rev Garrard was most enterprising for a vicar in those days and learned to drive a coach. Once he had gained his PSV licence he would hire a coach from the local Bere Regis Coach Company and take the youth group for several rides. The motor company only hired out their oldest vehicle to us and I remember after a stop for fish 'n' chips in Wareham one evening, all the boys were pushing the coach round the car park till the engine coughed and spluttered into life again. He used to drive us all to Swanage on bank holidays, and we would walk what was to become our traditional Easter walk mainly over the cliffs to Bournemouth, sometimes almost being cut off by the tide, but we always got there. We would then all stagger in to a cinema where there would be a film showing from the *Carry On* series. After a good laugh, we then caught the last bus back to Wimborne.

The youth group, sometimes had organised visits to places such as the *Dorset Police Museum* in Dorchester. Rev Garrard drove us there. Far from being a stuffy old place we were all enthralled by it. Another time we were shown around the Bournemouth Telephone Exchange. Those were the days before automation and people had to sit manning the switchboards day and night, to be able to connect people to the numbers they asked for. At that time you were careful about what you said on the phone, just in case you were being overheard by the operator, hoping for some gossip.

In 1963 there was an unbelievable train robbery, when a gang of robbers somehow managed to rob a train at a level crossing and got away with over two and a half million pounds, promoting a nation-wide hunt.(Two of the robbers were never caught until they gave themselves up after living lives of luxury in Brazil when they returned to England to die many years later.) As a youth club that year our entry in the Wimborne Carnival procession was based on the Great Train Robbery as it came to be called. The boys had done a lot of carpentry and painting to the flat-bed lorry to make it look like a steam engine. Their hard work was worth it. We were awarded first prize!

Sometimes three or four of us girls would go ballroom dancing at the Pavillion Ballrooms in Bournemouth on a Saturday. Two of the girls had full driving licences and would persuade their father to lend them his car – or, as happened most often, Linda's father, Mr Higgins was happy for her to drive his old jalopy of a van. We would squash in with our huge skirts then spend ages in the *Ladies* sorting ourselves out on arrival. Sometimes we met interesting people, sometimes we didn't. Linda met her future husband, John Newman in this way. I knew the basic steps of ballroom dances but that's all. One time a guy asked me to dance what turned out to be a jive; something I had never got the hang of. However, his lead was so good, I was surprised myself as I twirled, spun, turned as if I knew exactly what I was doing. My friends were open-mouthed when I joined them back at our table.

"I didn't know you could dance as well as that!" they said.

"Neither did I." I replied.

It just shows what a woman can do when she has a good lead from her partner.

I started work as a junior clerk with ARO Foster Ltd in September 1961 after leaving school. It was here that I gained the nickname of Dolly (short for Dolly Daydream) from the other girls. (I wonder with hindsight whether I was slightly deaf in those days to gain such a tag.) However, this nickname was preferable to Porky, the one I had gained at school. That was during the early sixties when two pig puppets *Pinky and Perky* apparently made records that got into the charts. My friend Irene blushed a lot, so she was dubbed Pinky and I became Porky because of my tendency to puppy fat at that time.

Returning to my first job; at first I found it very hard working an extra hour in the afternoon, especially as I still had to make the dash home to help with the lunch trays. There were four of us girls around the same age and we got on well together. Twice on a Saturday we would catch the train from Wimborne station, change at Brockenhurst and go on to Southampton for a day out shopping. It was very sad when Dr Beeching closed the line in the early sixties and we could do this no more. Coach rides just were not the same. It was whilst working for ARO Foster that I learned a couple of alternative version to a carol, such as this one when the Beatles were shooting to stardom, another song could be heard, namely;

> *We four lads from Liverpool are,*
> *John in a taxi, Paul in a car.*
> *George on a scooter honking his hooter,*
> *Following Ringo Starr*

During the winter of 1962/63, it snowed more than we had ever seen down south. Waking up on Boxing Day morning, everywhere was white and there was no way we could use the car. I remember walking to church and the snow coming over the tops of my wellington boots. It was a long freeze. This meant it was out of the question to go home for lunch and I stayed at work for a full day eating lunch from Middleditch's fish 'n' chip shop opposite. Needless to say, I gained a lot of weight.

After three years I went to work with British Drug

Houses at Parkstone in their Personnel office. I loved it there, but first one person, then the other who used to give three of us a lift to work from Wimborne, left the firm. Walking down to Wimborne, then catching a bus part way and waiting for another connection took far too long so I reluctantly gave in my notice.

My mother worked hard all her life. Even when she gave up Niger Lodge as a nursing home she rented the top floor out to a couple and lived downstairs with her last and only patient, Miss Digby. When Miss Digby died, she sold Niger Lodge and moved to a small flat in Wimborne. For the last three years of her life my mother was in The Magna nursing home before her death in November 2003, just three weeks away from her ninety-fifth birthday.

I often wonder if she eventually thought that perhaps she had been too hasty in marrying my father. She and Alan had obviously very much in love. I know she always wanted children of her own, and this would probably not have happened had she waited to marry him. Living together in those days was just not done. She had also been strictly brought up. The way she seemed to want to erase my father from her life once he had died and getting rid of everything he possessed, even his war medals, (he had served with the Liverpool Scottish regiment during the First World War) seemed strange to me, as they didn't take up much room. It was something that I know annoyed Daphne when she realised what had happened. Both of us would have liked some small keepsake of him.

Not long after my father had died I noticed a dainty little china figurine on the mantelpiece which I had not seen before so I quizzed her about it.
    "That's Priscilla." she said. "Alan gave me that."
    Later, when given the opportunity, she told me about him and happily explained over a period of time about their love affair, the likes of which I hadn't heard before.

She often referred to him when recounting the past as naturally as if I had known him too.

Epilogue

It must have been in the mid-1960s whilst my mother was out shopping when she met Dorothy Bates, a nurse with whom she had trained at Middlesex Hospital. They had later met up again in West Africa. She was asked back to Dorothy's home for a cup of coffee.

Dorothy was also a widow by this time but had kept in touch with all the people my mother had known since my parents had left Warri. Having kept in close contact she was able to tell my mother that Alan had retired to the Cayman Islands suffering from heart problems.

My mother was immediately concerned that she personally may have been the one to physically trigger this by rejecting his love.

"Oh dear," she remarked before asking casually whether he had ever divorced Gwen.

"Oh yes, as soon as he could. Then he met and married a woman who was waiting for her own divorce to come through."

"So everything's all right now then?"

Dorothy made a grimace. "Well, no, I believe he has stomach cancer, but I don't know how far advanced it is."

My mother had to leave at that point to relieve whoever was on duty at Niger Lodge.

Dorothy had given her Alan's address so she sat down and wrote to Alan as soon as she could, apologising for leaving him, especially in the cowardly way of writing to him. She told him what she was doing these days, hoping he was all right. She ended with a request for news of him and again asking his forgiveness.

A letter arrived ten days later having been posted from the Cayman Islands. In it Alan remembered exactly how long it had been since he had last seen her in Warri and assured her there was nothing to forgive her for after such a long period of time.

Marjorie gave a little shudder as she recalled hearing

how upset Alan had been after their final parting and her subsequent letter telling him that she intended to marry John. He went on to recount how he had finally re-married in 1949 after eventually getting a divorce.

(Author's note - My mother sometimes told me that she often wondered if she could have held out so long in order to marry Alan, despite their deep love for one another).

Alan's letter continued by saying that he had retired from Nigeria in 1954 and after a few administration posts in England had landed a plum job on the Cayman Islands. He had now retired there.

As he described his surroundings, Marjorie could almost hear him conversing with her. He explained about his stomach cancer and that he hoped to return to the UK in the near future for surgery and to find a cure.

He added that he had kept in touch with several mutual friends, so was aware of Marjorie's situation and suggested that now he had her address that they kept in touch. *When I came to England* he wrote, *I would like to meet you again.* He ended by thanking her for writing and for all the happy times they had enjoyed together, telling her not to reproach herself for anything.

Marjorie read the letter several times over before replying to him by return of post. She mailed the letter.

Two days later she was completing the crossword in the *Daily Telegraph* as she did every day, when a name caught her eye in the obituary column. It recorded the death of Alan McKenzie on the Grand Cayman Island. He had probably never received her second letter and his to her was no doubt the last one he wrote.

At that time I was trying to help with some housework as Mrs Hoare was unable to come that week. While I was dusting, the *Priscilla* figurine got knocked off the mantelpiece and smashed beyond repair in the hearth.

I don't know which of us was more horrified by the coincidence.

About the Author

Diana wrote her first short book when she was just 6 years old. Although unpublished this was well received by her close family. Writing has always been her passion but it was not until she took early retirement that Diana was able to devote more time to writing. She had several articles published in national magazines before writing her first book then two others soon followed.

Raised in Wimborne, Dorset, Diana moved to Southampton in 1976 after her marriage to James. Both are committed Christians. They have two adult children, three grandchildren, and are servants to two cats.